WILLIAM CHRISTIAN is a member of the
Department of Political Science at the
University of Guelph.

The many published volumes of the writings
of Harold Adams Innis testify to his extraordinary grasp of the ordering principles of
human history. The notes that he left at the
time of his death provide a new and revealing
profile of the inner workings of this restless
and relentless mind.

Innis maintained, added to, and corrected,
in the last seven years of his life, a single
system of cross-referenced notes, which came
to be called the Idea File. Before his death in
1952 he collected these notes into a single
numbered collation. In this edition the material has been arranged in chronological order
to give a sense of the development of Innis's
ideas and concerns.

Innis's interests were many and varied,
and this collection of some 1500 notes
covers an encyclopedic range of topics. The
different lines of Innis's investigations
converge, however, in his interest in basic
political and cultural issues and in his fundamental concern for the preservation of
individual freedom and creativity. At heart
Innis was a moralist whose hatred of oppressive social institutions led him to examine
them from many angles. It is a fascinating
odyssey. Every reader will be refreshed and
enriched by sharing Innis's life-long intellectual adventure.

University of Toronto Press / Toronto Buffalo London

the Idea File of Harold Adams Innis

introduced and edited by
William Christian

© University of Toronto Press 1980
Toronto Buffalo London
Printed in Canada

Canadian Cataloguing in Publication Data

Innis, Harold A., 1894-1952.
The idea file

Includes indexes.
ISBN 0-8020-2350-9
I. Christian, William. II. Title.
AC8.I55   082   C79-094751-X

This book has been published
with assistance from the
block grant programs of the
Canada Council and
the Ontario Arts Council.

Contents

Preface

What Anglo-Saxons call a Foreword, but gentlemen a Preface.

HILAIRE BELLOC (29 / 40)[1]

Anyone who knew Harold Innis well could attest to his acute sense of humour. It was an essential part of the man and it was equally a vital part of the scholar. Innis could see the juxtaposition of incongruous elements and laugh; but more often than not the apparent incongruities of Innis's juxtapositions dissolved on closer inspection – there was after all a connection between the invention of the bored rifle and the rise of responsible government in Nova Scotia. It was this ability to see patterns and relationships that had led Marshall McLuhan recently to describe Innis as a right-hemisphere thinker. Innis took pains to cultivate this talent; Donald Innis remembers that his father often worked at reading several books in different areas, a bit of one then a bit of the next, the better to see connections that might escape the more single-minded scholar.

Those who had visited Innis in his office at the University of Toronto or at his study at home carried away the distinct impression of a chaos which they presumed to be creative on account of the stream of publications that Innis generated. S.D. Clark recalls that Mary Innis once gave her husband a file cabinet in an attempt to introduce some order into his filing system, but it stood in splendid emptiness in the corner of his study, while the floor was covered with open books and piles of notes, each pile with a scrap of paper on the top containing an index to the contents. It is likely that some of these piles constituted what Innis himself called the Idea File.

There were, of course, other notes – reading notes, and more important, the travel notes. Wherever Innis went, the Mackenzie River, the Maritimes, the Soviet Union he looked around him and recorded his observations and speculations. Section 27 in this volume, the notes Innis made during his vacation to the United Kingdom and France in 1951 are just a small and tantalizing sample of Innis's amazing powers of observation and speculation. The Idea File, however, stands by itself among Innis's unpublished works as both a temptation and a challenge.

The committee that was established after Innis's death to decide on the possibility of publications from his papers rejected conventional publication of the Idea File. This was an odd decision and probably stemmed from the chaotic form of the original, as well as the lack of resources which the committee had at its disposal. I describe this decision as odd because it was argued at the time that the material was too impenetrable by ordinary readers to be published. Yet the Idea File is no more opaque than most of the material that Innis himself published; and what is more, because it sits in note book form rather than fully articulated sentences as in the published works, it is more obvious that the reader has to fill in the lacunae in the observations. It does not take the reader very long into the Idea File to get into Innis's style of thought, and the process of filling in the gaps in argument becomes exhilarating.

If the founder of a school can be forgiven anything but his school, Innis is safe; he had few followers in any direct or immediate sense. This is not surprising, since his genius was probing and penetrating, but not of the system-creating sort. As an economic historian he had dealt with considerable tracts of time - over three hundred years in the fur trade, and over five hundred in the cod fisheries. He had not restricted himself to narrowly economic phenomena. When he set his mind to outlining in 1929 the skills that a student of Canadian economic history ought to possess, he suggested that, in addition to a detailed knowledge of French, British, and American economic history, he ought to 'have a knowledge of French, German, and Latin, and of certain of the sciences, electricity, metallurgy, and mechanics with relation to Canadian development'.[2]

Innis himself had struggled to expand the traditional compass of his discipline. He abjured political boundaries and followed the logic of his investigations wherever they took him (25 / 23). Geology and geography were important to the economic historian of the fur trade, especially the river routes; so he travelled to the mouth of the Mackenzie by canoe and by river steamer. The biology of the cod was an essential factor in understanding the Newfoundland fisheries, and so the reader is introduced to a discussion of the salinity and temperature of the Grand Banks and the specific gravity of cods' eggs at the beginning of the *Cod Fisheries*. Political activities, related economic events, technological discoveries all receive their fair share of attention. It was Innis's driving ambition to penetrate behind the surface economic facts that made him such a difficult model for others to imitate. His was a singular genius.

But how did this man who had spent most of his life to the age of forty-five contemplating the economic exploitation of beaver pelts, square timber, wheat, and fish transform himself into a critic of his civilization? The usual answer given to this question has been that the link was the staple products of pulp and paper. Innis, it is suggested, turned his attention naturally to these as he pursued the history of staple production in Canada, and in the course of his investigations followed the topic from the production end to the consumption end – that is, to the newspapers in the United States, the main consumers of Canadian newsprint. This new interest led him to inquire into the mechanisms of newspaper production and from there expanded to include all forms of communication. Such an explanation is adequate on the surface, but it is shallow and incomplete. By concentrating on the communications aspects of Innis's later writings it impoverishes our understanding of a man whose very claim to enduring greatness was his refusal to allow his speculations to be restricted (5 / 201).

Moreover, the raising of theoretical questions was not as unique to the post-1940 period as this explanation would suggest. Innis had begun to explore the theoretical and philosophical implications of contemporary social science in the 1930s, especially around the height of the Depression. 'The Role of Intelligence', 'The Canadian Economy and the Depression', and 'For the People' published in the period from 1934 to 1936 suggest a mind that was beginning to show dissatisfaction with the limitations of the merely phenomenal, with the writing of economic history, and the analysis of contemporary economic problems.

The Depression had ravaged the economies of the western world. It had also posed a challenge to man's understanding of the mechanisms of his social order, since contemporary economics appeared unable to respond to it with any effective remedies. As well, the reaction in Europe had, for the most part, been horrifying, especially in Germany and in Italy. As the Second World War made the very survival of his civilization look doubtful, Innis was drawn back to the role of the scholar, and especially that of the social scientist, in preventing catastrophe. Although not a philosopher himself, and having little in any way that could be described as philosophical training, Innis was fortunate in enjoying the friendship of another colleague at the University of Toronto who, like Innis, was a product of Protestant rural Ontario, the great classical historian, Charles Cochrane. Innis and Cochrane often met for lunch, and Cochrane would chide Innis for his interest in such base subjects as fish. That Cochrane's conversations, and especially his masterpiece, *Christianity and Classical Culture*, (1940) influenced Innis deeply can be seen in the central position Innis attributes to Cochrane for Canadian social science:

the significance of the volume for social scientists is in its philosophical approach. In classical civilization reason asserted its supremacy and in doing so betrayed its insecure position with disastrous results ... The sweep of the Platonic state in the nineteenth and twentieth centuries and the spread of science has been followed by the horrors of the Platonic state. The social scientist is asked to check his course and to indicate his role in western civilization. His answer must stand the test of the philosophic approach of Cochrane.[3]

At about the same time as Innis was writing this memorial to Cochrane he had noted in the Idea File the paradox of a need for a universal or comprehensive theory of civilization and the difficulty that prevented the development of one (5 / 181). He was not the man himself to achieve this kind of theory – his mind was too restless for that sort of thing – but he understood well the importance of trying. This concern remained with him. Even toward the end of his life, in 1951, he still insisted that it was necessary constantly to attempt a synthesis in order to offset the influence of mechanization; it was civilization as a whole, and not just parts of it, which ought to be studied (26 / 7).

Although the twentieth century had produced a number of attempts at a universal and integrated approach, such as Kroeber and Toynbee who figure with some prominence in the Idea File, and Spengler and Sorokin whom Innis mentions more elsewhere, this phenomenon as well as Innis's own interest in universal themes represents a bias which in itself has to be accounted for. To some extent these efforts represented the working out of possibilities that had been created by the development of mechanized printing: Toynbee, for example, Innis characterized as the factory system applied to learning. The printing industry had generated a 'constant pouring out of words' which had led to 'bewilderment' because of the 'inability to break through them'. There had been a 'steady cumulative pressure on [the] modern mind' (5 / 12). Even scholars had difficulty in resisting technological advance (14 / 8) and had become as a consequence captives of new developments in communication.

Image worship had crept over civilization (2 / 24) because the injunction not to worship any graven image had not been interpreted to include 'the printed word or those words themselves' (1 / 1). Rather than serving as a liberating force, a possibility that was inherent in writing and printing (24 / 45), the worship of print had broken up western civilization into aggressively rival national units each organized around a particular written language. This technology had proven to be particularly adaptable to the needs of militarism and had been suborned by established power to the service of vested interests (15 / 7).

For Innis the predicament of his civilization lay in its lack of self-consciousness. This insight was another he had garnered from Cochrane, an idealist historian who had been influenced by the distinguished British philosopher and historian, Collingwood. The tragedy of the western world was that it had allowed itself to become the plaything of forces or causes (6 / 35, 50); indeed, though Innis never puts it in quite this way, it had become a society suitable for study by social science and particularly by economics, the social science which had been responsible for inflicting ever more distortions and misery on mankind.

Innis saw himself clearly as out of step with developments in his discipline. As a graduate student at the University of Chicago he had been influenced by the writings of Thorstein Veblen. In 1929, the year before the publication of the *Fur Trade in Canada*, the work that was to establish his reputation as one of the leading economic historians in the English-speaking world, Innis contributed an appreciation of Veblen to the *Southwestern Political and Social Science Quarterly*. This article is particularly instructive because Innis points to many features in Veblen's work which were later to become of central importance to the line of argument he developed in the period covered by the Idea File. Veblen had come to economics from a background of interest in philosophy, and this had contributed to Veblen's strength as an economist. He had also been influenced by the German historical school, which looked closely at the influence of institutions. Veblen's most popular work, the *Theory of the Leisure Class* 'was a direct and devastating attack on the marginal utility theory. It was precisely a clash between the viewpoint of the German historical school with its stress on the evolution of institutions and the classic theory.' If Veblen's approach could be summed up simply, it would be an interest in dynamics: 'he insisted upon the existence of laws of growth and decay of institutions and associations. His life work has been primarily the study of processes of growth and decay.'[4]

The interest in institutions and the laws of growth and decay formed the central core of Innis's own writing on empires and cultures and their attendant forms of communication. He asked the following questions: what factors accounted for the fact that some large-scale political organizations survived for a considerable period, whereas others faded rapidly? What connection was there between the brilliance and fecundity of a particular culture and its longevity? How were cultures and empires overthrown?

Neither in his published writings nor in his Idea File is there any indication that Innis had arrived at firm answers to these questions. Indeed it is his failure to arrive at definite conclusions which have lead many to look to the titles of his works, and to conclude, mistakenly, that they are studies in communications and the effects of different media of communication. Innis's real interest lay in the underlying political and cultural issues, and the studies in communication were to a considerable degree a device for getting at more important questions. At heart Innis was a moralist whose hatred of oppressive social institutions led him to examine the manner of their subversion from many angles.

Empires survived, Innis thought, when they avoided a condition he termed monopoly. Although he was aware of the dangers of borrowing terms from his own discipline of economics for the analysis of politics and culture, Innis thought this a useful concept to point out that societies have a tendency to fall into the hands of small organized groups who try to mould society for their own purposes. In taking this line Innis showed sympathy with the Italian theorists Pareto and Mosca who argued that societies will always be run by an élite and that social change consists primarily in the circulation of élites.

In order to strengthen its control and to enhance the likelihood of its survival, an élite should be constantly taking steps to recruit able individuals from all social classes and geographic regions of the society. For example, Innis wrote of the centralized educational system in his native Ontario that it 'fails to secure mobility in moving from outlying areas to [the] centre and thus [fails] to secure the most efficient structure' (9 / 4). This observation applies more widely, and it is probably fair to suggest that Innis's ideal society would be one ruled by competing élites, each scouring society to find the most talented individuals in order to recruit and train them for social leadership. Innis realized, I think, how very fortunate he had been in his progress from farm boy to department head, dean, and royal commissioner; and it was not immodesty but compassion for others not so fortunate as he had been that led Innis to understand the great human waste when talents were not properly developed and deployed.

Competing monopolies were better than a single monopoly for another reason: they prevented rigidity and in the process fostered cultural creativity. It is important to note here that Innis comes at the problem from the political and cultural ends, and not from a study of communications. The mechanics and influences of different forms of communication were important, but Innis was no narrow communications theorist. He used his interest in the forms of communication to make the point that societies became moulded, set in their ways, and as a consequence it was extremely difficult for an individual to escape from the dominant forces of his society.

Civilization, he argued in one note, was at its peak in the period of a shift from the oral to the written tradition, or when the society is shifting from poetry to prose, or from oral to written law (10 / 5). Art Innis saw as a means of escape from the limitations of the organized hierarchies that necessarily dominated any society, and it was a fear of contamination that led him to condemn the politicization of works of art (15 / 5, 27 / 12). In any event in the contemporary world this release from domination was likely to be checked by nationalism, paraochialism, and the bigotry of the church. Even the great humourist Stephen Leacock had allowed himself to be debased by writing a history of Canada under the auspices of a distillery (12 / 4). On the other hand, occasional opportunities arose in which pressures were almost evenly balanced. For instance, James Joyce had possibly 'developed break through English language by familiarity with Celtic or Erse or realization of [the] significance of another language'. An additional advantage which helped to account for the vigour of Irish writers was the 'clash between English and Roman Catholics and Celtics' (27 / 47).

A balance between contending hierarchies and competing media of

communication allowed thinkers and writers to escape from the settled
traditions of their culture. A long-standing and successful hierarchy was
most likely to purchase stability at the price of sterility.

On the final question, namely that of the destruction of monopolies
of knowledge, Innis thought that he had discovered an important error
in previous thinkers such as Schumpeter, Cole, and Wissler who had be-
lieved that the key to social change lay in understanding that the centre
dominates the outlying regions. The contrary, Innis argued, is true; it is
those areas that have escaped the restrictive influences at the centre that
retain the possibility of development. Technology has its impact first in
frontier areas which are more open to social change, and then works in
to the centre in an attack on the more conservative elements (2 / 1). The
frontier is associated with two other key Innisian ideas: the vernacular
and the oral tradition. Both these concepts have a much broader significance in Innis's notes and published writings than they would ordinarily
bear. A successful élite of long standing was very likely to have lost contract with the vast mass of the populace it controlled. Hence each society
would develop an authorized version of that society's life, which would
be protected by the dominant media of communication with their associated vested interests. Existing simultaneously but continually evolving
would be the social, cultural, and religious concerns of the people, and
that people's own self-understanding of their situation.

Ultimately it was the forces in society which had been open to new
developments in commercial, industrial, or military practice which
proved to be of decisive importance. Whether empires were overthrown
from within or without, the agents for change would most likely be elements that had been marginal to the empire. It is at this point that Innis
invokes the concepts of the vernacular and of the oral tradition. The
vibrant life of the people, especially where it has been allowed to develop freely and creatively, is now separate from the required practices
and orthodox beliefs of the hierarchy. It has been the beneficiary of
new developments and, if the empire is ready to fall, it will seize the
advantage and press home its superiority. If the technological developments have taken place in military science, or if there have been associated military developments, then the success of the new class is more
likely. Whatever happens, however, there is likely to be social disruption; social change usually has untold and unforeseen costs.

For Innis the most problematic element of the modern world was
mechanization and the associated battery of beliefs and practices that
mechanization had called forth. If he were to point to one salient cause
of the character of modern civilization, it would be the printing press.
In the Middle Ages the church had been the pre-eminent institution of
learning and had held the central place in the dissemination of knowledge. The development of the printing press had offered the newly
emerging states of modern Europe the opportunity to challenge the

church's monopoly over the development and spread of knowledge. But when the state took advantage of the opening offered by the printing press to challenge the dominance of the church over the opinions of men, it did so by concentrating its attention on expanding and consolidating its control over a given territory - what Innis called control over space. The church in the Middle Ages had many weaknesses, but it had lent strength to the medieval realms by supporting dynastic continuity; it had exercised its influence by a concern with control over time, manifested by such phenomena as the reform of the calendar, and the insistence on religious holidays.

As the state, with the aid of the printing press, diminished the church's role, the question of the organization of time was left open. The vacuum created by the defeat of the church was quickly filled first by commerce and subsequently by industry. Business and the state had created the modern era to suit their own particular needs:

Significance of revolution in politics is preparation for revolution in economics - preparing people for discipline of machine - communism in Russia, fascism in Italy a device for compelling undisciplined people to accept discipline of machine - probable that revolutions have much of element of preparing for discipline - printing industry a part of disciplining process - includes disciplining of language. (15 / 6)

Universities, rather than maintaining a stance of neutrality towards the organization of space proposed by states, and the organization of time proposed by the needs of business enterprises, had abandoned their true responsibility, which was to train men of character and judgment. Instead of making students aware of the biases implicit in their civilization, they had allowed themselves to be co-opted by its dominant forces. 'Universities systematically register effects of ground swells or affected by major waves in disturbances of civilization. Excess of religion paralleled by excess of commerce and finance' (12 / 4). Instead of holding to their proper function which was to be 'a creator and destroyer of ideas' (21 / 5), universities had become dominated by political and business concerns and had been induced to turn their attention to professional education, and consequently to neglect the problem of the university tradition (19 / 35).

Innis's own discipline of economics had been particularly guilty. In the first place it had been active in aiding the triumph of the price system, a process which invaded every sphere of social relationships, often with disastrous consequences. Yet the limits of the price system were shown in the 'necessity of corruption at top levels - pressure to secure friendships and exploit friendships' (5 / 49). Economics had further allowed itself unwittingly to be trapped by two contradictory trends. The first was to become impregnated with mathematics. To the extent that this contributed to the internationalizing of economic science, it was a

desirable development. But it had a more powerful tendency to restrict
the interests of economists to those things which could be measured,
and to turn their attention away from the most valuable aspects of human life. The other aspect of economics which had been strengthened
by the Keynesian revolution was to link economics even more closely
than before to existing political units, since Keynesian economics required not only governmental activity, but relied on statistics that were
collected on national bases (4 / 23).

All these factors contributed to the stultification of a civilization and
needed to be fought against. The existence of a free society could not
be assumed or taken for granted. It needed to be created, and once in
existence, steps needed to be taken to preserve it: 'humorous periodicals
characteristic of free societies - humour a desire for breaking rigidities
and keeping societies flexible' (5 / 81). As he put it in relation to his own
country in one of his most famous aphorisms, the 'social scientist in
Canada must have a sense of humour' (5 / 88).

This aspect of Innis's concern is also paralleled by a element he saw
and admired in Veblen. 'Like Adam Smith, [Veblen] is an individualist,
and like most individualists in continental countries, in which the industrial revolution made such rapid strides, he is in revolt against mass education and standardization.'[5] This fear of mass education and standardization returned again and again to haunt Innis. When he was sitting as a
member of the Manitoba Royal Commission on Adult Education, he
noted bitterly that adult education was 'a grinding down of large ideas
to suit men's minds - part of cramming system'. It had been generated
to fill the 'vacuum created by industrial revolution - designed to stop
socialism and competitor of socialism but both concerned with their
own type of poison' (5 / 88). And when he visited a France that by 1948
still had not fully recovered its strength after the ravages of the Second
World War, he warned against the threat 'of mass production of North
America to French culture and taste', and suggested that the future of
Europe depended on its capacity to evade 'strangulation by Anglo-
Saxon barbarism - especially North America - and by communism'
(16 / 50).

How then are we to understand Innis? First of all, we must accept
him as a liberal. For Innis, without doubt, the most important moral
fact was the value of the individual, and his Idea File is filled with observations which stem from Innis's concern to allow the individual to
lead a free and creative life. Because of this deep concern, Innis opposed
monopolies of knowledge both because they inhibited creativity and
also because, for the most part, they did not seek to develop fully the
human potential in the territories for which they were responsible.
Secondly, his liberalism led him to be hostile to fanaticism, whether
this was the fanaticism of the church, in the form of a demanding religious orthodoxy, or the fanaticism he found most dangerous in the

modern world, namely that of nationalism demanding a narrow, exclusivist intolerance based on ethnic or linguistic considerations. Innis's liberalism found a further expression in internationalism. He participated in the drafting of the 'Preliminary Draft of a World Constitution by the Committee to Frame a World Constitution' published by the University of Chicago Press in 1948. No one who reads his 1948 or 1951 travel notes on the United Kingdom and France can fail to observe his deep commitment to the values of European culture.

The reader of the slightly fewer than 1500 notes in this edition of the Idea File will have an easier time once he realizes that concern for the dignity and the freedom of the individual lies at the heart of almost every note. Although the range of Innis's interests was vast, and the collection of notes spans the whole period of recorded human history until Innis's death, the material is much more accessible if we remember that Innis's ordering principle was not a doctrine or a dogma, but a belief that it was not truth, but the search for truth that made men free (26 / 1) and that a university was a place where men had both a right and a duty not to make up their minds (5 / 105).

One final word about Innis. The reader of these notes cannot fail to come away with the thought that they have been fortunate to see something of the inner workings of the mind of the first social scientist of international repute who was a native son of Canada. But I think that they will be even more struck by the joy in thinking and speculation that informs this whole work. Innis, as I suggested earlier, had a sharp sense of humour, and although the jokes are sometimes obscure, and difficult to find, they are there in abundance. If, in many cases, the reader suspects that Innis had his tongue in his cheek, he is probably right.

Innis was a lucky man, and he continued working in the way he had chosen to spend his life almost right up to the end. I cannot help thinking that Innis had himself primarily in mind when he transcribed the following passage from Robert Louis Stevenson: 'If a man love the labour of any trade, apart from any question of success or fame, the gods have called him' (17 / 34). This Idea File is clear evidence that Harold Adams Innis was truly a man with such a vocation.

NOTES

1   References in this Foreword / Preface are to sections / notes in this edition.
2   'The Teaching of Economic History in Canada', in Mary Q. Innis ed. *Essays in Canadian Economic History* (Toronto 1956), 16
3   'Charles Norris Cochrane, 1889-1946', *Canadian Journal of Economics and Political Science*, vol. 12, 96f
4   Harold Innis, 'The Work of Thorstein Veblen,' *Essays in Canadian Economic History* (Toronto, 1956), 24, 25

A Note on the Text

Manuscript Collection #845, Innis Papers, Archives of the University of Toronto, Thomas Fisher Library, Box 8

The early history of the material that came to be called the Idea File is obscure. Innis's son, Donald, recalls that his father used to keep notes on card files, and that there were, at one point, about eighteen inches of white cards, with another five or so inches of white cards containing an index. This index, according to Donald Innis constituted 'a cross referencing system so that one idea might be referred to under several headings and vice-versa'. These cards appear to have been in manuscript. However, at some point or points, Innis had these notes typed on sheets of paper, and near the end of his life collected the typed notes into one collation which he numbered consequently from 1 to 339.

The cards themselves appear to be lost. It is possible that they still existed at Innis's death, for there is a second typed version of part of the Idea File. What might have happened is that in the process of preparing Innis's posthumous material for limited circulation, a typist began working from the cards; then, during the typing, the family discovered the typed version and stopped the retyping.

The typescript we possess was certainly used by Innis himself, and there are manuscript additions and corrections on it which demonstrate that he used it actively in preparing papers for subsequent delivery and publication.

After Innis's death, a committee was formed, consisting of Mrs Innis, his son Donald, and Professors Donald Creighton, W.T. Easterbrook, and S.D. Clark to supervise the collection of Innis's papers, and to decide which of these ought to be published. It was decided at the time, as S.D. Clark put it that: 'Given his cryptic style of writing, and his tendency to make great leaps in his thinking, there was clearly no way in which these notes could be prepared for publication. But there was much here too valuable to be lost completely.' Hence the committee had Mrs Jane Ward, for long Innis's assistant in the Department of Political Economy at Toronto, prepare a version for typing, and subsequently had it microfilmed for limited circulation. (This edition can be found in the University of Toronto Archives, Ms. Collection #77, Innis Papers, Box 25.)

This version did great violence to the text, since it reorganized the material under a series of alphabetical headings. The consequence of this reorganization was to lose completely any notion of the chronological span of the material, covering about eight years. In addition, notes encompassing a range of material were sometimes broken down and indexed under different headings, thus losing the force of the sweep of Innis's observations. Perhaps the most unsatisfactory aspect of this reorganization was the violation of the spirit of Innis's later work. He had noted in 1951 the 'Extent to which encyclopedia may tear knowledge apart and pigeon-hole it in alphabetical boxes - necessity of constantly attempting a synthesis to offset influence of mechanization - possibly basis for emphasis on civilization as a whole' (26 / 7).

If Mrs Ward's edition were unsatisfactory, then what was the best way to make this material available? There were three solutions considered.

First, it was possible to reorganize the material in broad topic headings under Innis's main areas of concern. This would allow people interested in one area of Innis's thought to contemplate that material with a minimum of trouble. But this advantage was also a disadvantage. After all, had not Innis been preoccupied with the dangers of specialization and struggled heroically, as the Idea File is witness, to avoid just such narrow concentration? As well, this method would lead either to the break up of notes, or else to considerable duplication of material. The concession to the needs that this form would satisfy is to be found here in the topical index. The inconvenience of using this index should serve as a warning to those tempted to do so. Print, as Innis taught, has its biases, and it is a matter of vital importance to our civilization to find ways of offsetting them.

The second form was to print the material as it stood in Innis's typescript. To have done so would have pleased a number of scholars who view authenticity as the paramount virtue in an edition. Indeed, when I thought that the material stood in relatively straightforward reverse chronological order (page 1 being the most recent and page 339 the earliest), I leaned in this direction. But Innis's editor at least has Innis to chide him and urge him on. As the first note in this version puts it: 'Thou shalt not worship any graven image - not interpreted to mean the printed word or those words themselves' (1 / 1). As well, I had Innis's own example of editing available, most clearly in *The Diary of Alexander James McPhail* (1940). There Innis had taken considerable liberties in reorganizing the material to make it more accessible. When I worked on the material in detail, I discovered that the last sections, rather than being the earliest, probably dated from 1949; I concluded that there was less to be said for this form of presentation. However, anyone wishing to reconstruct the order of the typescript can do so by consulting the accompanying table.

Section	Date	Typescript Pages	Section	Date	Typescript Pages
29	1951 / 1952	1-19 (1-19)	1	1944 or 1945	317-19
24	1950	20-31 (1-11)	2	1945	303-11
28	1951	32-54 (1-23)	3	1946	312-3; 314-6
27	1951	55-82 (1-28)	4	1946	292-5; 296; 297-8; 292-302
26	1950	83-93 (1-11)	5	1946	181-234 (para's #1-141)
17	1948	94-98	6	1946	164-80 (1-17)
15	1950	99-106	7	1946	242-55
21	1949 or 1950	107-111	8	1946	256-61
22	1949 or 1950	112-117	9	1946 / 1947	262-68
18	1949	118-30	10		269-71 (1-3)
16	1948	131-147	11	1946 / 1947	272-85 (1-15)
15	1947 / 1948	148-163	12		286-91
6	1946	164-80 (1-17)	13	1947	235-6
5	1946	181-234 (para's #1-141)	14		237-41 (1-5)
13	1947	235-6	15	1947 / 1948	148-63
14		237-41 (1-5)	16	1948	131-47
7	1946	242-55	17	1948	94-98
8	1946 / 1947	256-261	18	1949	118-30
9		262-268	19	1949	320-30
10		269-71 (1-3)	20		331/331-33
11	1946 / 1947	272-85 (1-15)	21	1949 or 1950	107-111
12		286-91	22	1950	112-117
4	1946	292-5; 296; 297-8; 299-302	23	1950	334-39 (1-6)
2	1945	303-311	24	1950	20-31 (1-11)
3	1946	312-3; 314-6	25	1950	99-106
1	1944 or 1945	317-19	26	1950	83-93 (1-11)
19	1949	320-330	27	1951	55-82 (1-28)
20		331/331-333	28	1951	32-54 (1-23)
23	1950	334-39 (1-6)	29	1951 / 1952	1-19 (1-19)

The third choice was to attempt to present the material in chronological order. The advantage of this form was that it would allow the reader to see development in Innis's ideas and concerns. However, and this is a very important reservation, the reader is warned that this chronological ordering is tentative at best. There are some clues such as internal dates, publication dates of books Innis used, and use of the material. Indeed some of the sections cannot be dated with any certainty at all. In the absence of more information about the original form of the notes, when they were typed and how they were assembled, the present arrangement must stand as one order among many, though I hope it is a broadly reliable one. Should I turn out to have been mistaken, then this edition will have to count as one among a mathematically very large number of possible random orderings, which, considering Innis's concerns over the last decade or so of his life might not be such a bad thing after all.

The section numbers and the note numbers are entirely my own creation, and are meant for ease of reference. Except for Section 5, in which Innis had numbered the paragraphs of material from 1-141, there is no way in the typescript to refer to individual notes. I have broken the material where there was a natural break in the text, and also in individual blocks of material where the material fairly clearly related to two distinct topics. However, where there was doubt, I left the material as it stood since, as any student of Innis knows, one of the hallmarks of his style was the discovery of relationships between phenomena which might not be otherwise obvious.

Some of the sections, namely 5, 6, 10, 11, 14, 23, 25, 26, 27, 28, and 29, were separately paginated by Innis, probably before he collected them all together. These sections have been kept. In other cases there is some sort of break in the typescript, either a blank space or a change in typewriter. However, sections 3 and 4 are both collections of relatively short sections in the text which could have been presented separately. Again, the table contains the detailed information about the relationship between the editor's sections and the pagination of the original typescript.

In addition, I have taken some liberties with minor matters in the text. Innis's punctuation was erratic, and I have attempted to impose some order, feeling free to replace dashes with periods and to capitalize words where the text warranted. I have silently corrected spelling mistakes and other typing errors, as well as attempting to standardize the use of capital letters in cases that I thought this did no damage to understanding. I have also added question marks where appropriate. Any other additions to the text have been made with square brackets. There have also been subtractions from the text, mostly in the form of references (e.g., Thompson, *Here I Lie*) which have been more fully identified and given in greater detail in a note. In one case I have eliminated a note that is entirely repetitive of an earlier note. And in two cases I have

deferred to reservations Mrs Innis expressed in a note she left in the
Innis Papers, and have eliminated the names of men still living.

One final word about Innis's ubiquitous 'i.e.' In some cases it does mean i.e.; in many others, e.g. And in some places it serves as a dash. Tempted though I was to change these, I have left them all as they stood, trusting that the reader will be able to sort them out easily after a little practice.

William Christian

University of Guelph

Acknowledgments

In the course of preparing an edition such as this, the editor acquires more debts than he can properly discharge. I would at least like to express the lineaments of my indebtedness as follows: First, to the Innis family, especially Donald, who have been friendly, co-operative, and helpful from the very beginning. Second, to the archivists at the University of Toronto Archives, especially to David Rudkin, the Chief Archivist, and to Mel Starkman. Third, to Peter Russell, sometime principal of Innis College, who originally suggested this project to me, and helped get it on its way, and to Art Wood, Assistant to the Principal at Innis and invaluable secretary to the Harold Innis Foundation, for his consistent co-operation and support. Fourth, to the Canada Council which was prompt and generous in its funding. Fifth, to Barbara Christian and Julie Beatty who helped with proofreading. And lastly, I must express my enormous gratitude to Blair Dimock who worked as my research assistant throughout most of the period that this edition was underway; and to Marty and Lorna Davis who did heroic work near the end, and also helped prepare the indexes. It would not have been completed without them. W.E.C.

The Idea File

1

By 1945 Innis had decided to resist the blandishments of the University of Chicago and to remain at Toronto. He was about to become Dean of the Graduate School, while retaining the headship of the Department of Political Economy. He was also to serve on a provincial and a dominion royal commission before his death in 1952. None the less he was dedicated to the proposition that the scholar's chief concern was with research and reflection. The notes that follow bear witness that he was faithful to his calling to the end of his life.

1   Thou shalt not worship any graven image - not interpreted to mean the printed word or those words themselves.

2   Sismondi, Saint-Simon and Simonians represented continental point of view and opposed classical orthodox tradition of economics in England.

3   Growth of Roman code reflected increasing power of lawyers, and of landholding aristocracy - decline of middle class - breakdown of municipal system, corruption in army and in civil service. Decline of trade - problem of taxing land - corruption in administration - lack of devices for effect of public opinion, absence of public debt.

4   Concept of Trinity important to development of philosophical discussion.

5   Significance of family to royalty - kings of France only one son to succeed for generations. Germany - emperors without heir leading to decentralization. England - place of women after Henry VIII.

6   Absolute ownership of Roman law failed to provide basis of expansion of possession of German law and of common law - essential to growth of economics and commerce.

7   Political science, economics, history expanded as result of demands of journalism. Conception incidental to corporate income tax, seen in growth of advertising accounts and reluctance of press to attack evil. Press reluctant to mention features needing reform yet detrimental to its interests.

8   How far clash of written language with oral creates symbolism? Cassirer claims Akkadian attempt to understand Sumerian written character led to understanding of meaning of abstract symbolism and discovery of symbolic algebra by Babylonians - was this also true of Greece and Mycenae, Rome and Etruscans, French and Normans?

9   Power of theocracy evident among Jews and ability to throw over kings reflected the Babylonian tradition. Writers and prophets weakened kings - Hebrew writing simpler than Egyptian and more effective against monarch.

10 How far element of disciplined force reflected by Normans in England and in Sicily became an element in destruction of power of papacy and reinforced power of law from Byzantine empire in growth of nationalism in Europe?

11 Tendency of publishers to advance money to writers who have something fresh and to direct their writing - development of plot and structure - evident in movies and adaptation of book - using book for advertising purposes. Process pushed to books - written with view to expected trend in interest and large sums advanced. Art tends to be moulded to suit demands of monopoly group and conforming of artist to taste a result of influence of fixed capital. Encroachment of commercial factor in direct fashion in production of artistic work - concern with wide sales. Canadian publishers flourish by discovering fresh writers on which large New York publishers able to feed. Schapiro of Maclean's magazine discovered by them and taken up by New York publisher.

12 Influence of press on religion - necessity for large capital makes for large-scale death rate and amalgamation or publication of diverse religious papers by same press. Ryerson Press handling *Canadian Baptist*. Pressure of secular interests. Attacks of religious press on J.G. Bennett for reporting annual gatherings an indication of resentment of secular encroachment. Purely religious papers generally fail - demand for variety of news by reader. Spectacular outburst of advertising by Robert Bonner - *Ledger* 1850s - recognized demand for fiction with emphasis of newspapers on news after telegraph - also exploited antiquated advertising system and able to sell paper on large scale. How far interest in fiction built up as result of lags in newspaper development incidental to concentration on news and communication? Income tax system permits exploitation of expense accounts by those publishing small comment sheets. John Atkins' small farm paper and Erie *Letter Review* charge very high prices and profitable because paid out of company expense accounts.

13 Dominance of church followed by dominance of lawyers in parliament. Break of American Revolution meant dominance of commercialism and public opinion.

14 Fictions developed in Roman law followed by fictions developed in church and growth of religious ceremonial.

15 Hierarchy of oral tradition developed with limited written tradition – elaborate ceremonial an indication of limited written tradition. Church ceremonial and university ceremonial to reflect influence of oral tradition. Gradual decline of influence of church in university compels latter to emphasize its own ceremonial as a device to preserve oral tradition. Weakness evident in influence of church, army, business – difficult for university to find a footing.

16 How far does celibacy involve intense interests of priests in active movements and division in church? Franciscans vs. Dominicans – activity in province of Quebec split between Montreal and Jesuits and Quebec and Dominicans.

17 Shift of external affairs to Wartime Prices and Trade Board – essence of work in arranging bilateral trade agreements – fats with Argentina in return for paper. Actual problem of negotiating of trade agreements handled by department of trade and commerce rather than department of external affairs.

18 Spread of printing in 19th century – compilations of historical material – calendars, etc. basis of positivism rather than reverse. Positivism mastery over small-scale problems and weakness in mastering large-scale problems.

NOTES

2 Jean Charles Lénard Simondé de Sismondi (1773-1842) was a Swiss historian and economist. The Comte de Saint-Simon (1760-1825) was a French philosopher and social scientist whose theories formed the basis of a powerful strain of French socialism.

8 Note on Ernst Cassirer, *An Essay on Man* (New Haven, 1944)

12 Probably note on A.B. Paine, *Thomas Nast: His Period and His Pictures* (New York, 1904). See also, 2 / 21, 31, 43; 4 / 11. Bennett (1795-1872) founded the New York *Herald* in 1835. For Bonner, see 2 / 23.

2

In 1945 Innis visited Russia as part of a contingent invited to celebrate the two hundred and twentieth anniversary of the Academy of Sciences. As usual when he travelled, Innis made detailed observations ('Russian Diary', Ms. Collection #45, Archives of the University of Toronto, Box 106).

1 Significance of geographic factor in language - technology tends to have impact first in frontier areas and to push inward to break up conservative factors. Oral tradition more powerful on frontier and penetrates press and newspaper which cuts under conservative elements - vulgar encroaches on vernacular and on learned language. Struggle between organized elements with vernacular, i.e. Latin and church with nationalism and vernacular - printing spreading from Germany as frontier. Printing essentially mass phenomenon beginning with Buddhism and spreading to Europe - significant to religion as a factor bringing together masses and political organization, i.e. Buddhism in contrast with Confucianism. Rise of Roman Catholic church with collapse of Roman Empire - reestablishment of rational, i.e. legal and political, organization to offset irrational dangers of religion. Problem of rationalism in difficulties of understanding and communication leading to outbreaks of irrationalism. Church tempered nationalism and facilitated free trade. Military factor strengthening or weakening political organization and influencing role of religion.

2 Significance of expansion of advertising after last war in emphasis of media on success stories and success media. News and stories adapted to sale of goods and general emphasis on mass consumption and spending. Belief in prosperity cult part of increased advertising - emphasis on better world and avoidance of problem.

3 Clash of languages with conquests may promote freedom, i.e. French and English in Canada, Dutch and English in early New York. Jury system a device for bringing administrative reforms without legislative aid, i.e. trials as to freedom of press. Legal advance of common law in courts may be ahead of legislatures - building up of prestige of lawyers - rise of legislatures reduce power of lawyers - parliament in a sense a revolu-

tion against legal caste as protestant reformation a revolution against ecclesiastical class.

4   American Revolution – clash between freedom of press in colonies and restriction in England, church in New France and press in colonies – weakness of class in colonies opened way to press. American Revolution changed attitude of public to point of loud insistence on freedom of press. Press made revolution basis for continued freedom – effectively sold public. How far American Revolution essentially a struggle for freedom of press? Press appealed to people and regarded by aristocracy with contempt – in itself it undermined authority of aristocracy and destroyed rigidity of class structure. Inability of politicians to appreciate danger of interfering with freedom of press – indignation over Alien and Sedition Laws defeated [President] John Adams and destroyed Federalist party – changing character of American politics – successive waves of incidental to technological change, i.e. American Revolution, destruction of federalists, party of good feelings destroyed with [Andrew] Jackson and newspaper interests, Civil War, and later wars. Revolutions in technology of communication bring political change. 'The printers can never leave us in a state of perfect rest and union of opinion' (Jefferson). Importance of intense political journalism – Weed, Greeley, Raymond in breaking up Republican party – place of journalists in politics made for divisiveness and activity. Newspapers active in starting Republican party 1854 – joining Free Soil and Whigs – destroyed Whig party – power of journalism.

5   University presidents giving each other degrees. A university not an institution designed to that end, or to give members of boards of governors degrees.

6   Too much made of Greek slavery and not enough of wage slavery under development of capitalism.

7   Significance of communication to development of new ideas – general lack of new ideas in U.S. associated with popularization of knowledge. Impact of European ideas – Darwin, Spencer – energy in diffusing ideas at neglect of originating them. Improved communication smothers ideas and restricts concentration and development of major ideas. Mechanization and sterility of knowledge.

8   Constantine in Council of Niceae [325 A.D.] made Christianity religion of conquerors. Europe christianized by Constantine rather than by Christ.

9   Troubadours (1071-1294) and ladies of Middle Ages developed concept of romantic love.

10 Trade essentially based on growth of cities and assumes break of ecclesiastical control and rise of state or struggle between ecclesiastical and state as basis of political liberty and in turn of trade. Political liberty – residuary legatee of ecclesiasticism.

11 Linking of hierarchy of church to that of business, i.e. Luce family using church to serve larger circulation among Catholics.

12 How far alphabet and its convenience facilitated constant linking up between spoken and written language in west in contrast with India and east? Consequently prevented long-term development of learned language and made for constant shifting of ideas in western world. Rise of abstract philosophy in Greece at expense of place of women and largely limited to men.

13 Enormous importance of news to American publishers and emphasis on lives of politicians. G.W. Childs, George Jones – former publishers became owners of *Public Ledger* and *New York Times.* Childs capitalized on Franklin tragedy in book by Kane. Raymond wrote life of Lincoln after assassination – emphasis on news brought enormous sales. Journalists wrote books – Greeley, Raymond, Bryant, Weed. Great emphasis on dictionaries and compilations – involving heavy outlays of capital and wide sales to schools and libraries. Lack of copyright arrangements meant very close relations between English and American firms. Collections of newspaper paragraphs by witty authors watched for by publishers and books brought out. American enterprise also republished essays of English authors – Macaulay's Essays for *Edinburgh Review*, also De Quincy and Thomas Hood from newspapers and periodicals. As in newspapers – family played large role in publishing industry – carried on in partnerships or by descendants. Large-scale printing industry – J.F. Trow, New York *City Directory*, 1852 – had published Leavitt and Trow and printed books for New York University, also Putnam and publishers – protection in favour of avoiding unused capacity. Scribners with no printing plant used plant of various printers, i.e. a sort of broker.

14 Books made widely accessible in U.S. through serial publications and enormous demand of large numbers of newspapers and market for written material – drew heavily on England and Europe – probably books more available to Americans than English.

15 Constant reference to crises in writings of social sciences a result of necessity of appealing to fear and influence of news appeal.

16 Probable difficulty of Europeans in writing on Anglo-Saxon world – weakened by failure to realize interrelation of economic and political development.

17   Place of learned class - universities to prevent domination of various
      groups - church, army, state - appreciation of necessity of limited
      power of groups.

18   Essential problem of commercialism in complete neglect of standards,
      i.e. lack of evaluation of headlines. Commercialism in advertising em-
      phasizing anything which attracts attention or news.

19   Ivory tower essential if universal point of view to be attained - necessity
      of resolving conflicts and contradictions.

20   Significance of economic theory of modern economy or extent to which
      conclusions become a basis of action and consequently making for
      more accurate prediction. Nature copying art.

21   One man, one vote produces monopoly of politics, i.e. machines of
      parties. More political monopoly than economic monopoly ([Frank]
      Knight). More losses than profits - indicating inability to secure effec-
      tive accounting system or proper appraisal by individuals of their own
      capacities.

22   Significance of distribution in publishing, i.e. dominance of printer fol-
      lowed by dominance of publisher in 18th and early 19th centuries and
      by dominance of writer after Dickens. Rise of sensational writing in
      fiction to meet demands of enormous numbers gave writer a new posi-
      tion. Instalment plan of producing and selling tapped lower-income
      groups particularly with monopoly conditions of three-volume novel.
      Monopoly of high price accentuated development of low price but new
      type of fiction (sensational Dickens) necessary to overcome monopoly
      element linked to class structure. Class structure accentuates disturb-
      ances in classes by making jerky development. Stage driven into novels
      of sensationalism of Dickens.

23   Fear and sensationalism devices driving literature to lower levels of read-
      ers. Enormous importance of newspapers to publishing in U.S. - political
      figures centre of authors' interest and of public. Bonner capitalized ad-
      vertising by advertising and using advertised names - concentrated on
      advertising paper - paid large amounts to Dickens, Fanny Fern, etc.
      Publishers watched for newspaper writers of promise. Sold material
      concerning political figures - advertised by newspapers in political strug-
      gles. School books of enormous significance to publishers - large market
      - concentration on small number of books - significance to homogeneity
      and uniformity of training - explains discipline of people and breaking
      down of particularism. Literature as opposed to writing imported from
      England to an important extent.

24 Significance of Jaeger in restoring significance of oral tradition after being overlaid by written tradition, poetry shifted to dialogue to lecture and prose and philosophy. From listening to reading, rise of authority of literature - Plato used Socrates as device to screen his position. Necessity of realizing importance of continued thought not acceptance of written authority. Image worship crept over civilization particularly with printing and influence of sacred word.

25 Cowan claims as result of Security Exchange Regulations speculation clamped down and market very unsteady - jumping back and forth in sudden fashion without long-term speculative support.

26 Toronto *Star* supported by [Sir William] Mulock and others but by 1911 Atkinson had bought majority of stock and refused to write any editorial on streetcar strike at Mulock's dictation - Mulock told he was no longer in control of paper.

27 Nova Scotia thought of Confederation as device for opening American markets whereas St Lawrence thought of it as protective device.

28 Newspapers attack patent medicines - also periodicals as device for weakening position of lower-grade newspapers and periodicals dependent on that type of advertising and increasing the possibilities of stronger papers dependent on higher brackets of income. Increasing circulation and demands of advertisers for income drove out patent medicine advertising.

29 Little Brown encouraged English publishers of standard works to dump on American market.

30 Repression of literature dangerous in making for accentuation of oral tradition. How far revolution a result of suppressing conservative written tradition and necessitating overemphasis on oral tradition? Written tradition unable to have its effects. Intense conservatism of written tradition - revolution necessary to drop letters of alphabet.

31 Greeley campaign of 1872 primarily a battle of caricatures - Nast opposing Greeley - cartoons reach lower levels, can be handled in weekly for wide circulation, more brutal and devastating and unforgettable and unretractable.

32 Significance of written word as basis of division in interpretation - Christianity - division of Communists - oral tradition always breaking down position of written by building up modifications.

33 Conflict between pressure of advertising toward savings in insurance
    salesmen - leading to increased investment and turning out of goods
    particularly those adapted to advertising. Consumer's goods advertising
    must pull off funds in competition with insurance advertising.

34 State regarded as instrument of oppression by European writers - Lenin
    to substitute worker for bourgeoisie - cessation of class oppression
    means disappearance of state. Place of state, i.e. tradition of Roman
    Law - patriarchal set-up - Lenin's *State and Revolution* [1917] -
    Lenin's influence in writing - undermining position of state. Theory of
    state essentially appeals to revolution or necessity of shifting violently
    to bring about change - role of authority of state - revolution setting
    up of new authority or device for bringing about gradual or more or less
    gradual change.

35 Significance of stereotypes, i.e. turn of Republican papers to support
    Cleveland or Butler injured *Times* and started *Sun* on downgrade. Break
    in goodwill built around politics facilitated penetration of Pulitzer with
    new tactics. Later break in goodwill centred around advertiser - Simp-
    sons in [Toronto] *Globe* during Price Spreads Commission [Royal Com-
    mission on Price Spreads, 1934-35].

36 Overwhelming importance of break between eastern and western empire
    - eastern empire saw continuation of alliance between church and state
    - Russia a second Rome for Greek Orthodox Church and centralization
    - probable source of fascism and totalitarianism in contrast with separa-
    tion of church and state in west.

37 End of exploitation of common man - death of Mussolini [28 April
    1945] and difficulties of Hitler and fascist leaders - by high command
    and centre of military power and force.

38 Difference between pre-literary and literary culture - anthropology as
    social science.

39 Russia absorbed traditions of Greek philosophical and metaphysical
    interests of eastern empire - Greek Catholic Church and relation to
    state - background of development of Russian novel - Tolstoi [Dostoiev-
    ski's], *Brothers Karamazov* (see chapter on Grand Inquisitor [Book V,
    Chapter 5]) - disturbance of concept of power as represented by Napoleon.
    Western Europe dominated by Roman Law - code and common law, to
    be redressed with rise of Russia or triumph of Greek over Roman -
    natural law concept developed by Romans as means of securing adapta-
    tion to force. Query how far a part of Russian tradition?

40 Improved methods of communications facilitate repetition and build up ideologies which become extremely difficult to break down - position of defence in knowledge strengthened at expense of attack - with resistant ideologies necessity of resort to force - irreconcilable minorities reinforced by new propaganda technique make possibilities of philosophical attack difficult - inability to secure common ground. Necessity of universities to withstand pressure from irreconcilable minorities. Small islands in rising sea of barbarism. Inquisition of religion followed by inquisition of nationalism.

41 Emphasis of writing and authority in Roman law in Europe - constant necessity for revolution to destroy position of patriarchy based on authority. Late penetration of writing and authority to England accentuated possibility of oral tradition - use of jury - common law, etc.

42 Problem of testing authority - tolerance - factors influencing extent to which authority tolerated - tendency of extension of communication weakening its position but offset by decline in rationality accompanying improved communication - inability of rationality or of thought to keep pace with communication and consequent entrenchment of authority and inability to offset appeal to irrational element at lower levels. Power of print to serve as opiate and strengthen position of authority. Price system and necessity of relying on personality or ability to get along with people. Power to keep organization running smoothly and make contacts essential to large-scale organization - implication to clubs, church, etc. and devices to bring people together, make contacts, news as advertising devices - emphasizing contributions to goodwill - charity, relief, etc.

43 Lack of international copyright gave New York and Harpers a tremendous advantage with access to European literature - led to enormous expansion - concentration on their own printing plant and dominance of magazine field with cheap serial material. Probably explained difficulties of Harpers after international copyright and ease with which Morgan and financial interests came to dominate - appointment of Harvey with journalistic background and failure to appreciate problems of books - indication of journalism and finance dominating books and publishing - though English literature widely diffused with absence of copyright. Interest of Harpers probably explains antagonism of Putnam to lack of international copyright.

44 Childs with money from publishing built up Philadelphia *Ledger* and becoming annoyed with comment of Dana in *Sun* bought presses for *World* under Pulitzer which helped to defeat *Sun* - but *Sun* continued whereas *World* came into difficulties. *Sun* had passed through family stage into tougher financial problem but *World* scarcely survived family stage.

45   Problem of goodwill in price system or of advertising to build up reputation of individuals in politics or business. Increasing importance of
administration means emphasis on factors other than price system –
getting names in news – belonging to organization – growth of organization incidental to interest in prestige, goodwill – managers of banks, etc.
Politicians constantly alert to importance of news as means of building
up prestige – necessity of speeches in House of Commons to impress
public. Reach public ear by extravagant statements – press seizes on
extravagant speeches to belittle speaker. Possibility that fanaticisms of
Christianity essential to stirring up western civilization and preventing
growth of monopoly of thought. Dangers of commerce in wearing off
edges and reducing stiffness of belief – essential to have sharp hard edges
to cut through civilization and keep it flexible. Made impossible dominance by any single group.

NOTES

4   Note on F.L. Mott, *Jefferson and the Press* (Baton Rouge, 1943). Thurlow Weed
      (1797-1882), Horace Greeley (1811-72), and H.J. Raymond (1820-69) were jour-
      nalists who were leading figures in both American national and New York state
      politics.

11   Henry Luce and his wife Claire Booth were leading figures in American publishing
      and politics.

13   Reference to E.K. Kane, *Arctic Explorations: the Second Grinnell Expedition in
      Search of Sir John Franklin, 1853, '54, '55* (Philadelphia, 1856)

21   Note on Frank Knight, *The Economic Order and Religion* (New York, 1945)

23   Probably note on Paine, *Thomas Nast* (see 1 / 12). Robert Bonner (1824-99) owned
      the *Ledger Monthly*. Fanny Fern (Sarah Payson Willis Parton, 1811-72) wrote for
      the *Ledger Monthly* from 1856 to 1872.

24   See Werner Jaeger, *Paideia: The Ideals of Greek Culture*, 3 vols. (Oxford, 1939)

25   Possibly Frederick William Cowan (1867-1949), a director of the Canadian Bank of
      Commerce in the mid 1940s.

31   Probably note on Paine, *Thomas Nast* (see 1 / 12)

35   B.F. Butler ran as the Greenback-Laborer candidate for the American presidency
      against Grover Cleveland in 1884.

38   Identified by Innis as a note on Green, *Philosophy of Art*. Possibly T.M. Greene,
      The Arts and the Art of Criticism (Princeton, 1947). If this reference were correct,
      then the section would have to be dated later.

43   Possibly note on W.F. Johnson, *George Harvey* (Boston, 1929)

44   Reading note not identified.

3

possibly 1946

1   Significance of boredom to constant change - resistance to sameness
    and demand for change, i.e. styles of women's dress - long cyclical
    change - Kroeber. Interest in cultural activity declined with political
    breakdown and period of writing down set in. Writing down in itself an
    indication of decline - Plato *Laws*. Advantage of varying languages in
    that only cream skimmed off in each culture, language and handed on
    to other culture, languages, but digestion of cream limited and borrow-
    ing limited - novels translated from French. Culture, language influenced
    by commercial considerations and difficulty of securing approach of
    universality. Divisiveness of Western Europe gives classical civilization
    an enormous advantage, i.e. influence of Greece and Rome. Cultural
    change in part a reflection of boredom.

2   Becker suggests philosophers of 18th century too sceptical and too
    credulous.

3   Constitution - the views at any time of five court justices in America.
    Constitution unwritten in sense that it emerges from divisions of
    Supreme Court.

4   Influence of climate of opinion on American writers - depression and
    war - Mumford, Becker, Knight - carried away by opinion in period of
    stress.

5   Wallas argues professions law, medicine, or church - trade union changed
    from prejudicial tendencies by pressure through parliament - impact of
    public opinion or oral tradition.

6   Aesthetic vs. theoretic cultures - Mexico is an illustration of aesthetic -
    St. Thomas - theoretic but science brings change - medieval synthesis
    upset by Newton, Galileo - Locke an attempt to provide new synthesis
    - theory of innate ideas - creating problems of philosophy, psychology.
    Positivists attempt to meet gap left by Locke - constant process of

correction - Locke makes for contradictory features by three terms -
Northrop favours two terms aesthetic and theoretic - opens gates between east and west - observer a third component to aesthetic and
theoretic - Northrop reduces these to two by eliminating observer. Kant
attempted to meet problem - led to German idealism and Russian communism attempts to correct this - Locke significant to United States.
Eastern civilization - aesthetic. Conflict and contradictory elements in
the west favour penetration of trade whereas Byzantine, Russian unitary
state restricts possibility of trade - constant struggle in west destroys all
ideas and gives enormous impetus to trade. Religious struggles in west
destroying fanatical element and facilitating growth of law and trade
but law too much influenced by language, mechanized knowledge and
opinion - east and west incompatible because errors of western philosophy make understanding of east impossible.

7   Power of university - restriction of court in 18th century accentuated
emphasis of printing on encyclopedia. Learning tends to follow force to
move to centres in which force able to protect it. Greece to Alexandria
- later to Rome and Constantinople then to Italy and France - and to
Holland and Germany to England and United States. Force to take advantage of opinion develops on fringes near to vernacular - science and
technology linked more effectively in marginal areas. Flowering in
period of migration - cultural peak within force areas moves to fringe
areas and leads to cultural authority.

8   Learned class in China parallels position of learned class in Europe but
latter less able to build up monopoly and adjustments easier. Importance of Chinese relative simplicity serving to link vast areas of varying
dialects - alternative attempt to make language known to all population
but adaptation involves breakdown in separate vernaculars. Rome unable
to teach all population and growth of learned class - encrustment of
dead languages. Spread of parliamentary system to Europe a reflection
of the power of the press to link written to oral and success dependent
on penetration of learning or breaking down of monopoly of learned
class.

9   How far lack of clear division between possession and ownership in
England necessitated building up of common law, jury and parliamentary systems?

10   Monasticism an escape from the state; sects an escape from monasticism
and state - fall of monasticism coinciding with rise of sects. Monopoly
of church on oral tradition, i.e. in preaching weakens position of theatre,
for example, in Middle Ages - writing introduces egoism, makes for
harsher criticism than possible in conversation. Printing again impersonal
and suited to combat.

11 Hall and Knight's *Algebra* [probably *Algebra for Beginners* (London, 1892)] by far the most profitable of Macmillan's books.

12 Adam Smith - savage attack on philosophy - attempt to clear away myths and to favour spread. of science and industry - concentrating on production of goods.

13 Building of learning and interest in learning in areas protected by force - with weakening of force scholars put forward greater effort and flowering develops at point before collapse, i.e. Greece, Byzantium - Minerva's owl.

14 Printing in new areas involves high costs of labour and overhead and emphasizes unused capacity and concentration on smaller works in vernacular. This involves emphasis on improvement in technology which begins to spread back to old areas where old methods entrenched. In new areas also development on new ideas, i.e. American revolution. Lutheran reformation - England escaped Roman law tradition because of lateness in spread of printing and strong oral tradition. Complexity of Chinese alphabet gave power to class in whose hands writing concentrated. U.S. escaped book tradition.

15 Significance of oral tradition on outer edges of written, i.e. England common law. Oral tradition without records - written tradition an attempt to stake out areas which give stability - collective bargaining. Written tradition implies rigidity, conservatism, inhumanity of humanists. History of Europe - swing between Hebrew tradition and written scriptures in contrast with Greek oral tradition. Rise of universities meant struggle between them reflected in influence of geography and vernacular. Conversation - oral tradition, also common law. How far France never lost colony through revolt? Common law - jury system, parliament.

16 Patriarchal system persisted in Greek civilization, i.e. in Greek orthodox church, whereas celibacy tended to flourish in Roman law countries or in which individual separated from family by Roman law. This facilitated spread of Roman church and of celibacy and explained wiping out of celibacy in England. Dead languages created during periods in which media of communication limited. Limited media implies small group of scholars and learned language, or dead language becomes separated from vernacular with increase in media, vernacular becomes important and dead languages tend to retreat.

17 Printing creates powerful assumption of truth and facilitates building up of and elaboration to point of absolute truth - directs mental energy to points in which accumulations of manuscript largest. Becomes device for checking spread of scepticism.

1   Reference to A.L. Kroeber, author of *Configurations of Cultural Growth* (Berkley, 1946)

2   Note on Carl Becker, *The Heavenly City of the Eighteenth Century Philosophers* (New Haven, Conn., 1932)

5   Note on Graham Wallas, *Our Social Heritage* (New Haven, Conn., 1921), a revision of the Dodge lectures at Yale, 1919

6   Note on F.S.C. Northrop, *The Meeting of East and West* (New York, 1946)

4

probably 1946

1   Most forward-looking people have their heads turned sideways.

2   Drama reflected power of oral tradition reduced to writing and in turn
     makes advance exceedingly difficult - only achieved at greatest heights
     of oral tradition and written down becomes exceedingly difficult to
     surpass. Milton turned to epic poetry and prose as democratic in con-
     trast with court and drama. Literature and scholarship, according to
     [Samuel] Johnson designed to level all ranks - to build up tradition of
     escape from church, and law and state, e.g. [H.G.] Wells seized an es-
     cape via science - attack on royalty and Roman Catholic Church.
     Publishers support development along new lines but difficult to main-
     tain position.

3   Rise of publisher in seventeenth and eighteenth centuries emphasized
     importance of profit and search for markets and cutting off of pecuni-
     ary from technology, i.e. printer - drive of price system on literature
     with evident appeal becomes increasingly powerful.

4   Split between eastern and western empires - Greek and Latin, state and
     church - accentuated importance of Arabs and Mohammedans - weak-
     ened power of political and ecclesiastical organization - law bridged gap
     between state and church - strengthened position of state or growth of
     empire.

5   Importance of catchwords in describing period - normalcy, etc. Genius of
     journalist in touching off word or of politician - nature copies art.

6   [H.G.] Wells - illustration of danger from tremendous interest in reform
     and application of science following writing of novels - especially after
     Outline of History [1921]. Became in consequence extremely pessimis-
     tic in old age - notably in last book [*Mind at the end of its Tether* (Lon-
     don, 1945)]. Realization of relative ineffectiveness of attempts to influ-
     ence public opinion. Tragedy of puritanical liberalism and belief in

power of writing - and effects of demands of printing press. Attacks on Roman Catholic Church and on royalty - struggle between book and scriptures, or science and scriptures, in contrast with struggle between church and scriptures.

7   Expansion of coal industry latter part of 16th century and 17th century 1581 to 1680 - basis of English position at beginning of eighteenth century. Coal used to produce salt - attempt to build up salt industry under Stuarts.

8   In assuming men act from near rather than remote ends and prefer the present to the remote it becomes difficult to secure rational decisions with communication changes making for relative changes in remoteness over varying periods of time.

9   Political theory and economic theory a struggle illustrating and illuminating liquidity preference - more important liquidity preference the more important movements of trade and greater significance of equilibrium.

10   Size of paper implications similar to size of book - produced at certain size meant printing sufficient to fill it and selling it in various forms.

11   Break up of local party domination in Richmond, Washington and Albany with newspapers with rise of fast press in metropolitan centres destroyed single governing authority and brought civil war. Necessary to recreate a central authority dominated by military - only resistance in press - significance of Greeley campaign 1872 - Wright, professor of physiology at Melbourne, commenting on ill informed character of British people - newspapers reduced to four sheets - sports, advertisements, rapes and murders and little possibility of news on international problems - consequently rumours and suspicion - particularly as to role of U.S.

12   Vancouver *Province* lost seriously to *Sun* as result of strike. Edmonton *Journal* helped *Bulletin* formerly in bad shape as result of joining between papers during strike. Also *Tribune* and *Free Press* - latter reaching twice circulation of former and regarded as breaking point for papers.

13   French defence - fur trade linked to forts - neglected transportation - roads on St Lawrence - as contrasted with English attack and dependence on navy and in turn on trade - canals, railways. Emphasis on fortifications made for decentralized and military government. English - railways and canals made for centralization and responsible government.

14   Advertising - influence on climate of opinion - new era - always good news - Hoover normalcy recession.

15   Rapid extension of communication means improved devices for getting down to lower classes or of getting up from lower classes - constant churning of language - implies capacity to develop effective propaganda. Problem of Germany having never developed effective propaganda with control over newspapers and limited flexibility of language - military success offset by propaganda. Russia effective in propaganda as essentially in oral tradition. French bureaucratic development in New France taken over by British governors bringing out hangers-on and placing them in civil service - Ottawa or elsewhere. Responsible government essentially a struggle for jobs for native-born - still not achieved in Ottawa for French Canadians.

16   Common law courts - independence of common law broke attempt of Stuarts to centralize monarchy. Roman law brought into England to support monarchy resisted by common law jurists and parliament - checked crown prerogative. How far conquest of England meant elasticity admitting of types of government, i.e. acceptance of Stuarts (James I) from Scotland or Dutch (William of Orange) or Hanoverian? Capacity to absorb foreign influence and yet to maintain independence.

17   Interest in antiquity in renaissance a device to undermine power of papacy and position of scholasticism based on Aristotle. Provided ammunition with which to break down place of church in first stream of renaissance and with emphasis on Bible after discovery of printing a means of providing an escape from church by way of religion.

18   Frankfurt Fair in late fifteenth century and early sixteenth century offset restrictions of University of Paris by providing market for books but counterreformation compelled migration from Frankfurt to Leipzig and emphasis on Protestant rather than Catholic literature - Germany became a book culture.

19   Cremation and baths assume greater freedom from epidemics. Middle Ages interest in body and spread of disease means greater interest in hereafter and elaboration of religious ceremony. Greater influence of death, greater neglect of life and concern with hereafter - vicious circle. How far concentration on ceremonial and relation to births, deaths, and marriages a result of emphasis on individual and family and destruction of city state and empire? Emphasis on individual used by church to combat state - but Roman law enables state to seize on individual to support state. Inquisition and principle of holding individual responsible. Conditions under which individual able to feel free of domination imply

struggle between large groups or several small groups. Systematic weeding out of population during Middle Ages provided a basis of stamina
which responded with amazing rapidity to the influence of hygiene improvement after 1800. Expansion of population a reflection of the
influence of a drastically selective process of epidemics and plagues in
the Middle Ages and a sudden release of this influence.

20   Significance of cremation – probably involves emphasis on poetry and
types of expression other than by tombstones. Sarcophagus implies
position of family and individual as does tombstone in contrast with
state. Cremation involves reliance on poetry or devices to perpetuate
names of heroes – patronage of courts – public monuments emphasizing
abstract idea. Without cremation tombs used as centres of interest –
Lenin, etc. – trade in relics – pilgrimages, shrines, miracles – spread of
plague and epidemics – age of faith the age of diet. Enormous advantage
of Greeks in use of cremation in contrast with Egyptians worship of
kings – pyramids – Greeks cut relations with dead and culture not cluttered with monuments, protests against elaborate funerals. Death used
to perpetuate individual family – exploited by church – seizing on uni-
versals – also in reckoning of time. Christian year independent of state –
insists on broader base of reckoning – states maintain separate reckoning
in terms of date of celebration of ruling authority. Religion facilitates
cutting across national boundaries – law apt to be bound to state and to
differentiate and reflect interest of force in political boundaries. Worship
of cultural past – learning may provide basis of common appeal – possible check to religion, i.e. philosophical approach – also to law or may be
used to reinforce them. City state in Italy a strength of municipal development provided ground for absorption of printing whereas place of
university – copying, etc. – in Paris checked its expansion – accentuated
religious differences between France and adjoining countries. Press in
U.S. as against press in England – developments on margin. Plan to emphasize U.S. as marginal development – machine industry approached from outside – monopoly of knowledge compels development of external character.

21   Conscription destroyed Liberal party in Ontario with [Premier Mitch]
Hepburn's opposition to [Prime Minister W.L.M.] King and necessity of
attempting to secure Conservative votes. In Quebec Liberal party dam-
aged in provincial field but dominion-provincial relations imply voters in
Quebec and Ontario support national Liberals though supporting provincial Conservatives through feeling necessity of having strong opposition
as protection to bureaucracy.

22   Mathematics and music able to cross linguistic frontiers – science to a
lesser extent with military secrets – social sciences assume cultural background and cross with difficulty though impregnation with mathematics

may facilitate wider dissemination - Walras, Pareto, Jevons. Keynesian economics restricted because of link to administrative and national system.

23   Importance of telegraph in Europe compared to telephone in the United States - a variety of languages emphasizes resort to the telegraph and to the Morse Code as an international device to transcend language. Large English-speaking population in North America facilitates spread of telephone with little problem of language variations. Newspapers in England in provinces insisted on government control of telegraph, and becoming entrenched in telegraph and advertising, opposed radio as possible encroachment which brought government ownership of B.B.C. whereas insistence on freedom of speech in U.S. facilitated spread of broadcasting under private control supported by telegraph and telephone.

24   The church in counter-reformation tore Germany into fragments - or rather the printing of the Bible and Luther left a number of despotic principalities just as the publication of the Encyclopedia in France became dynamic which tore France into shreds in the revolution. Encyclopedia in France took place of Bible in England but emphasized scholar rather than sacred tradition. Attempt to restore culture meant separation from political life in music and invisible republic of letters.

25   [Auguste] Comte (1) theological - external causes
                    (2) metaphysical - assumed abstractions
                            - causes, entities
                    (3) positive - emphasis on facts doing away with causes and consolidation of time and space

26   [Oliver Wendell] Holmes - background of interest in common law - oral tradition - refusal to be bound by black letters - common law is experience. Emphasized rule of opinion expressed through decisions of legislatures.

27   Christianity sponsors fanatical interest in missions - in contrast to sense of balance of Greeks or classical civilization. Admirably adapted to economic activity with emphasis on specialization in over-emphasis on economics - inability to realize necessity of limitations - fanatical interest incidental to specialization - division of labour, industrialism.

28   Japanese and Chinese require long period of elementary instruction to master written characters and hence drain on intellectual energy in education - fondness for English and German explained by difficulties of own language, particularly in science - lack of flexibility. Eyesight of Japanese notoriously bad.

29   Printing industry - lack of scientific cost system until after 1900 -
heavy overhead - constant demand for filler to use up unused capacity -
this in turn drives down prices. Tremendous pressure to specialize and
keep monopoly of specialized product - possible to emphasize quality
with enormous number of variabilities. Tremendous importance of good
relations with employees if standard of production to be maintained
and striking success of skilled labour in securing improved conditions.
Use of book to advertise firm and suggesting schemes for keeping up
prices - prestige advertising, ink, etc. Paper firms come into possession
of printing plants result of price cutting - former also concerned with
quantity production and unused capacity. Business school histories part
of prestige advertising - histories of firms.

30   Hospital - enormous administration and use of hierarchy. Efficiency of
public ward as compared with semi-private or private. Constant interest
of large number of nurses, orderlies and doctors - testing of blood.
Young men in charge as interns means application of advanced knowledge but perhaps lack of experience - offset by position of senior doctors. Implications of new developments - penicillin probably means
larger number come to hospital for treatment and leave in shorter time
- increased numbers of patients and more rapid turnover. Extension of
hospital facilities by inventions - problem of adjustment to demands for
capital - size of building - character of illness and treatment. Tremendous significance of medical profession - Hippocrates - influence on
Socrates. Interest in observation - long training involving in particular
skill of hands as well as book learning - importance of professional
ethics - training in handling people after long years of discipline - contrast social sciences and talk of handling people in personnel management - little knowledge of technical skill - little professional ethics or
etiquette. Danger of loading medical profession with social welfare
work but importance of handling social welfare with professional background of medicine. Enormous importance of training to character
shown in nurses and doctors - ability to handle people and to dominate
situations and emergencies. Problem of keeping medical profession free
of political control.

31   Roman interest in precise ceremonial carried even into Roman Catholic
Church. Strategic place of Roman centurion in charge of 100 men -
sort of sergeant-major but influenced by bribery from men - problem
of corruption in standing professional army - similar to problem of
socialist state - interest in beating the government - reluctance to accept intermediary of price system - serves as buffer - buffer tends to
disappear with state ownership. Romans not effective in cavalry shown
in Punic war - depended on mercenaries for cavalry - Caesar using
cavalry raised in Gaul - ultimate problem with increasingly effective
use of cavalry by barbarians.

32   Interpretation of various civilizations in relation to dominant element -
Rome place of army - Middle Ages of church - modern period finance.

NOTES

7   Note on John U. Nef, *The Rise of the British Coal Industry*, 2 vols. (London, 1932)
11   Probably note on Paine, *Thomas Nast.* See 1 / 12.
16   Note on E.F. Heckscher, *Mercantilism*, trans. M. Schapiro (New York, 1935)
29   Note on C. Francis, *Printing for Profit* (New York, 1917)

5

In 1946 the Royal Society of Canada elected Innis as its President. He also served on the Manitoba Royal Commission on Adult Education, the Chairman of which was Dr A.E. Trueman, then President of the University of Manitoba.

1   Significance of conversation as nearness to reality shown in power of Socrates and Christ – neither of whom apparently wrote anything. But philosophical development from Socrates apparently served to check fanaticism of Christianity or of Hebrew. Division between east and west – Latin and Greek – sterility of west in Middle Ages – fertilized by recovery of Greek in Renaissance and emphasis on importance of individual. In Byzantine civilization state dominant over church and latter more democratic in councils unless made part of hierarchy. Return of Russian influence may mean second Renaissance – compelling of west to recognize narrowness of its base. How far church in east able to temper influence of Asia? Importance of literature – Tolstoi in east.

2   Dangers of inflation lead to activity in building. American capital attracted to Mexico and South American countries to participate in building activities – also South American capital interested in building as a hedge. Problems of price system and government bureaucracy in necessity of determining policies – involves clash in personalities or devices to prevent clashes. Promotions in universities and ecclesiastical hierarchies without use of impersonal force of market or price system – difficulty of preventing nepotism, family influence. Price system tones down fanaticism –in avoidance of religion by financial journals, radio – constant watch of editors for possible offence. Query whether development of headline by wars responsible for improvement of advertising typography – suggests wars with emphasis on news or catastrophes improves headlines and widens circulation in interest of advertisers.

3   Role of oral tradition in church in Middle Ages emphasized with Latin but unable to meet impact of printing and emphasis on democratization. How far limitations of Greek state due to oral tradition and implied necessity of reliance on force? Development of written tradition and carrying over by Rome meant limitation of speculative activity and

emphasis on law and organization. How far rise of commerce, i.e. trade, in relation to media of communications brought decline of hierarchies in church and state? Use of paper meant weakening of authority and growth of commerce - printing at first largely concerned with hierarchies. Writing essential to imperial organization in keeping of records particularly public finance - may temper necessity of force. How far written traditions necessitated decline of polytheism, i.e. prose and philosophy, and monotheism growth of a central authority?

4   Constant pressure on savings of insurance men leads to pressure on supply of funds and lowers interest rate. How far insurance can go with steadily lowering interest rates - pressing on its own supply and requiring more saving to meet needs of life and saving features? Government using demand for funds to soak up insurance funds and keeping up insurance rates accentuates its influence on increased saving.

5   Vicarious interest in royalty in U.S., i.e. great interest in Hollywood movie actors - built up to take place of picturesqueness of royalty. Titles replaced by building up veneration for great leaders and figures - adaptability to advertising. Roman Catholic Church attempting to exploit movies - cardinals and pope, etc. - appointment of cardinals from Canada and United States.

6   Revolt of individual against state - in refusal to rear children to be killed in slaughter of war. [Gunnar] Myrdal a Swede with little appreciation of fear of war.

7   Problem of advance of physical sciences - use of inorganic material - inventions conflicting with relatively slow change of biological phenomenon - social institutions in part biological or result of inability of biological phenomenon to adapt itself to change incidental to inorganic materials. Break between biological adaptation and inorganic sciences.

8   Possibility of altering institutions in short period - Mohammedans with polygamy took wives of conquered and second generation entirely Mohammedan (B. Kidd). Ancestor worship adapted to military efficiency, social efficiency, or effectiveness of group to survive in competition with other groups. Powerful sanctions for conduct - Christianity and consideration of future gave basis for church - so strong as to weaken state. Modern western period - release from autocracy of church and growth of altruism and political emancipation.

9   Weakening of belief in immortality with strange wills calculated to keep interest in public people who have died, i.e. Miller will and Foster will. Canadian papers disregard item which might be regarded as news until

picked up by American medium. *Time* carried article - Brebner report -
immediately Canadian papers picked it up.

10   Substitution of newspaper and mechanical reproduction of works, i.e.
      radio for orators implies entirely new strategy or emphasis on tactics, on
      strategy - military element in political game - possibility of mobilized
      opinion - concentrating on certain areas, i.e. New York in presidential
      elections - Gallup poll indicates points at which strategic operations can
      be undertaken.

11   Learned languages, i.e. Latin or Greek. Latin culture serves as sort of
      poison preventing growth of human spirit or becomes part of disciplin-
      ing force, i.e. militarism in strengthening upper classes or aristocracy.
      Confusion of borrowing from earlier culture probably necessitates dis-
      ciplining force or dependence on armed force. Weakening of armed
      force - break up of Roman empire gives language of learned class cen-
      tring around law and rhetoric a peculiar position - supporting church or
      spiritual force. Argument of Jesuits restricting power of sovereign or
      state in favour of people or church. Development of Jesuits' argument
      led to contract theory and growth of liberalism. Distrust of both church
      and state (Lecky). Rise of trade and commerce - belief in tangible com-
      modities - undermining belief in intangible or spiritual, miraculous.
      Trade or industry involve rationalist scientific approach.

12   Constant pouring out of words by printing industry and bewilderment
      created through inability to break through them. A steady cumulative
      pressure on modern mind - unable to resist influence of Greek civiliza-
      tion which wrote on a fresh slate but with such force that marks never
      erased. Use of writing to restrain in Middle Ages by church - eventually
      writing restrains itself or rather rapid expansion of printing meant pro-
      duction of poison on large scale without necessity of checking it. Free-
      dom of press follows discovery that press a powerful opiate.

13   [Roscoe] Pound - law influenced 12th to 16th century by authority,
      17th to 18th century by philosophy - natural law daze - 19th century -
      history. Pound emphasizes jurisprudence as engineering.

14   Roman Republic - Cicero dependent on Greek literature - importance
      of political oratory. With Empire political oratory declined. Latin clas-
      sics replaced Greek - emphasis on rhetoric. Taken over by Christian
      schools. General neglect of upper schools by state and replacing of
      philosophy of Greeks by jurisprudence. Empire meant legal develop-
      ment and rhetoric as did restriction of political oratory.

15 Papyrus - philosophy; parchment - rhetoric. Decline of Greek through bad teaching meant split of east from west. Rhetoric exercised powerful influence on writing of history and made it subordinate to state - panegyric, etc. Rhetoric a reflection of continued importance of speech but neglect of search for truth. Significance to teaching of languages and division. Latin displaced Greek and unable to assimilate Greek contributions. Latin in turn displaced by vernacular - power of mother tongue potent factor restricting transmission of cultural contributions of learned languages.

16 Implication of idea and belief in idea, i.e. Schumpeter - factors determining monopoly position of idea and factors leading to breakdown of monopoly - necessity of new ideas in capitalism and avoiding belief in single idea or monopoly - rate of production of new ideas as against socialism. How far state education a systematic bonus to extend literacy and facilitating migration from lower to upper classes or how far a device for keeping whole rigid and strengthening class structure at top?

17 Slowness of girls schools in England meant great emphasis by women on schools and circulating libraries, and gave latter tyranny over moral fiction. Rise of girls schools meant girls stories of schools, magazines and weakening of position of circulating library.

18 Trade in rags for paper significant to modern civilization - abundance of linen rags in Italy facilitated paper industry - imports of rags from north in France and Spain - encouragement of collection of rags in new areas - attempts to check exports of rags in order to encourage manufacture of paper. Emphasis on paper in France and restriction of printing favoured Holland and Geneva. Holland developed paper industry which attracted rags from Italy - also English paper industry attracted rags from Europe. Capacity to take advantage of illiteracy in areas subject to church - poverty of nations contrasted with wealth of nations - implying abundance of rags and export to more intensively commercial areas. Commercial activity a powerful factor in demand and manufacture of paper. In France later 18th century restrictions on literature accompanied by market for wallpaper - also sold in U.S. Migration of rags from south to woollen areas - probably concentration on wool in England handicapped development of paper industry dependent on linen. But repression by church and state in Roman Catholic countries favoured export of rags and paper to literate countries.

19 Significance of military control in opening way for cultural diffusion - in Rome for Greek thought and Christianity. Importance of post-war

periods shown in sense of relief from fear of death and willingness to face any other fear as less dangerous. Freshness, originality, boldness, i.e. brilliance of 17th century England - especially execution of Charles I. Belief in capacity to accomplish a fresh approach and to defy authority. Marvellous release of energy with emphasis on individual. Significance of pressure of state education in providing readers and demand for writers, i.e. character of subvention in disturbing equilibrium of country.

20   Significance of constant change in capitalist society - compels administration to keep constantly on alert to protect themselves against and to take advantage of any particular change. Compels individuals on large scale to take active interest in business - avoids routine of administration, i.e. church, university, or institutions flooded with inefficient routine, i.e. government.

21   Problem of printing in perpetuating past achievements and strengthening necessity of imitation. Politicians' references to Bible and Shakespeare - an indication of the prevailing influence of 16th and early 17th century and of lack of interest in them. Maugham arguing that style of King James version created problem of English prose. Shaw - Irish and not poisoned by English views - complaint of pernicious influence of Shakespeare. Poisonous virus - drama short-lived - no later English development. Overwhelming importance of mandarin style - strengthens position of class - significance of conservatism of spelling to English - journalism destroyed influence of written language. Machine industry and industrial revolution gives tighter grip of nationalism over individual - no significant literature in western world since 1870 - necessity of aiming at advertiser's level - writing harnessed to enormous problem of selling goods. Power to build up sustained thought - dependence of philosophy on prose largely lost. Problem of schools of journalism to develop inoculation.

22   Enormous usefulness of price system as an impersonal factor - competitive examinations a partial check, i.e. in China - without check terrific pressure - personal patronage, charge of unfairness, family nepotism - hierarchy built on personal force and aggressiveness. Politicians generally a stop-gap to prevent the introduction of their own ideas. Appealed to electorate on general principles and compelled to recognize details and carry on in face of electoral demands.

23   Enormous significance of a speaking population - institutions adapted in relation to oratory - dialogue. Writing population or reading popula-

24 Political importance of newspapers - men make their own news and dominate them to keep public in hand. King on atomic bomb. Necessity of stressing continuous political and legal change as device for dominating news. Also liability of burghers for city debt strengthened position compared with princes, i.e. Florence and Italian cities - weakness of feudalism - significance of republics, i.e. Netherlands, providing basis for public debt - relation to military demands. Condottieri more expense [more expensive than building] walls. Rise of exchanges, development of opinion. Sale of indulgences not adequate to finance large undertakings of modern war - form of tax which could be easily overdone. Growth of market opinion - rise of price structure - Lyons, Antwerp, Amsterdam organization of news services as basis of opinion. Shift from political and ecclesiastical hierarchies - rise of state as instrument of credit. Role of Netherlands as republic in contrast with monarchies. Impersonal method of appointments of price system compared with competitive examinations, nepotism, etc.

25 Russia builds up resistant political organization pressing communities along the edge into national units - Greeks, Chinese, etc. - squeezing from Russia brings hardening of structure for defence.

26 Effect of tariffs and regional buying, i.e. no liquors in Evanston - giving new importance to commodities. Can touch commodities only on certain conditions - curious religious sanctity being attached to commodities - developing conditions of monopoly due to tariff, etc. Commodities given religious significance.

27 Tyranny of erudition - characteristic of American scholars - necessity of creating impression by knowledge - neglect of human relations with students in order to impress by knowledge. Defence against anaesthetic effect of democracy or appeal to newspapers - inevitable result in dullness and solidity.

28 Buddhism appeal to masses and existence of masses basis of development of printing, i.e. printing essentially a mass product carried from Asia or Buddhism to Europe. Writing at base of prose and philosophy. Buddhism after 845 [A.D.] pressed into lower classes and probably block printing hastened - leading to expansion to west. Conflict between Confucianism of classes and Buddhism of masses pushed latter to west, and east in Japan.

29   MacIver suggests that improved community facilitates possibility of dis-
        covering likeness among individuals and of forming associations.

30   Did old testament make headway in Roman Empire as having prose tra-
        dition when poetry tradition on decline in Graeco-Roman civilization?
        Did it make headway against, or parallel, prose of philosophy, and rhet-
        oric and New Testament? Did alphabet admit of poetry for Greeks
        whereas Egyptian and Palestine writing favoured prose particularly as
        dominated by hierarchy? Poetry reflected feudal tradition. Hierarchy
        favoured prose in Egyptian and Semitic alphabet but philosophy fav-
        oured prose in Greek alphabet.

31   *Chicago Tribune* emphasizes editorials as news – by consistently annoy-
        ing readers and compelling them to read editorials – gives them place as
        news completely subject to views of owners. Effect of movies on books
        – apparently more books sold up to time of appearance of movie but
        after appearance of movie sales fall off sharply – people no longer inter-
        ested.

32   How far [A.L.] Kroeber's approach sound in regarding religions as con-
        taminating influence in cultural activity – suggests that strong religious
        interest accompanies cultural deterioration? How far religious activity
        or organization assumes isolation of language at expense of vernacular
        and drains off intellectual resources to prevent cultural growth or how
        far religious activity a cleansing process burning off less desirable ele-
        ments but with tolerance allowing individual to escape and develop
        other interests?

33   Civilization – a struggle between those who know their limitations and
        those who do not. Adult education appealing to those with limited
        training in large numbers becomes advertising on a large scale – shift of
        interest of large organizations to development of goodwill destroys line
        between education and advertising. Pool elevators, etc. Advertising as-
        sumes appeals by visual education and other devices to large numbers of
        relatively illiterate – adult education becomes competitive to a large ex-
        tent with advertisers.

34   Liquidity preference principle evident in shift of control from industrial-
        ists to bankers – described by W.A. White about 1900. Also evident in
        emphasis of life insurance agents on savings – necessity of other types of
        advertising to offset effects of insurance agents or to offset tendency to-
        ward liquidity preference. Advertising of commodities uses wide variety
        of devices to increase consumption and to force down effects of savings.
        Avidity preference, i.e. emphasis on sale of goods in advertising, leads to
        extension of pulp and paper plants and development of power sites.

35   French Canadian insistent on language as conveyance of precise expression of religion and fearful that change in language means deterioration of religious ideas. Religion and language reinforce each other.

36   Provincial parties hampered in federal field - compelled to undertake measures in provinces unacceptable to other parts of Dominion - Social Credit, C.C.F. Adult education reaching lower levels of intelligence and concentrating on territory attacked by advertisers, newspapers, radio, films, etc. Films emphasizing goodwill engaged in adult education.

37   Significance of language as basis of continuity of thought - mathematics of Newton basis of interest in natural order and deism of 18th century. Working over language leads to development of philosophical systems or of great literature - provides anchorage for continuity. Use of scriptures to provide continuity - breakdown with bombardment of words. Breakdown of cultural strength implies reliance on force. Significance of law as centre of professional group concentrating on legal problems.

38   Slow extension of information about internal affairs of newspaper, i.e. knowledge of G.V. Ferguson resignation extended by conversation - to interest of paper to suppress information and other papers recognize courtesy of suppression. Power of politicians over journalism partly a result of the weakness of journalistic training - W.A. White captivated by Roosevelt. Advertising an intensive development of image creation - newspaper, radio, particularly film, magazine. Tends to displace images or to utilize experience with images developed by church. Competition between creation of images of commercial products and images incidental to religion. Cooperation - a device to combine religion and commerce.

39   Danger of another world war history to facilitate conducting of another world war.

40   What happens to agriculture in full employment?

41   Very much a library job - competent workmen but not geniuses. Shotwell experience.

42   Importance of Brebner report.

43   Useful work on history of civilization. Kroeber and Toynbee. Kroeber's comment on disintegration of civilization. Necessity of concentrating on work done in classical field - generally neglected.

44   Jews - avoiding images and concentrating on abstract, i.e. law, opened way for penetration beyond blood relationship to universal - empha-

sized ethical standards – enabled prophet to check tendency to absolute power on part of king. Persians, Empire, Zoroastrian good and evil, immortality – appeared among Jews after captivity. Power of Covenant god and lack of idea of immortality emphasized atonement. Christian religion developed by church used atonement (fall of Man) and immortality to develop its position. Greeks shifted from several gods to philosophy or poetry to prose – approached universal from philosophic rather than religious but not adequate to resist spread of religion and empire traditions – rhetoric and law in Rome.

45   How far assemblies permitted change in Greece but absence compelled use of fiction by Roman lawyers in adaptation of law?

46   Character of sensational development in news result of increased supply of paper and tone of sensationalism set by war – Hall Mills murder, Peaches Browning, Lindbergh – character of news determined by naturalist expansion. Hydro-electric power sites of considerable extent started through pulp and paper – size of sites sets rate of production – geographic factor of site plus large outlay implies lumpy pressure of product on market. But enormous scale of demand for paper with pressure of advertising led to development of large-scale power sites, i.e. demand for advertising created demand for power sites and lumpy developments.

47   Restriction on learning in France part of mercantilist development in emphasizing exports of paper. Restrictions on exports of rags and limitations on exports of books because of language problem gave paper an important position and explained interrelation between mercantilism and printing restrictions. Most translations only 25% accurate. Significance of Bible, Scriptures for teaching – dominates learning over long period and built up in relation to teachers – performs profound social function – Greek *paideia.*

48   Problem of Middle Ages – sudden shift from Homer and Virgil to Scriptures. Importance of writing in building up scriptures. Problem of an index authoritarian tolerance, i.e. how far unity of organizations depends on willingness of people to fight for it – stimulating fighting quality and emotional interest to keep parties, etc. intact.

49   Limitations of price system shown in necessity for corruption at top levels – pressure to secure friendships and exploit friendships – systematic déraciné principle. Importance of family connections in Canada – business firms concentrated on regionalism in order to maintain connections and avoid charge of centralization – Oxford Press – Robertson from west as editor; Ryerson Press – Flemington from Maritimes.

50   Role of gentlemen – device or weapon to strengthen position and attack those in weak position – used in most ungentlemanly fashion.

5

51 Development of professions a device for securing hierarchies - device for checking commercial competition - restraint on competition through professional ethics but this may lead doctors and lawyers to go into politics.

52 Collapse of Graeco-Roman civilization or of political organization facilitated spread of religious organization from east. As religion among Jews emerged [with] defeat of political ambitions - so it spread from Graeco-Roman civilization with defeat of political ambitions - but saved by organization of Catholic Church or contribution of Roman Empire from becoming dangerously fanatical. Religion a primary growth spreading in decadent political structures - decline of eastern empires followed by religion and of eastern ideas in western empires also followed religion. Rise in individuality under Christianity checked by belief in other world and emphasis on humility - Athens and Florence unchecked by Christian influence.

53 Patterns in society - development and background of pattern, i.e. religion or philosophy - dependence on rate of diffusion, conditions of diffusion, supported by change in methods of communication - overturn of philosophical and religious pattern or of habits incidental to pattern - breaking down of monopoly position of ideas and emergence of new system.

54 A posteriori - Aristotle explains lack of scientific development in ancient world. Windmill - Holland about 1200 [A.D.]. Printing marked difference between middle and modern world. Oral tradition dominated Bank of Barcelona in lending policy.

55 Rumours of suppression of attacks of newspapers on Germans - must not annoy them but this part of pre-war period. Young love, mystery, adventure - chief interest of publishers of short stories. Growth of separate monetary systems a reflection of the printing industry isolating separate countries - accentuating problem of exchange and trade. Narrowing of means of communication meant spoken Latin deteriorated into romance dialects - those taken up by printing and division solidified among European languages. Printing also facilitated coming up of Greek in face of European deterioration. Scarcity of parchment and durability - enhanced respect for scriptures - meant concentration on problems of thought by church. Support of authority. Period in which church worked out allegory and symbolism in ceremonies - architecture, philosophy, universities. Deterioration of papyrus weakened position of authority.

56 Significance of emphasis on news in deliberately preventing continuity of thought concentrating on desire to be free from boredom on part of readers. Headline becomes device for breaking down continuity - even the headline must be varied in interest and appearance - makes continuity of approach exceedingly difficult if not impossible, i.e. weakens intellectual effort and necessitates constant interruption. Real essence of news to provide interruption - device by advertising to get widest possible circulation - pressure of machine industry through goods on discontinuity but breaking up of stereotypes of thought may increase advertisers' difficulty in getting stereotypes for own products. Stereotype generally broken down and capacity to accept or promote stereotypes for goods greatly weakened. News may break down possibility of monopoly or create a monopoly.

57 Writing or methods of expression a device for building up hierarchies - on the part of those who write thus expressing their capacity and on the part of those who read. Power of thought to act as solvent of hierarchical groups. Function of writing on large scale or extension of communication to make hierarchies more flexible. Religion - puritanism - search for truth - importance of determination to face reality or honesty - hence intensely practical attitude - importance to science and industry.

58 Monasticism a protest against consorting of church with state - Wycliffe, Hus and later Luther, Calvin - retreat of individual from church, book. State pressing on Anglican Church in Ireland led Newman to desert to Catholic Church. Religious organization gives escape from state. Lollardy an Oxford movement - result of Wycliffe and Babylonian captivity of papacy at Avignon.

59 Publisher emerges in 18th century with growth of advertising and need of cooperation to utilize plant. Does this mean that printing plants becoming larger and more publishers necessary to push market and look after business details? Pressure from government on publication necessitated constant search for new markets and emphasized position of publishers particularly as to legal publications. Advertising probably important in leading to publisher - possibly a publisher handled output of several small presses and reflected increased demand.

60 Legislative bodies developed through administration or legislation. Administration simpler but politician chooses elements from administration calculated to strengthen his position if made legislation. Opposition must note how far he can meet tactics by opposing legislation or compelling legislation which will embarrass government. Game of hide and seek.

61   Augustine - following Ambrose, emphasizing organization of church and concentration on theological speculation, i.e. restriction to parchment and book. Concentration relaxed with coming of paper - return to Augustine by Luther and Calvin marks picking up of paper regime from papyrus and beginning of parchment.

62   Russell Leffinwell - J. Pierpont Morgan - claimed in business Americans accustomed to lying (commission). English to not telling whole truth (omission). French undependable up to moment contract is signed.

63   Confessional - a device for securing access to sources of public opinion and brought distrust to church. Politician has similar devices - keeping his ear to the ground - barber shops, smoking rooms - where people off guard and speak their minds difficulty of getting under guard. Gallup polls an attempt to measure prejudice - avoids names, etc.

64   Instability of public opinion as result of commercialism, i.e. advertising enables powerful groups to dominate - particularly governments which can manage the press by control over news, i.e. what is meant by leader-ship - Roosevelt, King. Truman lacked power to dominate news in press and radio. Did this give him strength? Kennedy Jones points to power of government over news and press and significance that it should be him [who does so] as he represented commercialism. Did press reach peak of influence in Spanish American and Boer Wars and Great War and decline following possibility of politicians exploiting it - Lloyd George, Baldwin, King, Roosevelt? Marginal period with influence swinging back and forth - radio bringing power to politicians.

65   Linking of goods to communication, i.e. advertisements, lead to banning of films from U.S. because they advertise European goods.

66   Knight suggests importance of heresy in present as contrasted with previous interest in authority.

67   Spread in use of horse - dismounting in Scotland - long bow in England spread to Europe (Crecy). With long bow growth of armour - too heavy - rise of infantry - English longbow - Swiss pike. Fortifications - pro-tection in Constantinople and in France - defeating of English. Use of cannon 1453. Return of cavalry with light equipment 1640. Authority with defensive; freedom with offensive.

68   Education apt to become a building up of mazes - teaching students to go through the maze and using the maze to test capacity. Examinations studied as system of mazes and various approaches covered by best teachers - emphasizes memory. Neglect of training of intellectual capa-city - ability to meet and solve problems.

69   Significance of sensation as compared with ideas – in dreams shift on
      margin of sleep from abstract to tangible and into realm of dreams and
      sleep, but on margin may slip out of tangible and back to abstract –
      waking up – margin sensation and ideas – sensation dominant in dreams.
      Abstract ideas a reflection of sensation (Plato) and problem of constant-
      ly adapting ideas to sensation – problem of science. Deductive vs. induc-
      tive.

70   Repression of press in France leading to emphasis on encyclopedia and
      attack through this indirect method on government rather than direct.
      Diderot encyclopedia answer to restriction on newspaper. Significance
      of Jews trading between Christians and Mohammedans – profit obtained
      from religious divergence – increased profits and capitalism – undermin-
      ing religious differences.

71   Borrowing of inventions, i.e. in printing illustrations – migration from
      Montreal (1872) and from Melbourne (Osbourne) to New York – full of
      large centres on fringes and speeding up of communication process in
      centre of dense population – significance of cumulative tendencies in
      large centres. Private enterprise a powerful factor in introducing innova-
      tion or adapting it to commercial use. Without profit, fortune – probably
      difficult to get practical use of innovation. Mechanized monopoly of
      communication – press, radio strengthen monopoly of advertisers – leads
      to growth of checks, i.e. English restrictions on newspapers.

72   Main Johnsen claims [Kansas City] *Star* began to shift very early from
      emphasis on news to magazine material as a result of the radio – the
      latter cut drastically into sport news.

73   [Ontario premier Mitch] Hepburn – irresistible and irrepressible – a
      prima donna – got Conant and McArthur into politics. Under Conant's
      premiership [1942-43], proposal all Cabinet resign in protest against
      Ottawa but at Cabinet meeting next day never mentioned it.

74   Pressure of improved means of communication on class structure –
      enormous profits to be gained by men entrenched, in particular break-
      ing through into next larger group below – increase in production, re-
      duced overhead costs and sales, accentuated by prestige of class above –
      tendency of modern society and production to proceed in lumpy fash-
      ion by sudden spillover to lower parts of class structure. Monopolies
      tending to restrict production and stop spillover to lower prices and
      lower part of structure – pressure of machine industry then appears
      from below, i.e. Donaldson decision effect on publishers – forced them
      into wealthier upper classes and other publishers developed in lower
      class.

75   Printing industry steadily burying work of past except for reprints of
        work regarded as more valuable - problem of libraries and index makers
        to keep ahead of flood. Universities and libraries a fight against pressure
        of steady output of paper and print. Text books, etc. tend to mean neg-
        lect of basic minds - models of arrangement and manipulation rather
        than emphasis on original thought.

76   Rates in relation to value - furs, specie, dried fish - Europe and N. Amer-
        ica - finally lumber - used as capital or defence; wheat - consumers
        goods. Implications of rates - skyscrapers. Legal profession - profits and
        personnel especially of lawyers dependent on frequency of disputes and
        amounts involved. How far friction result of property or business cycle?
        How far lawyers sought in explaining extent of dangers of breaking law?

77   *Language* - before printing various regions develop special language and
        unable to speak with each other, i.e. disputes in England. Printing pro-
        duces order in language and holds it in check. South Sea Islanders -
        rapid change in language - young generation unable to understand old -
        printing not available to hold it in check. Significance of alphabet to
        trade.

78   Significance of monopoly of position of newspaper - influence over
        long period rather than short run - monopoly and heavy capital invest-
        ment - mobilizes opinion as in case of parties - stabilizing influence.
        Competition with small sheets - parties follow imperfect competition in
        newspaper. Mrs. Hughes - drive of advertising to press circulation -
        stirring up sect attitude - mass paper as against class - story of anti-
        convivisection. Advertiser driving class or mass papers together stirring
        up prejudices to increase circulation - drive of commercialism.

79   Jury system in England - protection against worst features of code - use
        of terror to secure confession. How far jury system developed in an
        open system? Norman conquest opened language and effect of pressure
        to crack custom making it flexible but not to break custom producing
        a new set of rigid constitutions. Political flexibility a result of pressure
        against peoples from interior - those against sea.

80   Importance of difference in language to governing classes - Greek persis-
        tent under Roman emperors as device for enhancing their prestige and
        Latin in Roman church as means of strengthening position against ver-
        nacular. French in England strengthened court. Latin in eastern empire
        similar to Greek in west. Aristotle effected by experiment; Luther
        thwarted.

81   Humorous periodicals characteristic of free societies - humour a desire
        for breaking rigidities and keeping society flexible - *New Yorker.*

82   Beginning of use of birth of Christ for date system - probably in 8th
and 9th century - Christianity simplified problem of chronology.

83   Importance of old testament in creating problem of fall of man and necessity of salvation - use of miracles, etc. to strengthen position as against barbarians. Original sin.

84   Struggle between oral and written or printed traditions. Oral represents democratic revolutionary tendencies with possibilities of appealing to emotions and writing more conservative autocratic tendencies. Printing - influence of machine industry over production - strengthens aristocratic tendencies but with pressure on market leads to breaking up of conservative or autocratic interests. Outbreaks of liberalism tend to be function of overhead costs of printing industry.

85   Active printing in England under Edward IV - probably exports of books to Holland - again under Elizabeth after repression under Mary. Assisted revolt in Netherlands.

86   Tremendous importance of fall of man in emphasis on devices for salvation - impact of old testament - need for allegory. Use of birth of Christ about 7th or 8th century - Bede. Alcuin not grandson of Charlemagne - reflected weakness of empire.

87   Rise of mysticism with clash of one group of symbols with another, i.e. simplifying scriptures and scholastic philosophy for German nuns led to mysticism. Developed concepts difficult to get into simpler language - Latin abstractions into German or Greek into Latin - philosophy versus law - missionaries teaching hell to Eskimos. Impact of science and scientific thought on humanities produces social sciences or form of mysticism. But also makes for inventions and abstraction. Newton dynamics - American constitution. Darwin's evolution on social sciences. Hardness of scientific thought produces fuzziness at points encroaching on humanities. Limits of education as device to reduce gap between illiterary and abstractions of learned language - emphasized symbols of Middle Ages.

88   Social scientist in Canada must have a sense of humour. Adult education a grinding down of large ideas to suit men's minds - part of cramming system. Filling of vacuum created by industrial revolution - designed to stop socialism and competitor of socialism but both concerned with their own type of poison.

89   Problem of Canadian external policy - Conservatives fight for empire and Liberals for perpetuation of civilization but both end in participation in war - the one fights because Great Britain at war, the other because the United States at war. Little possibility of unified approach.

90   Danger of trend toward uniformity in large newspaper circulation contributing to sudden erratic outbursts - religion, etc. *Menace* - phenomenal increase circulation suggesting that religion being neglected by daily press - attack of *World* on Klan an attempt to check fanatical outbursts. Greater tendency to uniformity in Canada leads to migration to United States to accentuate fanatical outbreaks. Aimee Semple MacPherson, Father Coughlin.

91   Significance of land in England basis of aristocracy - opposing commercialism - influence continued in position of farmer in West - struggle with capital - Western political influence - a sort of Canadian House of Lords.

92   Machine industry in large book companies emphasizing large books as texts to secure monopoly position and making revisions to strengthen position.

93   Danger of any one point of view in university such as Toronto - precisely because it is a leading university it cannot afford to follow fads.

94   What is significance of volume to later development - influence of [W.C.] Mitchell? Business cycle [studies have an effect] on the course of the business cycle - accentuate intensity of great boom and depression.

95   Stalin - named after steel - significance of choosing names - Trotsky, Lenin, etc. - enormous importance of attempting to direct public opinion in area where public opinion not disciplined and where court has disappeared. Mercurial quality of public opinion explains Russian foreign policy - necessity of presenting firm front.

96   Problems of hotels, meals - expense accounts - very few individuals travelling on their own but have expenses paid by one institution or another.

97   Carver - could trust opinion of common man if he were not uninformed. English tradition - we must educate our masters or French belief in democracy and realization that we do not have final answers. Importance to scholarship and universities. Overemphasis on politics and economics. Importance of drawing in England and Europe - Denmark and Sweden. Adult education developed during depression period.

98   Distrust of private enterprise in advertising through news - Consumers gas in England favouring clearing of slums as advertising devices. University of Chicago studying freedom of press as means of capitalizing news interest. Press interested in booming its influence and stressing its

importance as education factor - part of advertising or influence of
commercial civilization. Consistent weakening of intellectual independence.

99 Deism in Anglican Church led to outbreak of Evangelicalism - Whitfield and Wesley - inability of established church to check fanaticism - break from influence and authority of writing to oral - speaking and preaching. Restriction of Roman Catholic Church based on parchment brought outbreak in Albigensian and Waldensian [heresies] and in turn to reliance on force as check. Writing of enormous significance in authoritarian tendencies and influence in damping down outbreaks of fanaticism - based on oral approach. Conflict between writing and oral.

100 Dafoe, Sir Clifford Sifton, G.V.F. [Ferguson] with sons - publishers continue with family concern - combination of exceptional stupidity with exceptional ability among editors.

101 Monopoly position of moving more important than standing still, i.e. mobility in caste system - ability to move from one area to the next partly monopolistic in character - Jews prevented from moving in various channels and Scottish in Canada probably able to move ahead more rapidly. Most wealthy people disliked and with anti-Jewish fervour. Anti-Semitism closely linked with anti-rich or anti-wealth. Attitude of journalists toward publishers - regard latter as stupid and narrow-minded and to be managed.

102 Toronto brick seriously handicap architectural development - impression of odds and ends attached to brick - brick never satisfactorily handled.

103 Destruction of Court in Germany and Russia and of prestige elements meant building up of leaders through machinery - Hitler and enthusiasm of radio and press. Also in Russia creation of vacuum meant constant emphasis on building up individuals; revolution meant importance of common man and distortion - deifying of politician as image of common man but in Germany deifying substitute of Crown. Machine-made prestige to take place of old forms.

104 Difficulty of emphasis on machination shown in diversion from interest in history - development of hierarchy in immediate interest and disregard of broad cultural interests necessitating study of civilization.

105 University - centre where one has the right and duty not to make up one's mind.

106   Problem of language - Norman invasion weakened English language and left it exposed to numerous words from outside. German language made more rigid by development of printing. Latin as a medium for philosophy or rather law checked expansion of Greek - how far did Greek contribute to growth of vernacular? Break down of Latin, mendicant orders followed spread of writing, i.e. paper. Chinese not adapted to legal possibilities.

107   Migration stimulates literature - means leaving baggage and remembering tales - see Toynbee. More difficult character of writing means that it becomes possession of special class and tends to dominate and protect autocracies until speaking or vernacular gets out of line and compels extension of writing in vernacular. Significance of divergence between speaking and writing - tendency of ruling class with writing caste to be absorbed. Writing supports caste - breakdown speeded by new inventions of communication - paper, etc.

108   *Readers Digest* accepts no advertising and attacks advertisers - *New Yorker* accepts advertising and ridicules pretensions of advertisers - advertises advertisers by exploiting pretences.

109   Problem of high wages during period of construction of capital equipment - wages passed on to capital and imply use of credit in future which is exceedingly difficult to calculate - competition with wages in consumers goods - increased demand for consumers goods but less slack in credit possibilities or emphasis on cash and short term credit.

110   Effect of belief in forest in Germany possibly explains migration of barbarians - England destroyed forests and took to coal - Germany worshipped forests and preserved them, i.e. destruction of primitive religion in England.

111   Printing advances designed to expand religion or to improve handling of language for less literate groups - involves large-scale production and mechanistic process. Role of monasteries to reach down from learned to vulgar languages. Rise of unintelligible fiction for masses - illustrated tendency toward incommunicability. Tendency of power to move from learning, i.e. Greek became learned also Latin, but Greek literature rediscovered. Army based on vulgar literature. Religion penetrates to lower levels. Extension of language by press, i.e. English brings internal strains - novels of intelligensia not understood by newspaper reader. Language not equal to demand for equality and cracks in relation to hierarchy. Increase in numbers of books and growth of book civilization makes for more extensive hierarchy - those who know more books than others and development of universities to foster book knowledge and

create hierarchies – difficult for adult education to make impression on
it and difficult to develop new points of view – cramps freshness and
vitality.

112 Cathedral sank behind press but nevertheless buildings continued to
exercise profound influence, i.e. through religion – churches – also ritual
built up in Middle Ages – mass, etc., so too case of cemeteries – opposition to cremation as pagan. Buildings as permanent bodies encroached
on printing as impermanent.

113 Significance of one-man books – writing centring around Lincoln or
Christianity – in monopolistic principle in ideas – cumulative effect
restricts writing on less dramatic figures or rational approach – distorts
views regarding civilization – Napoleon. Vested interest in Bible, etc.

114 Gallup poll takes place in radio with newspaper in A.B.C. [American Broadcasting Corporation?] Check on advertising influence by advertisers by
elaborate sampling.

115 Anglo-Saxon countries settled matters by odd-numbered committees
rather than principles – involves concentration on problem of getting
vote and ingenious efforts to control machine – mathematics and politics
– emphasis on statistics. Wears down prejudices – general acceptance of
results of majority votes – neglects qualitative factor in individuals.

116 Splitting up knowledge – paraphernalia of scholarship – difficulties and
dangers of attempting to make broad generalizations – worship of print
– decline of active thought, discipline of print and check to revolutionary activity, i.e. public opinion and puritanism with constitutional
change.

117 Spread of block printing from China – impact on production of images
in Europe – reflection of Buddhism in China – large-scale printing of
classics, i.e. Confucianism reflected in printing of manuscripts for
church or aristocracy – in Europe paper had been influential in writing
and rise of commerce – forced its way up from bottom – coming to
printing or stronghold of parchment and Latin – vernacular reinforced
by cheap material and breaking through in reformation – printing of
Bible. But large-scale printing of scriptures again in China as in Europe
emphasizes position of text. Religion barred trade between Christians,
and Mohammedans and Jews developed contacts – interstitial religion
essential to trade – fanaticism worn down by trade in all these groups.

118 Abbé Maheux – menace to Canadian nationality as involves suspicion
church behind the move and accentuates imperialism by Protestants.
Importance of emphasis on learning as a means of showing that a belief

in the exercise of the mind is important - it even has a ritualistic importance. Suggests necessity of rational approach.

119   Role of writing - involves impression at second remove as compared with speaking - reading at third remove and less effective in impression than writing. Problem of monastic civilization - limited writing and much reading - lack of creative writing.

120   Text-books - constant revision reflects news character of university education and pressure of printing press - necessity of rapid turnover with large overhead costs.

121   Printing an industry constantly emphasizing appeal of writing to large numbers of readers and tending to have a leftist tendency and to break down position of hierarchy. Responsibility of writers for Russian revolution - compelled to work against censorship and to write so as to reach active elements and to appeal to revolution against hierarchy - revolutions result of efforts of hierarchy to prevent levelling influence of printing. Role of theatre or drama important at stage where conversation being turned to printing or record, i.e. Shakespeare - English, Greek drama conversation of stage effectively represented in printing and printing makes for constant discipline of language and weakening of stage. Role of great books - crystallization by printing and capable of various interpretations in large powerful organizations. Roman Catholic Church emphasizes oral tradition but adapting printing to purpose - emphasis of Protestants on Bible - scriptures support hierarchy but effects weakened in suitability to varied interpretation - Marx *Kapital* used as scriptural text but susceptible of wide range of interpretations. 'Great Book' infinite possibilities for discipline but enormous restriction on intellectual effort - commentaries and readers chained to it and intellectual horizon narrowed. Tyranny of hierarchy and 'Great Book' and priestcraft broken only with infinite difficulty - vested interests of publishers, universities, etc.

122   Destruction of monasteries effect of technological unemployment. Enormous importance of cathedrals accompanying monastic system and expansion of church. Church emphasized cathedrals as against monasteries and writing. This has killed that English with emphasis on Greek - German or Latin. Mommsen - Caesarism of Rome versus republic tendencies of Greece. Significance to England of inability of any group to dominate - trade, land, Church, non-Conformists.

123   Emphasis on political equality in U.S. accentuates economic equality - price system used as device for developing hierarchy - high prices. Pullman, hotel meals, shops serve constantly to separate on basis of wealth -

also education in more expensive schools. Hierarchy of price system
distorts capitalistic development - effectiveness of price system in distributing hierarchy on basis of efficiency - how far estates and wills
necessitate influence and bankruptcy destroys them? Advertising on
large scale - skyscrapers - illustrate the pull on capital by hierarchy.

124 Importance of element of monopoly in publications - basic factor determining price of comic strips - refusal of newspapers to mention names
of competitors or to give them any advertising by indirection. Difficulties of price system in determining monopoly charges of publicity.

125 Science makes for rapid continuous obsolescence of its literature - each
new advance implies disappearance of old literature - humanities on the
other hand involve retention of the past - scriptural writings and difficulty of overcoming bondage of written word. Increases burden of religious institutions' rigidity even strengthened by influence of science,
i.e. increase in printing - U.S. - newspaper journalism means rapid dropping of tradition - humanities brought more clearly into line with science. Science compelled to pull enormous burden of humanities'
rigidities.

126 Lenin essentially a revolutionary organizer - used Marx in building up
philosophy and self-confidence and appealing to proletariat to soften up
peasants, labourers and soldiers and pushed system over at weakest
period. Organization of old regime compelled emphasis on close revolutionary organization - essentially military - this continued in new regime to take place of vacuum - Church replaced by new ikons. Bible
ineffective in revolution but Marx as Jew in old testament tradition and
German philosophy and emphasizing hatred and necessity of fighting
used with effect. French revolutionary tradition broke with Christian
tradition and opened way to penetration of Russian system where
Christianity had been particularly an instrument of corruption. When
Marx wrote you have nothing to lose but your chains in those words he
forged new chains.

127 Problem of building up reputations of party leaders over long period -
making for monopoly and inflexibility in political structure - radio
helps to build up prestige and electorate respond to effects of publicity
in long term. Increasing number of illustrations of meetings and circulation of papers designed to evade the press and keep out of news - fear
of publicity in sensational press leads to suppression or rather secrecy.

128 Russian revolution differs from others because of lack of development
of press - without press sharp lines begin to develop, i.e. Bolsheviks able
to bring out differences. With extensive press in France, etc. in 19th

century difficult to separate parties - bourgeois linked to workers and so on - easier to move up through hierarchy.

129   Civilization built on belief on part of man that he differs from apes - act of belief makes difference.

130   Spread of printing and lack of authorship in England brought rapid growth of translation in 16th century and development of drama with Shakespeare. Period of new techniques - papyrus to Greece - printing to England brought cultural outburst. Scottish lagged and no stationers company grew up giving Scottish printers advantage in competing with monopoly in London.

131   Newspaper and publicity separating presidents from scholars who do not get publicity - reflection of character of news.

132   American branch factories capitalizing [on] nationalism in Canada and accentuating regionalism by compelling agitation against central group exploited by branch factories.

133   Significance of national advertising to various economic theories - Social Credit advertised Alberta, C.C.F. Saskatchewan - New Zealand - experiment - advertising by getting into news. Accentuating of regionalism result of regional advertising.

134   Importance of advertising in novels shown in resort to contemporary questions to secure wide interest - an attempt to get into the news as a means of attracting attention also in politics - with newspapers orators spoke throughout country in order to get into news - changed character of political organization.

135   Demand for new developments with industrial revolution brought pouring in of romantic movement from Germany via Coleridge, Carlyle, etc.

136   Significance of Puritanism in emphasizing importance of individual in spiritual world - reacting on political world and producing tendencies toward equality or emphasizing mobility of society. How far it accentuates mobility to point of danger in society? Destruction of hierarchies.

137   Defensive policy - historical background - late spread of revolution - division of Roman Empire - English, American, French, Russian - repression in Germany - Karl Marx - breaking out in Russia and crushing of Germany and Japan. Political revolution opens way for industrial revolution. Lenin student of revolutionary technique - cumulative trend. Difficulty of Canada in appreciating revolution - refuge of counter-

revolution in loyalists and in church. Counter-revolution checked in
Russia except within movement - rebuilding defensive mechanism
against war. Significance of printing on language - Rabelais wrote before French language simplified. Russian language young - suited to
oratory and not fully chastened by printing.

138 Significance of uniformity of men, horses in military parades as result
of training and undisciplined character of machines - tanks get out of
line. Constant effort to build up machines to meet possibilities of discipline among man. Continuous evidence of limitations of machines -
wrecks, etc. but these evidence also of inability of man to stand up to
demands of machine - a constant balancing or attempt at equilibrium -
machines built up to new discipline and man built up to meet it.

139 Danger of immodesty in nationalistic science and importance of making
it international as a means of checking artificialities in contribution of
Russians. Printed word entrenched in languages - Bible in Germany and
English-speaking countries unable to make impression in France and
Italy and Spain with institutions based on oral traditions. French revolution meant clash of printing and intellectual effort not dominated by
Bible as in Germany. Russian revolution meant toppling over of oral
tradition in church and state by printing - Bible made little headway
against Greek Catholic but Marx and revolutionary tradition broke into
Russia through printing. Revolutions result of conservatism of state and
religious institutions built around languages coming into contact with
printing. Language in printing offers escape from religion particularly in
large area of illiteracy such as Russia and with strong bureaucratic tradition in church and aristocracy. Printing in Russia meant leaking through
and overwhelming oral tradition in religion - Marx outside religion and
emphasizing dictatorship of proletariat - gave the key to rapid expansion. How far radio a return to oral tradition to support revolution
based on printing? Significant Germany and Italy base of development
through radio susceptible to control by state and reaching larger numbers than printing.

140 Advertising partly based on cheapness of paper in relation to selling
valuable goods - innumerable letters can be sent out and if one order
materializes overhead cost is slight.

141 How far existence of purchasing power an incentive to intense advertising activity which paves way to development of newspapers? Possibility of making profit by pressing demand for goods for which demand
can be pressed creates demand for newspapers. Newspaper development
essentially a reflection of the growth of trade and the demand for advertising to market goods. Barnum capitalized selling of intangible - lottery
tickets, bibles, museum, Jenny Lind (singer).

142   Adam Smith developed from law to political economy and necessarily depended on natural law or device for going beyond ordinary conceptions of law - seized revolutionary concept as basis of political economy - abandoning of natural law means return to historical principle and emphasis on authority.

143   Importance of Roman law and Greek philosophy as check in social sciences to reinforce humanities against pressure of science and dominance of mathematics and influence of price system. Carrying over of word law to physical sciences and destroying it in its old sense.

144   Factors influencing civilization

Military and Law	Rome
	Germany
Philosophy	Greece - Aristotle reinforced Church.
Religion	Roman Catholic
	Greek Catholic
	Lutheran
	Calvinist
Political Institutions	
Commerce	relation to navy in Great Britain as against army and continent.
Common Law	social sciences
Code Law	significance to religion and revolutions.

145   How far newspapers given away and money made through advertising - sales or small subscription price largely designed to assure delivery to proper people rather than bring in revenue?

146   Organized hatred, i.e. politics, religion, organization of church - restricts fanaticism. Organized industry restricts intense cut-throat competition.

147   Politics, law, morality - non-economic keeping capitalist system intact. How far economics result of extent of overlapping of power and ethics the basis of law? - but politics part of law - weakening of power - military facilitates growth of law and growth of trade. Paper and printing weaken position of naked power or force and open way to law and trade. Political recovery extension of law in handling of complex relations. Land and nobility and rent and militarism against communism but may be favourable to industry for military purposes.

148   Publishers regarding themselves as authors and backscratching their own clientele. Some most distinguished authors compelled to seek American publishers. Warm fetid smell of nationalism the breeding ground of the pestilences of the west, the worship of which kills its millions where the

worship of the church in the inquisition killed its thousands. Strikes at
root of letters, the chief element of escape from the modern pressure of
power.

149   Free trade in 19th century accompanied by factory legislation and by
       rise of tariffs in Canada as protective devices. Canadian nationality and
       break into regionalism accentuates back scratching small groups - Mari-
       times, Western Canada, Quebec - necessity of university making avail-
       able standards of western civilization.

150   Political economy as extension of law - enormous advance of order un-
       der commerce and industry in 19th century - success leading to enor-
       mous increase in productive capacity and problems of power. Decline
       of religion and check to growth of power of state. Law ceases to be ade-
       quate and begins to encroach on political economy with rise of bureau-
       cracy. Necessity of fanaticism to burn encrusted framework of old insti-
       tutions - Aberhart improved educational system where previous minister
       of education unable to carry through reforms. Revolutions necessary to
       reduce alphabet in Russia, or metric system in France. Role of men of
       letters in breaking up rigidities of law, religion etc. - George Moore at-
       tack on circulating libraries.

151   Idolaters of British North America Act and of sayings of FATHERS -
       failure to allow for flexibility of law and necessity of adaptation. Danger
       of making British North America Act more rigid. Interpretation provid-
       ed for in Judicial Committee of Privy Council decisions - danger of
       looking for consistency in decisions.

152   Impact of continental framework on rapid development of pulp and
       paper industry - drive of newspapers against monopoly price of Inter-
       national Paper Company stressed migration to Canada and this possibly
       retarded by Ontario policy of embargo encouraging Quebec policy of
       exports. Pressure of newspapers on public opinion keeps down price of
       newsprint and accentuates influence of advertising on lower levels of
       intelligence. Drive of machine industry toward commercialism and im-
       pact of continental production on sudden extension of opinion media.
       Advertisers press for production of goods sold on mass scale and mono-
       polistic element in advertising drives toward goods with rapid turnover -
       emphasis on number of middlemen and provision of outlets. Produc-
       tion of goods for consumers on vast scale paralleled by development of
       production of capital goods for war purposes - capitalization of com-
       mercialism versus capitalization of industrialism. Pressure on govern-
       ments in armament industry and large-scale capital undertakings to off-
       set drive of commercialism and consumers' goods. Militarism versus
       commercialism in form of capitalism and industrialism versus commer-

cialism. Drive of paper industry and printing industry - wedge of commercialism - ease of distribution, stirring up of sensations, political agitation, wars, widening breach for markets and communication system for other goods - advertising. Printing industry expanding in relation to war, and politics turns to advertising and goods. How far censorship a sponsor of advertising and trade, i.e., driving paper toward trade rather than opinion? Trade centre of disturbance - newspaper publishing dominant over paper production in U.S. but struggle with International Paper Company trust prices. In England publishing interests against protection of paper in 19th century. How far paper production factor driving printing into other than censorship countries - ease of handling?

153   James Joyce - flies by nets of nationalism, religion - last inarticulate gasp of western man under pressure of nationalism.

154   Great influence of Greek thought followed crystallization of period of rapid growth before writing. Great difficulty in overcoming power of youth of civilization during prewriting period caught in writing period. Writing facilitates growth and elaboration of system or is at basis of whole concept of law of uniformity. Philosophical systems and laws a reflection of writing and its influence on human mind - laws a part of writing and printing technique - even Marx product of technological background. Writing stresses sovereignty with emphasis on language as basis of public opinion and propaganda. Science and laws also result of writing - observation and recording but applicability to mathematics implies introduction of element of certainty in social science and eliminates speculative and philosophical side; law from natural scientific side influences approach to social sciences - rationality tends to become mathematical - particularly serious for legislation and lawyers - with importance of authoritarian approach and reliance on force. Law absorbs rigid and not creative elements of science.

155   Significance of masses after mass army of Napoleon - large-scale manipulation of conscription. Interest in mass education, health, rise of statistics. Manipulation of masses rather than aristocracy in earlier period. Technique of control over masses - how far Marx part of trend of penetration to masses? - whole range of fanaticisms - single tax, bimetallism, etc. - [these represent] processes of boring to lower levels of intelligence - appeal to proletariat - lower classes.

156   Importance of writing and literature to improvement - few malevolent books - all interested in making society better - essentially ethical and religious and consequently fanatical - individualism or egotistic - belief in possibility of improving society. How far law keeps writing in check or hampers and restricts growth of fanaticism - even law gave way after 1832 with enormous emphasis on legislation?

157   Science in England had impact on industrialism and government and re-
       duced possibility of speculative interest in law of Continent. Conse-
       quently political economy emerged as part of practical problem of com-
       merce and industry in relation to law. Religion weakened by church
       under control of state. England consequently borrowed and influenced
       by continental movements. Adam Smith began with influence of law
       and extended to philosophy and political economy - elaboration of law.
       But economics and social sciences exposed to influence of natural sci-
       ences - equilibrium, etc.

158   News or incitement of interest tends to break down rigid stereotype in
       religion, etc., but sets up patterns of its own - significance of catastro-
       phe or technical development - steady change - population, technology,
       etc. all point in same direction.

159   Significance of North America and especially of Canada and St Law-
       rence - organization and production on large scale of raw materials and
       impact on Europe. Specie from Central America - impact on European
       prices more important than hiring of mercenaries in religious wars. Furs -
       attempt to check increased production - cost of imports and inflation.
       Timber - resistance of shipbuilders and end of navigation acts. Wheat -
       revolution of English agriculture. Paper - on U.S. - change in character
       of production of public opinion.

160   Mind of proletariat apt to dwell upon omnipotence of God and mind of
       dominant minority on supremacy of law.

161   Concentration on goods following Adam Smith - capitalized by Marx -
       emphasis on exploitation then by stress on full employment - but for-
       getting narrowing effect of materialism and neglect of artistic and philo-
       sophical interest. Gradual breaking down in England of feudal honour
       by trading spirit.

162   Language built up as part of aristocratic system - objection of Eastman
       to revised spelling - hierarchy implicit in language. Facility of English
       language as medium for trade - trade wears down aristocratic texture.

163   Ideologies, race, nationalism, pressure groups of ideologies far more
       serious than pressure for advertisers. Drive of advertising part of duo-
       poly of department stores - latter influencing advertiser and paper in
       pushing circulation stirs up exploitation of sects. Dana - stirring up the
       animals - in city, conflict between various opinions. Paper instrumental
       in breaking up opinions as against class paper attempting to build up
       monopoly opinion. Influence of Bible with varying possibilities of inter-
       pretation in disintegration of uniform belief and rise of sects.

164   Tendency of radio to dominate news - selects spot news and these writ-
        ten up at great length in the papers because of the feeling that people
        wish to know more about it even though it is not news.

165   Influence of labour on politics through journalism - [Whitelaw] Reid
        helped introduce linotype and antagonized newspaper men in election
        in which he was defeated [in] 1892 [as vice-presidential candidate].

166   How far mechanical change, new presses in 1880s, responsible for shift
        of partisan journals to independent newspapers? - mugwumps - coin-
        cided with defeat of Blaine. Pressure for circulation necessitated break
        from party affiliations and collapse of Republican party. Comparable to
        Roosevelt and radio. Restriction of circulation precipitates political cor-
        ruption and party fanaticism. Civil war and Grant regime with Boss
        Tweed - increase in circulation of paper and advertising means increased
        criticism - fight of *New York Times* against Tweed. Expansion of popu-
        lation and relatively slow rate of development of press facilitates politi-
        cal fanaticism and party alliances - Civil War - particularly with relative
        divergences between north and south - how far thesis could be pushed
        to Revolution? How far Republican papers supported by industrial
        interests favouring protection - break from party suggested retailer be-
        coming more important - department stores claim attitude of Dana of
        Sun on G.W. Childs led to war by which Pulitzer bought press for
        World?

167   Danger of focusing change in language, i.e. of public opinion, with new
        technological developments shown in Germany and Italy - radio. Ideas
        slow to change in spite of technological pressure - power of thought
        weakened and with it power of resistance and effective organization.
        Importance of languages exposed to major incursions and increased
        flexibility in making for mobility of classes, rapid diffusion of techno-
        logy and rapid adjustment to change, i.e. Latin took over from Etruscan,
        Greek (Ionic) from Minoan, English from French. Culture absorbed by
        language without destroying latter makes for stronger development and
        more flexible language adapted to expansion intensively and extensively.
        Marx pointed to importance of interrelation between technology and
        classes and made for emphasis on closer coherence or in a sense des-
        troyed or weakened class struggle. Absence of Bible and priesthood gave
        Greeks advantage - not dominated by learned language. Sacred literature
        and priest assume language unable to absorb previous cultural contribu-
        tions - dead language acts as poison restricting growth of living language.

168   Oriental empires dependent on army under king largely unstable be-
        cause of existence of conqueror and conquered - implied infliction of
        conqueror's language and development of administration and official

language adapted to writing but without training in schools - spoken
language contributed to difficulties of control - people tended to get
out of hand - or break increased between spoken and written particularly with emphasis on force - Sumerian emperors.

169   Bible in Anglo-Saxon countries contributed to fanaticism of sects and
constant struggle which facilitated economic and political development.
France without influence of Bible able to build up literature - so too of
Italy and Spain but church a restraining factor. Church and Bible in
Germany a factor supporting state. Significant tenacity of language -
helped divide Greece in Pelopponesian war - Ionic and Attic vs. Doric
Spartan; divided Rome - Latin and Greek - east and west - checked
Greek in east and Arabic in west. Enabled English to absorb Rome and
French. Moulded and hampered application of machine industry -
growth of nationalism.

170   Necessity of constant pruning of language to prevent growth of dialects
and keep channels of communication open - state support of education
device for keeping large area with uniform language.

171   Ionians absorbed Minoans and earlier civilization and Athens - clash
with Dorians at root of Pelopponesian War - Dorians invaded from
north. Latin absorbed Etruscan culture. Rich cultural background -
absorbed by peoples of different language but facilitated growth of an
adaptable language. Tendency of literature to develop and lose touch
with people - result settled by war. Literature maintained contact with
technological change, gives hierarchical strength, but losing touch in
elaborate development becomes handicap in technology at basis of war.
Cities developing civilization but losing touch with country lose control,
i.e. Etruscans. Significance of force greatly enhanced with more efficient language or uniform spread of language accompanying literature.
Literature as a military factor greatly neglected - speeches of Churchill.
Enormous significance of absorptive capacity of language and consequent flexibility and extension to lower classes.

172   Significance of alphabet to trade, i.e. Phoenicians, and to language -
flexibility and permanence of Greek civilization. Facilitated development of ideas - enabled closer approximation to reality than crude pictographs or images of organized religion. Printing and paper brought
widespread flexibility - divisive character of religion and language -
breakdown of Latin and limitations of parchment in Middle Ages.
Science facilitated industrialism and spread of information essential
to marketing. Significance of trade and alphabet to expansion of Europe
based on science result of possibility of approximation to reality -
facilitated appeal to philosophy and natural law. Radio accentuates

emphasis on patterns but increases competition to emphasis on appeals to largest common denominator with other media - newspaper, etc.

173 Writing basic to trade - alphabet - Phoenicians. Permanent records - transaction in land and later basis of credit. Improved communication essential to development of trade. Engineering and science training involves tremendous emphasis on memory and neglect of capacity to reason. Middle Ages - force and discussion, i.e. universities, parliament, common law - lack of writing facilities - emphasis on architecture in church.

174 Spread of national advertising with purging of dubious advertisements and building up of confidence in advertisements.

175 Evening paper meant rise of newsdealers - developed with demands of working classes. Morning papers essentially aristocratic - evening papers meant to appeal to new levels - support of labourer.

176 Darwin *Origin of Species* [1859] destroyed doctrine of original sin and led many, i.e. [Leslie and Fitzjames] Stephens, etc., to turn from church. Religion susceptible to influence of appeal to natural law, i.e. of science but more difficult to combat - contrast with social sciences particularly susceptible to influence of hard facts of science.

177 Overhead costs of printing means running off large numbers - encouragement of waste and relative neglect of improvement in design. Erratic influence of price system and monopoly. Young writers do best work and get low pay before prestige built up and after prestige get high pay for poorer work. 'It makes me laugh at what the *Times* pay me now, when I think of the old days and how much better I wrote for them then, and got a shilling where I now get ten.' (Thackeray)

178 Buddhism - impact of borrowed religion on China - consequent emphasis on printing to bring about wide distribution of charms. Spread to Europe - penetration to lower strata of society through influence of Church but alphabet sufficiently simple and effective to result in literacy and beginnings of trade especially with paper and its spread from China. Possibility of adapting contributions of Greek civilization but difficulty of advancing beyond it except in science and mathematics - rise of Aristotelian philosophy - reworking of cultural contributions and discarding in relation to science or adapting them to science - speed of scientific point of view - objectivity - absorption of individual in collectivism - mass dissemination of knowledge - mobilization of technology in interest of force. Greek science and Roman law - latter sharpened by philosophy and particularly by acerbities of Christian religions necessitating powerful devices to keep it in hand.

179 Tendency for successive languages to become poisoned by dead languages used to bolster class structure - Greek in Rome, Latin in Italian -
burden of two languages prevents freshness and probably accentuates
role of force. Vernaculars break through in vigorous aristocracies -
poetry and drama. Dead language deadens intellectual vigour and drains
off resources provided in media, i.e. papyrus supported expanding administration in Rome and two languages but inadequate for extensive
education - apt to be combined with slavery even in Greece. How far
break from oral tradition to written shown in freshness of Greek civilization paralleled by growth of oral tradition in development of universities and emergence of Aquinas and Abelard? Tendency to crystallize
in written tradition. Augustine at beginning of parchment tradition.
Renaissance of paper and printing. Each new development of communication giving freedom to develop new point of view.

180 Significance of decimal system on history - fingers and toes - overemphasize role of centuries and of chronology and neglect of spatial factors - spatial factors emphasized by military leaders - also technology.
Poetry a device for building up cultural stratification with a language or
of separating languages - represents specialization between languages -
point at which language matures. Most significant that Greeks did not
have a second learned language - stood on their own feet - no energy
absorbed in confusion of a second language. Widening of communications and reaching to lower strata makes for vested interest in large-
scale printing and publishing and accentuates difficulty between nations -
means increasing departure from common language of small number.
Printing weakening grip of capital on language and increased differences
between language.

181 Logical positivists claim thought dependent on expression - complex
ideas result of communication. Implications of mechanization to language - intensive commercial and capitalistic development involves wearing and adaptation of language to particular demands and consequently
difference with countries of different commercial and capitalistic development - difficulty of understanding enhanced, i.e. Russia at different
level in terms of language than Anglo-Saxon countries. Words mean
something different in one than in the other language. Confucian -
writing scholarly class - left open way to rapid spread of Buddhism with
use of charms for printing for large numbers - aristocracy versus classes.
Increasing closeness between written and oral tradition with modern
newspaper increases difficulty of universities in developing, say, theories
of social sciences - rigidity of social science leads to obsolescence and
constant shifting demands of 'average public opinion of radio' or 'newspaper'. A conservative rigid approach to serve as guide. Paradox of need
for universal theory and difficulty developing it.

182   Extent to which depression result of nationalism built up on accentu-
        ated emphasis on vernacular and consequent growth of tarrifs. Cartels
        developing outside nationalism result of restrictive power of vernacular
        accentuated by machines.

183   Alphabet facilitates ease of learning - compulsory education. Rhetorical
        tradition weakened by emphasis on vernacular - facilitates rapid spread
        of science - dissolution of social structure by science. University sub-
        jects very largely an extension of modern languages - each subject has
        its type of words - course designed to develop special vocabulary - eco-
        nomics, sociology - vested interest in mutual unintelligibility - reference
        to fields. Class structures more difficult to maintain on basis of lang-
        uage with spread of means of communication. Significance of brush to
        China contrasted with stylus developing to pen. Propaganda developed
        so effectively in Anglo-Saxon countries that it brought immunity but
        suddenly introduced in Germany and Italy and Russia produced totali-
        tarianism. Implication of closing gap between written word and vernac-
        ular with newspaper to university - tendency to reduce significance of
        learned language - Latin, Greek and reduce possibility of class based on
        language - emphasis on science - difficulty of understanding literature
        of past - obsolescence of great books except for prestige purpose. In-
        creases difficulty of securing universal approach in face of nationalism,
        communication, etc. Machine industry emphasizes regional civilization
        and difficulties of broad understanding. Emphasis on vernacular of
        printing press accentuates problem of university in maintaining bridge
        between world view and a shifting base of vernacular. Universities over-
        whelmed by vernacular and common interest with little prospect of
        maintaining interest in problems of civilization. Machine, i.e. radio, em-
        phasizes language as against nationality - ease with which Germany at-
        tacked Austria and Czechoslovakia through German. Concentration on
        vernacular weakens liberal tradition.

184   Growth of ideas and recognition of history of ideas first in Germany -
        latter a definite implication of objectivity and mechanization incidental
        to printing industry. Problem of extent and intensity of growth of ideas
        supported by machine industry and consequent adaptability to demands
        of force. Conflict of intellectual activity with ideas.

185   Overhead costs fundamentally opposed to equality - hotels favour im-
        portant people because they pull other people and tend to have adver-
        tising value. Capitalizes commercial value of hierarchies by giving special
        advantages to upper levels. Significance of women to force and rhetoric,
        i.e. omission of women by Thucydides. Government by eunuchs - break-
        down of dynasties with rigid principles of descent and shift from kings
        to queens - Cleopatra - palace politics - Henry VIII. Church attempt to
        isolate women and emphasize virgin. Role of women in vernacular.

186   Danger of history of ideas and concern with furniture apt to distract
       attention from basic problem of inadequacy to meet problem of lack of
       contact between abstract ideas and technological development. Concern
       with minutiae of research – archeology, etc., tends to contribute to be-
       lief in knowledge of change and therefore to exercise a conservative
       influence. Assumption of knowledge of character of change makes for
       less violent change. Trotsky – revolution intended as artistic formulae
       according to which revolution carried out and continued – again makes
       for conservatism of revolution.

187   Significance of news as device for breaking down hierarchies – spreads
       information quickly and undermines aristocracy. Newspapers not inter-
       ested in freedom of speech but in getting advertising from organization
       interested in freedom of speech. Civil liberties union.

188   Effectiveness of communication in destroying hierarchies offset by
       facility of organization – price system, accounting, administration. Cre-
       ates position of relative imperfect competition – shift in hierarchies
       within organization may facilitate continuation of organization, i.e.
       business firm into a sort of hierarchy – relative efficiency dependent on
       relative rapidity from top to bottom. Efficiency may be offset by influ-
       ence of advertising or stuffed shirts – creation of special positions –
       chairman of boards, etc. honorary position. Problem of overhead costs
       in large-scale technological development in communication implies
       imperfect competition in communication and imperfect competition
       between industries and commercial firms particularly through advertis-
       ing – growth of monopoly result in part of monopoly of communication.

189   Significance of Gothic architecture to universities – developed in cathe-
       drals and facilitated development of education in contrast with monas-
       teries.

190   Spread of printing and use of paper result of attempt to introduce a
       foreign religion, Buddhism, into China, i.e. use as tool for diffusion on
       mass scale – adaptability to images – consequent impact on Europe.
       Papyrus less adapted to images and implied handwriting and with de-
       mands of trade made for cursiveness.

191   Significance of crossbreeding – large horses of Franks defeated Moham-
       medans 732 [A.D.] – western civilization based on cross-breeding – bio-
       logical implication. Disappearance of armour by 1700 meant heavy
       horse turned to plough agriculture and transport – implications of tech-
       nical military change to agriculture. How far survival of fittest used to
       interpret human institutions – how far they are result of cultural, i.e.
       mechanical, scientific change? Alphabet at bottom of scientific growth –
       but alphabet a check on science.

192   Common law basis of common politics. King's court brought common law and parliament in contrast with French Estates General. Law developed into flood after reform acts of 1832. Limitations of writing brought growth of large assemblies as basis of parliament. Papyrus limited by restricted range of growth. Spectacles meant work of scholars at more advanced age and consequently scholarly work. Spread of printing accentuated poisons of Middle Ages and probably restricted penetration of science through ultimately encouraging it – made for break into ecclesiastical groups from Roman Catholics to Luther, Calvin and sects – diversification of religion hastened by printing and decentralization of authority. Division between east and west shown in fertility cults of east and interest in virgin in west – latter connected with monasticism and restriction of birth rate in contrast with emphasis on births in east. Restriction on population in west and emphasis on Virgin opened way to machine. Virgin a step in trend toward dominance of industrialism. Roman Catholic Church concerned with birth control shift from fertility cults to sterility cults.

193   Musson's *Birds of Canada* [by P.A. Taverner (Toronto, 1944)], [Dale] Carnegie's *How to Win Friends and Influence People* [New York, 1937], [H.M. and A.S. Stone's] *A Marriage Manual* [New York, 1935] – money makers dislike fiction.

194   Decline of oratory with cessation of printing of speeches. Printing of political speeches meant a wide public and great care in statement and method of speech. Decline in reporting of speeches meant lack of criticism and general disregard of form.

195   Development of administration in business and generally probably accentuates lag of industry. Administration constantly concerned with changes in organization even though underlying technique remained relatively permanent. Administrators concerned with activity in contrast with routine of industry. Even irrational spend much time in acting rational so as not to appear irrational.

196   Church-developed hierarchy and concern with power meant neglect of proletariat – consequently Marxism spread as new type of religion and reached group not recognized by Christianity or placed in subordinate position, i.e. tendency for religion with language to drift away from immediate contacts. Attack of Roman Catholics on communism and rallying to Roman Catholics and other churches of capitalists aligned with hierarchy on one hand and development of communist hierarchy on other hand. Difficulty of maintaining independent position in struggle between two groups. Utopias a result of the increasing efficiency of the civil service and the consequent necessity of the politicians resorting to the impractical.

198   Reckoning by time rather than mileage in driving cars long distances and travelling at uniform speed.

199   Commercialized printing and paper – nationalism in contrast with church. Newspaper clash with book – England. Continued cultural stability, i.e. time and space. Trade – pressure toward socialism. Newspaper civilization – U.S. – obsession with space. Monopoly of newspaper – U.S. – pressure toward armed power – neglect of problem of time – planning – administration.

200   West profoundly influenced by fall of Roman Empire and deterioration of idea of state and emergence of idea of church or religion – emphasis on book or Bible and on elaboration of symbols of unity. Architecture made for division as influenced by localization. Pushed forward with printing of Bible and evolution of church to Protestantism and sects – worship of book – great emphasis on literate clergy and schools capable of interpreting book – necessity of having tools with which to do thinking.

201   Importance of broad generalization as an approach to civilization and its study – avoids discouragement of details and emphasizes unity of approach. Attack of church on tribal and family relations – emphasis on individual by widening appeal along universal lines – emphasis on sex.

202   Passion for participation and organization – search for objections and part in hierarchies. Important thing in developing administration among executives and ways and means of keeping organization active. Commercialization of literature, drama (radio), etc., means cutting off best literature from average man and probably from hierarchy of wealth incidental to commerce. Hierarchy of literature without support of commercial court.

203   Russia escaped Reformation and Renaissance – unnecessary to escape from control of church as in west – state developed at later stage – constant struggle between church and state facilitated democratic development.

204   Universities developed with basis of science and compelled to emphasize elaboration of learning, i.e. Ph.D. theses take place of Roman Catholic ritual in Roman Catholic Church – worship of learning rather than church.

205   Technological advance in communication assumes narrowing of range of dispensation and widening range of reception in increasingly large

numbers [who] receive but unable to make any response. Books, radio, newspapers handing it out but little possibility of giving back as media of expression narrowed – prevents healthy vigorous vital development of people on receiving end of centralized technological system. Decline in influence of church and in numbers of highly trained clergy leaves problem of humanities to university and necessitates importance of scholarship. Problem of irony and other forms of literature with mechanization of communication – impossible to be ironical with enormous numbers – assumes sophistication.

206 Printing industry tends to make nationality parallel language, i.e. in east separate languages persist in nations and religion a factor perhaps reinforcing language preventing assimilation in national boundary. Printing facilitated dissociation of religion from language and growth of nationality. Mohammedans' restriction on printing accentuated importance of language and religion. Introduction of radio implies emphasis on language and intensification of religion and nationalism. Radio intensifies pattern of language which has not been naturally influenced by printing and enhances importance of language as national factor as built up with printing. Emphasis on language as national factor as built up with printing. Emphasis on language suggests learned and vernacular influenced by printing will tend to move farther from reality – even newspapers abandon extras – learned languages tend to drift farther from reality but possibly more necessary to provide stability accompanying emotional possibilities of strict appeal by radio to language.

207 Commercialization tends to make for imperfect competition between levels of reading public and to fix various groups within level. Average man cut off from literature. Problem of making fiction a channel of communication between levels. Commercialization prevents development of efficient channel – reading public disintegrated by imperfect competition in publishing industry. Problem of fertility of ideas moving more rapidly than science and machine industry or machine industry more effective in creation of ideas than of goods – cultural lag not of ideas behind machine but of machine behind ideas. Physics and chemistry accentuate rapid spread of communication and dissemination of ideas ahead of science, i.e. newspaper scientific stories far ahead of knowledge of actual facts. Problem of check on fantasy and restriction to reality to avoid confusion of ideas.

208 Importance of attacking aristocracy in spread of newspaper circulation – Dafoe happy when Manitoba Club annoyed with policy of paper – an indication that right line being followed and paper appealing to large numbers – advertisers watch circulation and type of appeal to readers.

209   Corporations make for more effective law enforcement - case of check-
       ing accounts and accepting government regulations in contrast with ease
       of individual fraud, but difficult to check personal accounts. Also ac-
       counting systems designed to show loss.

210   Spread of printing industry in Nova Scotia particularly migration from
       New England reflected in rhetorical nationalism (Harvey, 'Age of Faith').
       Regional patriotism a reflection of spread of innovation in technology.
       Rise and fall of science and technology - science in Greece declined as
       result of slavery and neglect of technology - science linked to techno-
       logy in arts (sculpture, etc.). Spread of rhetoric and law in Rome - em-
       phasis on rhetoric in Church and dark ages - rise of science - astronomy -
       Galileo - Newton - Darwin - technology increasing influence on rhe-
       toric (nationalism) but mechanical implication - advertising - impact on
       government policy.

211   Use of concepts bad and good, Devil and God facilitates emphasis on
       struggle and device for accentuating monopoly of those emphasizing
       good. Church attacked and built up idea of Devil to strengthen position
       and gain monopoly control by emphasis on frightening. Duopoly easier
       to support than monopoly.

212   Softening of science - effect of pressure groups on location of weather
       stations - nationalist influence - Empire scientists, Canadian scientists -
       influence of military, refused to exchange information - Russia. Social
       institutions becoming harder than science particularly nationalism -
       formerly science tougher but scientist without adequate training - tend
       to be conservative or to be influenced by fads - Marxist and so on, com-
       munists held to be exploiting universal interest in science - perhaps
       contributing to nationalism.

213   How far restrictions on imports of books in Nova Scotia to 1850 res-
       ponsible for literary activity? With import of books local talent stran-
       gled. Importance of protection to literature. Harvey, 'Age of Faith',
       Haliburton, etc.

214   Problem of improvement in densely populated areas - far east, etc. with
       emphasis on sex in contrast with populations of western civilization
       declining following emphasis on standards of living and small families -
       implies constant future difficulty on pressure of population from east
       on west - inevitable imperialism conflict. Russian pressure on west.

215   Significance of science in undermining religious factor in government
       and emphasizing democratic principle as against autocratic religious -
       but strengthens autocratic via control of technology or control of cen-

tres of capital characteristic of mechanical development of communication - weakens position of individual or controlling individual by emphasizing individualism.

216   Fred Allen - *Fifth Chair* a film with stars at various moments primarily a film to advertise radio - illustrating indirect influence of advertising consumers' goods in building up of radio and in turn influence on politics.

217   Saint John, N.B. - Librarian refused to allow Marx's *Capital* to circulate - also discontinued *Life* because of criticism of Empire - Chairman - retired Indian officer - bans books critical of India (Trueman).

218   Miss McKay claims groups divided in rural Manitoba - dominated by men or dominated by women or work cooperatively - latter most effective. Cooperatives a device for re-establishing community sense to offset divisive effects of individualism and trade but cooperatives tend to become commercial in character.

219   'He who is secure is not safe.' Poor Richard['s Almanack]

220   Editorials essentially news - used in early period to announce views of editor or publisher regarded as news and continued as such but forced to compete with abundance of other news and became less consistent in keeping with news.

221   Flin Flon shift system prevents continuity sufficient to develop adult education interests - demand of continuous operation tears cultural interest to shreds. Enormous power of company shown in grants to people and to town - keep relations sweet in spite of difficulties.

222   Popovich - teacher for Ukrainian Canadian Association in periods after school hours - say 5:30-9:30 in music, dancing and gymnastics. Built up orchestra of 85 pieces - work destroyed by government's closing hall but starting music with new group - young students have done eight months work - violin, concertina, etc. Popovich trained in Galicia (part of Austria) as teacher and carpenter. Reflects power of Greek Orthodox Church and emphasis on music - keep alive culture and community sense - children kept off street and engaged in intensive training - proceed to high school and university. Learn English and retain Ukrainian. Greek Catholic and others in Ukrainian Canadian Committee (Watson Kirkconnell type of organization). Greek Catholic - a result of attempt of Roman Catholic to break Greek Orthodox in Russia. Several groups of both Association and Committee scattered across country - Ukrainian farmers north of Dauphin and the Pas - wooded country - difficult to break and clear.

223   Typographical Union - older than other unions and rather haughty - looks with contempt on sympathetic strikes - consequently not supported by allied unions.

224   Importance of training leaders to teach people to avoid becoming leaders. Trueman as Superintendant of Schools, Saint John 1942-5 - extremely low salaries - beginning $550 going to $1150 but in spite of this large numbers anxious to get on staff. Depression reflected in devices for keeping down salaries. Illustration of rigidity of boards in municipalities as a factor in keeping down salaries and in checking response of public expenditures to income changes. Members of board opposed to increased taxation - difficulty of stirring up public opinion to favour increased salaries. Problem of low salaries in Maritimes - tendency to nepotism with damming back of salaries, i.e. Trueman and Trueman family. Explains resort of boards in other provinces to Maritimes for presidents - not accustomed to high salaries and acceptable to boards. Problem of enormous number interested in organization and holding of offices - leads to endless activity in setting up organizations and in agitating for reforms. Boards apt to be made up of professional groups - lawyers, doctors, etc. with narrow outlook toward education or with outlook concerned with taxation.

225   The Pas - Indians a weak, colourless group - illustration of impact of Anglo-Saxon individualism destroying vitality. Half-breeds spoke and Indians write but under domination of Anglican or Catholic Church and no vitality of their own. Contrast with Ukrainians - abundant vitality - resistance to Roman Catholic Church - strong sense of community - insistence on music and teacher - community persists with little dependence on church - illustrating significance of music as cultural factor - religion. Christianity penetrates to proletariat but in west took place of state with fall of Roman Empire and built hierarchical system. In Orthodox Church penetrates to proletariat but in same language, with married clergy and without independent hierarchy but subordinate to state and subject to political conception.

NOTES

8   Benjamin Kidd's *Principles of Western Civilization* was published in London in 1902.

9   Reference to J.B. Brebner, *Scholarship for Canada: The Function of Graduate Studies* (Ottawa, 1945). Miller was a Canadian businessman whose eccentric will continued to have an impact into the 1930s.

11   Note on W.E.H. Lecky, *History of the Rise and Influence of the Spirit of Civilization* (London, 1865)

13   Note on Roscoe Pound, *The Spirit of the Common Law* (Francestown, N.Y., 1921)

16	Reference to J.A. Schumpeter, *Capitalism, Socialism and Democracy* (New York, 1942)
24	On 6 August 1945 Mackenzie King announced to a Dominion-Provincial Conference that an atomic bomb had just been used against Japan.
28	Possibly note on T.F. Carter, *The Invention of Printing in China and Its Spread Westward* (New York, 1925)
29	Note on R.M. MacIver, *The Modern State* (London, 1928). See also 25 / 7.
32	See 3 / 1.
34	Note on W.A. White, *The Autobiography of William Allen White* (New York, 1946)
38	White (1869-1944) was a politically influential American journalist whose Emporia *Gazette* was widely respected.
41	J.T. Shotwell taught history at Columbia University from 1900 to 1942.
42	See 5 / 9.
54	Note on A.P. Usher, *A History of Mechanical Inventions* (New York, 1929)
57	Note on H.M. Robertson, *Aspects of the Rise of Economic Individualism* (Cambridge, 1933)
59	Note on Marjorie Plant, *The English Book Trade* (London, 1939)
62	Note on *Reprints of Statements Submitted by Members of J.P. Morgan and Co. to the Senate Committee on Banking and Currency ... May 23 to June 9, 1933* (New York, 1933)
64	Reference to Kennedy Jones, *Fleet Street and Downing Street* (London, 1920)
66	Frank Knight reviewed Keynes's *General Theory* under the title 'Unemployment: And Mr. Keynes's Revolution in Economic Theory,' *Canadian Journal of Economics and Political Science,* III (1937) 100-23. Innis draws attention to footnote 22, p. 112.
72	Note on Main Johnsen, *William Rockhill Nelson and the Kansas City Star* (Kansas City, 1935)
73	G.D. Conant and Duncan McArthur were Ontario lawyers who had varied and distinguished careers before entering electoral politics.
74	Donaldson is possibly N.V. Donaldson (1891-1964), an American publisher who headed Yale University Press from 1919.
90	MacPherson (1890-1944) was a Canadian-born pentacostal evangelist who rose to prominence in the United States. Father C.E. Coughlin was a Canadian-born Roman Catholic priest whose radio broadcasts in the United States critical of the New Deal had a considerable following.
97	T.N. Carver (1865-1961) was an American professor of economics.
107	Reference to Arnold Toynbee, *A Study of History*, Vol. II (London, 1934)
118	J.T.A. Maheux (1884-1967) taught history at the University of Laval.
122	Reference to T. Mommsen, *The History of Rome* (London, 1862-75)
160	Note on Arnold Toynbee, *A Study of History*, Vol. VI (London, 1939). Innis refers to p. 18.
162	Reference to Max Eastman, *Journalism versus Art* (New York, 1916)
163	C.A. Dana (1819-97) was nationally famous as editor of the New York *Sun*.
166	Possibly note on A.B. Paine, *Thomas Nast*. See 1 / 12.
175	Note on W.G. Bleyer, *Main Currents in the History of American Journalism* (Cambridge, Mass., 1927)
208	J.W. Dafoe (1866-1944) is best known as editor of the Winnipeg *Free Press*.
210	Reference to D.C. Harvey, 'The Age of Faith in Nova Scotia', Royal Society of Canada *Transactions*, Third Series, Vol. XXX, Sec. 2, 1946, pp. 1-20

213   T.C. Haliburton (1796-1865) was a Nova Scotia author. D.C. Harvey was Nova Scotia's provincial archivist and a contemporary of Innis. See also 5 / 210.

217   A.W. Trueman (b. 1902) was superintendant of public schools in Saint John from 1942 to 1945. Afterwards he was President of the University of Manitoba and then of the University of New Brunswick.

218   Frances McKay sat with Innis on the Manitoba Royal Commission on Adult Education.

221   Flin Flon is a mining town in Manitoba.

224   See 5 / 217.

6

1946

1   Importance of large-scale circulation of books similar to that for news-
     papers or magazines, i.e. an attempt to reach largest possible number or
     lowest common denominator - Sears mail order or Haldeman-Julius -
     latter sell cheap books, former emphasize Bible and avoid criticism of
     Bible and emphasize happy ending fiction or lowest common denomin-
     ator - significance of large circulation to sales of other books.

2   Influence of printing on logical discussion, i.e. parliament speeches re-
     port meant a record of position and possibility of use by newspapers
     and enemies. Consequently speakers cautious and select words and use
     style designed to protect speaker - an elaborate game of chess with re-
     corded material. Difficulty of understanding language of another coun-
     try when built up in relation to different political stresses. Problem
     within country intensified and not possible for those in another lang-
     uage to understand implications. Selection of slogans of politicians by
     newspapers - care of politicians in avoiding vigilance of newspapers.
     Comparable to guard on private conversation in Hollywood lest rivals
     secure gags.

3   Tree of knowledge - building up of information over long period with
     use of mechanical devices - monopoly power of knowledge within cul-
     ture - contrast Greeks with emphasis on training rather than informa-
     tion - Socratic versus Sophistic. Educational systems, additional courses,
     insatiable demand for new devices to disseminate information - mechan-
     ical impact on knowledge. Tendency to break down of its own weight
     or under impact of force. Problem of economist to point to limitations
     of knowledge. Choice of tree of knowledge apt to mean neglect of prob-
     lem of character. Overwhelming influence of knowledge and instruction
     and necessity of appreciating limitation of tolerance. Universities impor-
     tant position in weeding out weaker students.

4   Character of impact of material in contrast with monopolistic character
     of knowledge. Papyrus cut off - place taken by parchment associated

with monasteries and monopoly of knowledge. Paper spread through
Mohammedan world with restrictions on image worship - restrictions in
regions dominated by church - accentuated importance of paper in
development of trade and commerce and vernacular use with printing
spread to religion in reformation - restriction of church in France and
Italy and Spain, but paper made for export meant break up of monopoly of knowledge in Holland and England. Mercantilism favoured
spread of paper production but restriction in monopoly of knowledge.
Restriction of market for paper brought outbursts of independence -
vernacular - development of colonies. Parchment determined format of
book through manuscript and type. Dominance of book in Christianity -
use of pamphlet for agnosticism and radicalism. Restrictions of papyrus roll of education - importance of libraries for fragile material. Paper
production increased importance of trade - speeded up transactions and
meant prosperity - comparable to effect of gold inflation.

5   Impact of increasing knowledge and number of facts shown in growth
     of libraries and increasing registration in universities - largely concerned
     with retailing facts. Government support to large-scale marketing of
     facts.

6   Significance of sacred books and emphasis on writing with attacks on
     image worship by Semites and Moslems shown in inevitable tendency
     toward monotheism and drive toward concentration on writing. Ex-
     tremely important with paper spreading from China - impact of media
     and writing on culture based on parchment - renaissance and reforma-
     tion. European civilization a result of concentration on writing and
     destruction of polytheism and interest in image - worship which detracts
     from power of writing. Drive of sacred literature, worship of scripture,
     emphasis on learning accentuates impact of science - adaptability of
     alphabet but limitations in existence of different alphabets and capa-
     city to adapt to dialects - making for division particularly with printing.
     New language in maturation partly arabic basis of science.

7   Knight emphasizes tendency toward inequality following increased
     power of demagogue or political democracy. Capacity of demagogue to
     exploit monopoly position - this true of all communications.

8   Libraries part of autocratic government - Pisistratus first library in
     Athens 537 [B.C.]. In Alexandria, Pergamum, Rome - supported by
     emperors and ruling classes - reinforces position of force and strengthens
     public opinion. Writing monopoly of priests and lawyers - power of
     lawyers in France - literature reaching out to new monopoly position
     in vernacular with improved communication, paper and printing. Law
     of Rome and written tradition left vacuum for spread of religion - oral

tradition. Monopoly position of learning weakens initiative and allows force to develop in new fringe areas and brings about collapse of civilization at centre, new monopolies built up - religion, later law - monopoly position of law in France brought revolution. In England oral tradition broke out, struggle between vernacular and French of conquerors and between court vernacular and that of people - Shakespeare vs. Milton. Science - spread of monopoly of knowledge to industry and professions and to military or force. Monopolies in printing industry - broken down by pressure of improvements on margin - also trade monopoly of advertising agencies. Revival of general thesis - pressure of technology of frontier.

9   Difficulties of parliamentary institutions in Europe because of strength of Roman law and written tradition in contrast with Anglo-Saxon countries. Italian writers - Mosca, Loria - appeal to laws or neglect strength of legal tradition.

10   Significance of family to governing classes - advantage in political training - importance of name in advertising for political purposes - Roosevelt, Taft, Dewey - family names in U.S. Significance of Mosca's ruling class to written tradition or learned class. Universities in relation to tradition. Oxford, Cambridge, Harvard. Tradition of courts and army. Oliver Wendell Holmes. In Canada Mackenzie King.

11   Contrast Wissler's concept of spread outward to fringe from centre with trend in communications with spread fringe to centre, i.e. in spread of newspaper technique from west to east. Pulitzer, Ochs, Hearst, monopoly of communication at centre reverses trends emphasized by Wissler.

12   Printing in Germany with position of copyists in Paris - slow development in France - rapid development in Italy with paper. Significance of vernacular - decline in influence and international position of University of Paris - nationalism meant narrowing of position to France. Papacy encouraged rival universities. Power of king increased in France through support of lawyers. Dominicans dominant in University of Paris. Franciscans in Oxford - free from dominance of capital or study of law and medicine - power of arts faculty - possibilities of theological speculation - Wycliffe. Suppression but spread to Hus in Prague. Reformation in areas not dominated by law. Significance of regional factor - Paris as against Oxford and law in Italy. Dominicans vs. Franciscans reflection of regionalism and vernacular. Aristotle vs. Plato and Augustine. Scotland dominated by Roman law emphasized philosophy in universities. Significance of Adam Smith - Scottish universities early to use vernacular - [Francis] Hutcheson - Scottish tradition not acceptable to common law. England - back of revolt of English against James [I] and Charles

I or Stuarts. Regional approach to intellectual thought – important with
decline of Latin and universal position of University of Paris.

13   Rapid setting up by linotype reduced cost of composition and led to
daily changes in ads – made ads part of news. Before mechanical invention advertisers established position and gained enormously with exploitation of cheap newsprint and composition – by large purchase of
space during period of intense newspaper competition. Cheap large-
scale advertising brought by Pulitzer from St Louis to New York and
overthrew *Herald*. *Herald* dominated by news policy and neglected advertising – advertising brought evolution in journalism. *Herald* and
Times affected.

14   Significance of ploughing back earnings in newspaper and dangers of
withdrawing funds. Significance of war advertising to general advertising – bonds, Red Cross, etc. Broad pressure of advertising evident in
changing of reading material – emphasis on women's interests prepara-
tory to advertising. Department stores capitalized advertising in newspapers – classified advertisements backbone of penny press – papers
emphasizing these grew by amalgamation with others. Emphasis on
advertising – newspaper advertising and pointing to possibility of improving its position in competition with other media.

15   Aristotle – library, written tradition makes enormous impact on developments in relation to oral tradition, i.e. Plato – rediscovery of Aristotle –
emphasis on science made impact on philosophy based on Plato –
Augustine – rediscovered and made part of Catholic philosophy, i.e. St
Thomas Aquinas. Paper facilitated spread of Aristotle – printing emphasized science element, but split with sacred scriptures, i.e. Bible vernacular – mendicant friars, universities – oral tradition in attempt to absorb
written tradition – Aristotle. Suppression of newspapers of political
character under Walpole probably contributed to concentration of
advertiser on advertising. How far intense political activity weakens
position of advertiser and trade?

16   Contrast continent and England or Anglo-Saxon countries – continent
emphasized written law, i.e. influence of Roman law and Anglo-Saxon
countries [emphasized] the Bible or written religion with oral tradition
in law. Religion becomes conservative though characterized by infinite
diversity in Anglo-Saxon countries and without influence of Bible in
Roman law countries offers little outlet, i.e. organization of church and
leads to explosion – protest against organization or hierarchy of [Roman
Catholic Church] – less conspicuous in Protestant countries.

17   Fabians – Irish home rule illustration of possibility of small determined
group to emerge and become powerful with instability of public opinion.

18   Influence of character on position in hierarchies – mean, vindictive, ego-
      istic apt to hold on lower rungs of ladder as upper levels make greater
      demands for character – magnanimity, charity, humanity particularly
      in large organizations of successful hierarchies.

19   Neglect of study of monasticism and capitalism – celibacy accompanied
      by high living and large-scale consumption of food and wine – problem
      of reform and setting up of new orders with poverty vows but constant
      tendency to become wealthy – energies concentrated on other than
      family interests implies wealth and power. How far monasticism anti-
      clerical and how far does it reflect influence of vernacular as against
      clergy?

20   Success of agnostic literature sold by Haldeman and inability to sell
      Bible – evidence of success of publishing houses dominated by book
      tradition in excluding agnostic literature – agnosticism compelled to
      seek another medium, i.e. small pamphlet – Tom Paine. People expect
      Bible to be expensive and bound in black. Roman law and philosophy
      on continent reflected written tradition – Marx and Lenin opposed to
      state and attacked it as part of class structure – Marx provided base of
      revolutionary approach – taking place of Bible in common law coun-
      tries. Class struggle adapted to oral tradition – avoided rigid character
      of law incidental to written tradition. Limited influence of Marx in
      England – common law background. Reflected breakup of written tra-
      dition or impact of technological change on influence of writing.

21   Enormous increase in competition – production and sale of pocket
      books – possibly result in part of effect of taxes on cigars and decline in
      sale of tobacco and resort of cigar stores to pocket book. New techno-
      logical changes lead to revival of dead books on large scale – so-called
      classics as no copyright involved – how far this involves penalty on
      modern authors and enhances place of books with large sale – best
      selling advertisers using songs to widen market for product. United Fruit
      Company song about bananas in refrigerator won top place in Hit
      Parade. Illustration of dominance of advertising in radio and in song.

22   Radio means building up personal reputations especially during war –
      Churchill, Wallace – these continue like disembodied spirits or pestilent
      corpses after power gone – also Roosevelt – power of a single individual
      enormously increased.

23   Emphasis of Protestantism on individualism and disappearance of con-
      fession meant that individual in a position to buy and sell or to profit
      by hiding or giving information – no longer compelled to give informa-
      tion in confession to priest.

24 Loyalists in Ontario left U.S. in revolution but forced back to U.S. through dominance of emigrants from other provinces.

25 German obsession with scholarship a result of hold of printed word and early development of printing industry and Protestantism - Anglo-Saxon countries slow to develop printing industry and used censorship to guarantee oral tradition and parliamentary tradition.

26 Acton gave very little attention to importance of law and probably overemphasized religion - [John Henry, Cardinal] Newman knew little about Germany and neglected Protestant contribution.

27 Importance of sales of space for news - playing up of crime in Chicago a device for selling space over vast areas - as an inland centre compelled to capitalize on special form of news.

28 British Empire and emphasis on political organization as bulwark against Roman Catholic Church.

29 Follow significance of overhead costs, i.e. paper mills meant pressure of paper on writing - printing press meant pressure on paper and pressure on public of books and later other media. Basic element of disturbance in capital equipment and overhead charges incidental to it. Elaborate development of public relations - agencies suggesting to groups and organizations devices by which goodwill can be built up in return for substantial payment. Influence in magazines shown in articles written with strong indirect influence.

30 Danger of romantic belief in action rather than thought (Knight) a reflection of significance of action to news.

31 Instantaneous communication strengthens position of bureaucracy.

32 Idea of Plato - possible with shift from oral to written tradition and working out of thought and plan to which society can conform - use of force, rise of industrialism destroys possibility of working out of Idea or plan. Problem of later history of west in inability to work out Idea with power to mould society. Greece - emphasis on unity of approach - later civilization seized at various points with significance of an element of culture. Arabic literature and Persian literature excluded influence of Greek literature but absorbed science transmitted in west. Rome absorbed rhetoric but excluded sciences. Middle Ages absorbed artistic development of Greece in worship of images.

33   Significance of property in anchoring population and checking migra-
      tion - with barbarian invasions property became loot and disappeared.
      [Subsequently] as concepts of property reestablished, Roman law be-
      came more powerful and population became settled in feudalism.
      Cavalry probably assumed settled conditions and growth of wealth but
      migration also assumed reliance on land mobility - use of horse.

34   Roman law made more or less permanent following edict under Hadrian
      of 132 A.D. Written tradition dominated and law ceased to be flexible -
      contributed to spread of religion as oral tradition - in turn latter became
      written tradition - outbreak of vernacular but church attempted to
      dominate education rather than use of force.

35   A writing age - an egoistic age - becomes absorbed in mastering tech-
      nique of writing with little possibility of studying implications of
      technique.

36   Possibility of U.N.O. [United Nations Organization] with restoration of
      oral tradition - written tradition, i.e. treaties, etc., inflexible and diffi-
      cult to adjust - U.N.O. brings discussion immediately before people and
      makes for continuous adjustment and response to public opinion.

37   Broadcaster advertising various products concerned with improving
      their own goodwill as well as that of products sponsored, i.e. emphasis
      on stars - Jack Benny, Fred Allen. Individuals emphasize their own
      names.

38   Religion gained by the use of new technique in publishing, i.e. Christian-
      ity in book and parchment as against roll and papyrus. Emerged from
      writing area - Palestine and Arabia as against worship of images and
      worship of books. Emphasis on books meant gaining control of mind -
      dominance of education. Book a device for capturing rational approach.
      Chinese - dense population but limited division of labour and trade and
      consequently limited demands on communication or on a more efficient
      alphabet. Trade implies efficiency of alphabet.

39   [Emile] Durkheim holds the chief drive in society biological. Pressure
      of population leads to division of labour and technological change
      rather than maximum emphasis on technology.

40   Problem of price control in Canada - rumours as to scarcity of various
      items leading to systematic hoarding - lack of effective means of dis-
      seminating information - constant danger of inadequate information
      and need for devices to check spread of rumours.

41   Church apt to become menace to morals in struggle for existence. Women inveigling men and compelling them to marry them as means of getting them into church. Tendency to wink at loose sexual relations when results shown in addition to church membership.

42   Extent to which scholastic philosophy had sapped intellectual energies particularly as it was followed by spread of printing and revival of classics - thus making possible enormous impact of mathematics on political thinking and philosophy in 17th century.

43   Problem of controlled public opinion in dictatorships - ambassadors in other countries send back to home country information which they think will please dictators and thus give latter a distorted and fatal impression of developments abroad - Hitler completely deceived by attitude of England. Written constitutions provide check to usurpation of supreme bodies, i.e. writing down of customs - emphasis on custom in written constitution and on public opinion and ceremonial in unwritten as in England - power of class structure. With written word elaborate system of interpretation as to meaning of words in courts - precedents, etc.

44   Business fluctuations result of increase or decrease of intensity of belief in possibility of predicting the future - influence of communication. System of interest rates mathematically impossible - with increasing rigidity due to influence of publicity and communication inevitable pressure to lower rates of interest. Contracts or treaties between nations incapable of permanence and necessity of system providing for constant change in constitutional set-up. Political machinery built around interest rates and necessity of resorting to monetary manipulation.

45   Semantics - study which follows poverty of language in relation to demands. Words in relation to particular situation fail to apply to others - sense of humour because of increasing complexity and burden imposed on words. Words inadequate to meet strain of industrialism. Crucial place of language and its content shown in attitude of religion. R.C. [Roman Catholic church] opposed translation of Scriptures from Latin holding that vernacular not adequate for translation - also French Canadians insist on religion. Problem of monopoly position of one language and difficulty of punctuating it. Translation of scriptures into another language and for different class apt to produce heretical literature. Bishop Colenso and attempt to teach Zulu chief led him to realize that he had only a metaphorical belief in the Book of Genesis - so translation into German for Dominican nuns produced mysticism.

46   Toleration most ardently supported by intolerant individual. Universi-
       ties exploited by those exploiting the prejudices of civilization - suffi-
       ciently shrewd to sense prejudices of community and use it for protec-
       tion. Those also [exploit] who exploit the exploiters.

47   August 4, 1946. Alex Dadson - employed by government to check lum-
       ber shipped by small firms at exorbitant prices or without attention to
       grades. Price ceiling encourages over-grading with enormous demands of
       building industries and necessity to step in to prevent increase in price
       through this device.

48   Importance of capacity for conversation in development of politician
       and parliament - organization of oral tradition but restrained by print -
       crystallization of oral to written in parliament and laws.

49   Babylonian priesthood - power of goddesses; Egyptian king - emphasis
       on pyramids. Palestine influenced by priesthood and spread through
       Christianity to west. Roman Catholic Church in Babylonia[n] tradition
       particularly with combination of fertility religions and priesthood.
       Cathedrals. Weakness of Oriental king in Alexander and Roman emper-
       ors but strength in laws. Patriarchal system destroyed power of gods
       and magicians in Grecian religion and became basis of legal develop-
       ment in Rome. Power of force and appeal to sea against religion but
       decline of Mediterranean meant rise of Roman Catholic Church and
       feudalism and of Mohammedanism. Pressure of church on knowledge -
       control of media - broken down with impact of paper from China.
       Images - crude form of print worship.

50   Mankind constantly being caught in his own traps - language and sys-
       tems developed and most difficult to break down - significant that re-
       forms come latest in control of communications, i.e. paper duty last to
       be removed - interest in monopoly of A.P. [Associated Press] the last
       to be recognized. Control of methods of expression makes improve-
       ment more difficult. Greeks had advantage of debating without control
       but with development of written tradition control of systems followed -
       used by Romans. Communication limited to small number - hierarchy
       of philosophy - egoism makes it more difficult to secure relief - man-
       kind's belief in his own contrivances.

51   Development of prose in Greece meant objectivity and breakdown of
       Greek society as contrasted with rise of individual - facilitated growth
       of law and empire under Romans. Writing meant emphasis on individual
       or author and weakening of Greek concept of polis. Without the discip-
       line of printing the mob or democracy becomes irresponsible - hence
       attacks on democracy by Plato and Aristotle and the failure in securing

effective military leadership. Alcibiades expelled because of religious prejudice and generals changed with various reports of defeat – absence of consistent policy.

52 Silberling – strategic points – steel. Toynbee – place of pressure, movement of population, rather than trend. Danger of looking at earlier period with spectacles emerging from period after last war – Marxists. Significance in showing importance of ideas to which goods could be hooked on by which they were carried to consumers. Relativity slips into scientism, limitations of relativity.

53 Propaganda departments and popular press enabled war to be carried on much longer and left communities more exhausted after war and made for greater difficulty in maintaining peace. Peace a period with over-expanded propaganda development. Slow development of attacks on trusts in fields of communications an indication of difficulty of securing competition in fields of knowledge. Printing industry – large-scale production necessitated rise of distribution organization, i.e. publisher compelled to predict market and assume control over printer. Price system became effective in publisher's drive to extend consumption and to keep printer under control. Publisher tends to flourish as result of overhead cost of printer and to press production on market.

54 Priestcraft and relation to writing – use of written word and emphasis on *ipsissima verba* explains Catholic interest in writings of Fathers and concern of Middle Ages with authority and the text. Administrative hierarchy uses written word to strengthen position – Protestantism took over printed word. Great advantage of Greeks in being close to oral tradition. Catholic Church administered through system of reports from select individuals in the diocese and recommendations for bishop based on these reports. Vatican becomes centre of information and decision but once bishop appointed he has jurisdiction over diocese.

55 Ottawa civil service and union government of [Prime Minister Sir Robert] Borden administration came under control of an independent civil service commission. Present commission to investigate service [The Royal Commission on Administrative Classifications in the Public Service, chaired by Walter Gordon] recommends a swing back to more effective treasury control and less independence.

56 Extension of printing divides reason and emotion and overemphasizes reason. Significant power of close relations between vernacular and written speech – Norway and Russia.

57   Print - newspapers serve as enormous blanket to public opinion - broken around edges where less effective - Huey Long [in] Louisiana and Aberhart - also Hitler.

58   Oratory in 19th century brought to front men with powerful lungs - radio implied a sharp decline in this sort of individual - Bryan - Gladstone.

59   With barbaric invasions Romans continued with hereditary rank but retreated to church. How far religion a reflection of cultural disparity, i.e. used by Romans and appreciated by Franks - influence of missionaries to Indians? Emphasis on spiritual power a reflection of cultural difference. Enormous independent power of bishops in Gaul with acquisition of land - limited control of papacy - basis of Gallican temper of later French church.

60   Writing of books and persistent demand of printing press for author's names lead to development of individualism and to emphasis by individual on his own importance.

61   Enormous imperial significance of culture, i.e. Shakespeare in English-speaking countries - tremendous vitality essential to the production and influence continues over long period. Shaw's attack on Shakespeare significant in breaking up monopoly position of artificial interest. Emphasis on Ireland as pointing to weak spot in British imperialism - paving way in art to socialism and devolution of empire. Writing of books necessitates presenting case as final argument - consequently books contribute powerfully to closing of minds particularly of writer as he has strong vested interests in position which has been elaborated.

62   Greek - virtue is knowledge. Hebrew knowledge is crime. Latter reflects monopoly of prophets rather than scribes - attack on scribes and monopoly of knowledge held by Babylonian and Egyptian scribes - Greeks not in rebellion against scribes - found it unnecessary to emphasize prophets but developed emphasis on dialogue and scepticism - virtue - knowledge that we know nothing. Constant danger of building up of monopoly of knowledge in terms of material - manuscripts, books, libraries - leading to revolt on fringes of new techniques - fanaticism of ignorance waged against fanaticism of knowledge.

63   Penetration of advertising to book - volumes written to order by writers after contracts with publishers and with firms about whom volume written to take substantial number of volumes to guarantee printing costs. Exploitation of prestige advertising by writers and using book to emphasize it. Pamphlets formerly great instruments declined with reluctance

of publishers to handle small items and with newspapers - Keynes made limited revival of pamphlets. Essay declined because of lack of depth of writers and of readers with enormous increase in output of writing.

64   Papyrus   Egyptian literature - hieroglyphics

Clay   Babylonian - religious

Semitic   alphabet - religious writing

Greek   improved alphabet - flowering of literature - drama, philosophy, art of conjuring with words

Romans force - demands of army making for equality and law - Beneventan script

Christians parliament - book - Old and New Testament - theology - France return from Ireland - minuscule spread to Italy - paper - commerce - Italian and German city states. Germany - printing - Italian and German cities - emphasis on Old Testament in Germany - classics in Italy - struggle with copyists - France. Emphasis on vernacular - England - flourishing of stage - court - Shakespeare - clash with vernacular-prose - Puritanism.

NOTES

1   Emanuel Haldeman-Julius (1889-1951) was an American editor and publisher.

7   Note on Frank Knight, *The Economic Order and Religion* (New York, 1945). See also 6 / 30.

9   Gaetano Mosca (1858-1941) and Achille Loria (1857-1943) wrote on politics and economics.

11   Reference to Clark Wissler, *Man and Culture* (New York, 1923)

16   Note on Ernst Troeltsch, *The Social Teachings of the Christian Churches* (London, 1931)

20   See 6 / 1.

30   Note on Knight, *The Economic Order*. See 6 / 7.

31   Note on L. Mumford, *Technics and Civilization* (New York, 1934)

39   Note on Emile Durkheim, *The Division of Labour in Society* (New York, 1933)

45   John Colenso (1814-83), Anglican bishop of Natal, was found guilty of heresy in 1863 but was subsequently acquitted.

52   Reference to N.J. Silberling, *The Dynamics of Business* (New York, 1943)

7

1946

1 Hegel - worship of state - a concern with written tradition - significant that it developed in Germany.

2 Importance of trade in bringing science close to things and avoiding words. Importance of oral tradition among Greeks meant easy absorption with scarcity of parchment in scholasticism in Middle Ages - emphasis on oral tradition in universities. Words fostered philosophy in Greece and scholastic philosophy in Middle Ages - place destroyed with printing and emphasis on industry, science and observation. Mendicant orders attempted to bridge gap between words or learned language and vernacular by emphasis on oral tradition - but this inadequate with rise of printing and written tradition or emphasis on scriptures. Ruthless stamping out of pagan literature and magic by church created uniformity facilitating growing influence of state.

3 How far church interference with family strengthens political government on wider base than family?

4 Senate in Canada with entrenched position of party, i.e. in Maritimes possibly serves to foster rise of political parties in provinces not associated with old parties. Senate makes for less flexible government and breakdown of political flexibility in relation to economic demands.

5 Extension of communication to lower levels contributes to disturbances - moves in from outlying regions - printing in Germany. Development of science after Lord Bacon suggests importance of hierarchy.

6 Economics arose with interest of science in things rather than words - Adam Smith and Hume's attack on philosophy. Hobbes attacked emphasis on words as basis of ideas and demanded return of relationship between words and things as basis of ideas - impact of printing and vernacular gave ecclesiastical system position of very great importance in church and state.

7   That Hanoverian kings came from Germany may have meant bringing of
      influence of Roman law to England and leading to attitude of George III
      which brought American revolt.

8   Break on fringe - reformation in Germany, political revolution in Eng-
      land, American revolution, back to French revolution and to Germany
      and Italy - impact of printing on civilization centring around manuscript.

9   Speeches, writing, use of words designed to throw bridges from present
      into future - provide stability but periodically become inadequate and
      break down.

10   State essentially a reflection of force - latter compels peace accompan-
      ied by rise of individualism - reflected in growth of anarchism [in]
      latter part hundred years of peace 1814-1914. Improved [methods of]
      communication strengthens position of individual and weakens society
      as making communication [between individuals?] more difficult.

11   History of cruelty - use of lash up to beginning of 19th century in army
      and navy and influence of public opinion in leading to decline - influ-
      ence of Cobbett's writings - also decline of death penalty with revision
      of law in 19th century.

12   Significance of Keynes - used a style influenced by journalism in *Eco-
      nomic Consequences of Peace* [1919]. Significant power of writing by
      an economist in book form with distrust of newspapers. Keynes repre-
      sents Anglo-Saxon common law point of view emphasizing importance
      of free trade and economics and Mantoux the French Roman law point
      of view - continental - recognizing importance of force and political
      factors - in Keynes neglect of political considerations. Importance of
      law and order as basis of trade and tendency of trade to make for con-
      stant change and adaptation of law - social sciences developed as
      assistance to law.

13   Later development of geology probably a result of concern with
      astronomy and physics and influence of scriptures in checking an
      interest in development on the earth.

14   Development of belief in God largely an agricultural phenomenon -
      result of discovery of apparent plan in adaptation of man's work to
      influence of seasons - with rise of machine industry plan appears as
      more evidently a result of man's work or belief in man rather than
      nature and displacement of apparent plan.

15   Significance of written money, current accounts - use of cheques to
      explain character of crises since, say, 1890.

16   Significance of journalism as training for those exercising wide influ-
      ence, i.e. Henry George, Keynes in *New Statesman.* How far true of
      Bellamy? Power of journalism in making books effective and changing
      ideas of large number able to absorb simple ideas.

17   Chinese - 14,000 characters and 400 syllables - result difficult to under-
      stand conversations without getting context or beginning of discussion
      as same words with different meanings. Written language understood
      over wide area whereas oral language difficult to understand. Emphasis
      on classics in examination - systematic screening of ability - doing away
      with old system reduces efficiency of mobility - lack of effective screen-
      ing device and emphasis on cleverness - corrupt government. Taoism
      more widespread as religion. Pearl Buck and Pearl Habor greatest weak-
      ness of U.S. - difficult to get balanced picture of confused civilization.
      Dominicans appeal to Pope objecting to Jesuits admitting ancestor wor-
      ship as memorial service - objection to Pope's questioning of Emperor's
      word led to his banishing all Christian missions. Ritchie - powerful
      Jesuit - rights controversy. Rivalry of monasteries in Church weakened
      its position in China with strong Emperor worship and powerful family
      tradition and ancestor worship. China an illustration of a civilization
      based on scholarship - attempt to attract ablest in intellectual sense into
      field of government. Breakdown with neglect of essential function of
      scholarship and emphasis on cleverness rather than capacity.

18   Monopoly element in value of artistic products - death of artist and
      hence importance of originality. Also stamps never repeated have mono-
      polistic element. Value increases with recognition of irreproducible
      character of original. Also rise of reproductions - attempt to capitalize
      on monopoly value. All this tends to check growth of originality, i.e.
      importance of printing in relation to restriction of manuscripts - paper
      versus parchment.

19   Ancient empires absorbed in problem of international affairs. Greece in
      individual development - civilization concerned with absorption of two
      strands. How far writing began essentially as basis of administration and
      of empires - Babylonia, Egypt? Problem of marking out land in Egypt
      possibly at background of writing. Egyptian empire before 1390 B.C. -
      system of communication - Akkadian cuneiform - lingua franca. How
      far leather and stone developed as early medium in relation to law -
      papyrus in relation to literature or fugitive material - less rigid? Papyrus
      important to detailed administration of Egypt - this bureaucratic sys-
      tem spread throughout Rome in absolute monarchy. Significance of
      Alexandria as a created city in attracting diverse elements. Feature of
      empires in creating cities and destroying them. Translation of old testa-
      ment to Greek and Septuagint in Alexandria and taking over by Chris-
      tians led Jews to return to Hebrew scriptures.

20   Overwhelming importance of oral tradition in Athens - juries became
serious obstacle in efficiency of courts in handling disputes of Athenian
empire and weakened its federal possibilities.

21   [A.P.] Usher deplored decline in essay writing by students and consequent
illiteracy - problem of over-worked students in compulsory subjects and
over-worked staff. Administration fails to give proper attention to appointments with large teaching staff and staff overloaded with mediocrity. Probable effects of mathematics in social sciences - over-emphasis
on abstractions and neglect of writing and reading. Dangers of system
which emphasizes routine in education in dampening selective process
in relation to intellectual capacity. Probable that army efficiency due to
spacing of wars thus enabling younger men to dominate. Continued war
would probably imply increased importance of older men and consequent inflexibility. Significance of lower interest rate to increasing numbers of students and emphasis on teaching and fees to offset lower
income from endowments.

22   Complaint that enormous support of foundations to public administration had serious effects on position of political philosophy - students
turned from theory to administration. Weakness of economics shown in
absence of economists trained to understand other than western civilizations. Economists' interests narrowed by concentration with abstraction of mathematics.

23   Contrast between north and south shown in attitude toward printing.
Governor Spotswood in south opposed printing and this became typical
of aristocracy and slave economy. In north newspapers came to reflect
expansion of printing and literacy and emphasis on freedom of press.
Southerners claim negroes given religion and courtesy and these being
destroyed by contact with north.

24   Notarial documents in Italian business back to 1150 made of paper.
Municipal statutes prohibiting use of paper as not sufficiently durable
for government purposes. Business demands stimulated new industries.

25   Babylonia emphasis on star and astrology overcame physics and astronomy in Greece. Egypt emphasis on king and fertility cults - goddess Isis.
Mystery religions resistance against Fate and Babylonia - biology vs.
astronomy. Greek appeal to natural law limited by interest in experiment. Babylonia overwhelmed by natural law and astronomy or [in
other words] astronomy had stamp of religion.

26   In England interest in rural areas meant peasants little involved in Puritan revolution whereas in France lack of interest in peasants made their

concern with land important to revolution. Struggle between excesses of religion and the rationalism of price system.

27 Max Weber reversed Marx - the system of production grows out of the dominant attitude. Role of intellectual in revolution effected by supply of medium of communication and reward for service. Isolated event partly reflects demand for convenience of reference - apt to be overemphasized, i.e. starting point - Boston Tea Party, storming of Bastille - the revolutions in part belong to pre-literary stage, i.e. France, Russia, oral tradition and rumour extremely significant to technique - after revolution impetus of printing incidental to it makes for stability.

28 Problem of force to reduce number of gods and secure unity.

29 Papyrus in Greece gave freedom but not unity. Empire meant force and control of Egypt with supply of papyrus. Papyrus facilitated rise of poets and prevented control of priests. Rome - illustration of organization of force - west conquered east (Caesar vs. Pompey, and Augustus vs. Antony) but moved to Constantinople as more effective centre - latter effective through law which overcame religion in late Middle Ages. Problem of sex - destruction of female children - Greece emphasized perversion - opposition to celibacy among Jews and Islam - celibacy in monasticism Egypt and Rome. Contempt of Greeks for language of Latin in expressing views as to Trinity meant latter or Romans emphasized organization and dogma, and elasticity finally introduced with impact of Greek on Latin through Spain in field of science.

30 Empire destroyed city state - left gap between people and government and room for Epicureanism and Stoicism and Church. Greek principle personal law but Roman territorial - reflecting importance of element of force. Ptolemys in Egypt probably built up library to offset priests' influence at Thebes - also they established official religion. Christianity emerged with absolutism - following Alexander and disappearance of city state - rise of individual and powerlessness before government. How far Christianity a religion reflecting political impotence - monasticism, etc.?

31 Copying of manuscripts and translations emphasized bulky writings by single individual copyist. Size of books a factor in religion and priesthood - Indian Mahabharata - 100,000 couplets. How far does writing check religious extravagances? Great number of castes in India probably result of lack of influence of printing and of written tradition. Oral tradition of Brahmanism defeated scripture of Buddhism in India. In China Confucianism scriptures defeated Buddhism - conquered in Japan. Weak written tradition implies belief in superiority of intuition to

intellectual reasoning. Deeper experience a worldless [word-less?] doctrine, the self is silent.

32 Appeal to nature an appeal to Greece. Poetry essentially in oral tradition and uses meter and accent to be read aloud. Printing and silent
reading destroys beauty of music. Importance of handicraft to Greeks -
economy and conciseness in writing. Greek architecture - unrelated
buildings - Hellenistic and Roman - planned cities (city state versus
empire).

33 Assyrian success result of cavalry rather than chariots. How far administration in Persia weakened by dependence on papyrus? Did papyrus also
contribute to weakness politically of Greeks? Problem solved by Rome
with controlled supply.

34 Greek thought - Arabic translations - Jewish influence to Europe - had
significance for Christian, Jew and Muslim. Paper regime - beginning
with Muslim flowering under Abassids at Baghdad 749-1258. How far
church prohibition of usury a device for keeping down its own interest
rates? Persecution of Jews led to special devices to protect property -
public records of private transactions - copyright - hence over-emphasis
on property protection.

35 Struggle against Islam led to bigotry of Christianity in Spain - but centralized government supported Columbus. Paper gave impetus to Baghdad and in turn to Spain. Greek learning passed through Baghdad,
Spain, Europe. Geographic division of Mediterrean - Greek church
Hellenistic, Byzantine - West - Roman Church, Holy Roman Empire.
Crusades gave sanctity to laymen and to lay state. Emphasis on words
in religions concerned with written books - Cabalistic literature of Jews -
use of rhyme by Arabs - troubadours. Rise of mysticism with clash
between interest in words and older civilization - Arab and Persian,
German and Cabala. How far celibacy essential to church organization
in contrast with personal monotheism of Jews and Mohammedans and
insistence on marriage?

36 Party machine in U.S. after 1840 meant power shifted from Congress -
issues no longer settled in Congress and drifted to civil war. Constant
struggle of oral with written tradition in parliament, corporations.

37 Classes with flexible alphabet.

38 Natural law really an appeal to oral tradition.

39 Machine politics a reflection of power of oral against written tradition.

40   Rise of science reflects growth of language of mathematics and written tradition.

41   Court lyrics of erotic character contributed to growth of vernacular particularly with celibate clergy dominating administration and unable to cope with pressure against Latin.

42   Charisma – oral tradition; bureaucracy – written tradition.

43   Papyrus made Nile centre of empires and libraries for book production.

44   Importance of cathartic effect of literature – if sufficient flexibility [in literature, a country] may avoid revolution or compel use of major work, [such as] Marx's *Capital*, as in Russia.

45   Awful price paid by Jews for introducing flexible monetary system – church restriction on usury compelled Jews to become financiers.

46   Printing and accentuation of vernacular emphasized science and possibilities of escape from dulling influence of dual language – sharpening of language in relation to nationalism. Rise of dialectic oral tradition appearing in universities – emphasis on logic and disputation.

47   Cutting off of trade by Mohammedanism – lowering of standard of living in relation to population – weakening in relation to invasions of Vikings. General decline of civilization.

48   Babylonia – priestly tradition – Palestine scriptures, Roman Catholic Church, Reformation. Egyptian – king – emperor. Rome, Byzantine, Holy Roman Empire – nation state – machine industry – romanticism – Grecian civilization mediatory – culture – oral tradition – growth of science – mathematics – Renaissance – rationalism.

49   Brooks Adams – technology spreading out of population decentralization – absorption of energy – civilization comes with consolidation or pulling population to centre, i.e. rise of pecuniary system – price system – liquidity preference intensity of communication – bringing consolidation and civilization and conservation of energy – spreading out of population means loss of energy and decentralization.

50   Role of law and administration – women – cement of society and head of family – decline of family weakening of monopoly position of maternity. Adams – Calvinist position – people moved by energetic forces notably physical power – man having little to say as to direction – rise of Calvinism in students of civilization – Toynbee, Kroeber.

51   Second chambers assist in crystallizing oral tradition into law to remove emotional influence from law.

52   Significance of Associated Press shown in place of *World* - loss in *Herald* due to struggle against Western Union and Jay Gould. Problem of *Sun* in refusal to enter A.P. - tendency to reflect central power of A.P. and of Western Union or of telegraph.

53   Sombart regards Arabic numerals as extremely significant in spread of mathematics and rationalism.

54   Importance of disease in wiping out monasteries and nunneries - living together meant disastrous changes in distribution of population.

55   Problems of political boundaries worked out on basis of geometry or railroads (capitalism) and system of courts on territorial basis or language - difficulties of adjusting to technology - necessity of technology spreading over territory - extra-territorial government.

56   International cartels - difficulties of developing a system of government outside language or governmental boundaries - problem of spheres of influence.

57   Burckhardt - emphasis on art and culture as device for offsetting power of state and church and commerce - significance of great men in crises in relation to cultural advances - period in which great minds emerge. Power obsessions in church and state possibly checked by cultural growth or interest.

58   Growth of Marshall's work - systematization of economics - element of moderation - classical interest - enormous interest in growth of economic chivalry - Knight's sense of games - public opinion to be informal court of honour. Seldom possible to be a patriot and have a reputation for being a patriot. Codification of system - elaboration under Pigou - break under Keynes - obsession with democratic zeal - lack of sense of balance - Keynes' interest in art - over-emphasis and neglect of politics and law.

59   Significance of politics in scarcity value of oral tradition - crowding of written tradition leaves oral tradition as most exciting and attractive and implies obsession with politics. Art - culture - elements not involving compulsive power in contrast with church and state.

7

NOTES

12   Etienne Mantoux's *The Carthaginian Peace, or the Economic Consequences of Mr. Keynes* published in 1946 was a critique of Keynes's *The Economic Consequences of the Peace* (London, 1919).

23   Alexander Spotswood (1676-1740) was Lieutenant-governor of Virginia from 1710 to 1722.

49   Note on Brooks Adams, *America's Economic Supremacy* (New York, 1900)

52   Jay Gould (1836-92) owned the Western Union Telegraph Company.

53   Note on Werner Sombart, *A New Social Philosophy* (New Brunswick, N.J., 1937)

57   Note on Jacob Burckhart, *Force and Freedom: Reflection on History*, ed. J.H. Nichols (New York, 1943)

8

1946

1 Trading communities - Phoenicia, Carthage, Venice, Athens - Italy and Netherlands and Germany - England concerned with improvement of communication but obsession with short run and difficulty of long-run point of view - city state overrun by empire or large-scale unit. Struggle between urban and rural. Agriculture important in England with landed gentry - restrained communication - also spreading out of law, university, church, and trade meant that each tended to check the others.

2 Monopoly character of University of Paris made France inaccessible to Protestantism - again protest of nationalism developed on frontier in University of Prague and Hus and spread through Europe - preceded by Wycliffe on frontier at Oxford.

3 Character of borrowing or innovation in communication. Return of writing and books from England to Ireland, spread of minuscule from France to Italy - overrunning other elements. Intense element of conservatism requires innovation to develop outside and work toward centre thus overthrowing rigid elements. Printing in Germany held back by manuscript in France.

4 Veblen - pecuniary versus industrial but publishing, i.e. increasing accessibility of knowledge or mechanization of knowledge, at basis of pecuniary views - also implied in industrial problem. Significance of money economy to publisher and weakening of position of craftsman or printer - cutting across oral tradition.

5 How far oral tradition more accurate than written? Written apt to emphasize records and oral that which evaded law or unrecorded.

6 Spain - resistance in pressing out Mohammedans meant centralized control in church and state reinforced by character of support from new world in treasure and conflict with commercial and financial capital in Antwerp - collapse of latter. Power of monasteries, wool, and landed

gentry in England meant continued interest in agriculture – city life tended to destroy itself as in Italy, Flanders, and weakening of Germany in contrast with importance of rural area in England.

7   Printing industry – Bible reformation – Germany, Lutheranism and Calvinism – break of Netherlands. Common law tradition in England – clash with repression of church in Italy, Spain, and Germany. Freedom from monasticism in England and success of Henry VIII brought flowering of Elizabethan period but expulsion of Huguenots in France and 30 years war in Germany. Decline to savagery and return to classics – Erasmus, Grotius. New technique of printing released barbarism – leads to sudden boiling up of fanaticism and savagery ready to break through rule of law.

8   Great accumulation of manuscripts – durable, produced in monasteries during Middle Ages – available for printing and making for reading public before printing – development of schools and universities providing reading public.

9   Impact of printing on reason and logic in 17th and 18th centuries – but revival of romanticism with spread of oral tradition – Wesley and increased printing – in 19th century. 'It is written but I say unto you' conflict between law and prophets – oral and written tradition – tendency for law and printing to overrun – Christianity an attempt to check written or to combine written and oral tradition – church organization a reflection of limitations of parchment – Protestant – scriptures and oral.

10   Pareto emphasizes economic logical activity as factor leading to rise and fall of ruling class – neglect of force and emphasis on cunning lead to collapse of ruling class.

11   Recordings of phonograph records – political speeches heard long after death – Aberhart's records. Transcriptions facilitate work of politician. Aberhart – radio speeches – tactics emphasizing Christianity – attack on money changers semi-biblical language. Significant that semi-preachers capitalize radio – skill in mentioning people all over province – Bible texts, hymns. Pioneer character emphasized – attack on chain newspaper. Breaking out of oral tradition from suppression by print – use of Bible as combination of oral and written tradition. Scripture and classics near to oral tradition and consequently given power in periods when oral medium breaking through print. Attack on newspaper effective with celebrations. Teacher skilful with vocabulary. Attack on usury and interest and on debts – last a reflection of impact of written obligations. Attack of oral tradition on writing, i.e. debts. Enormous appeal of Bible

because of large amount of conversational content – emphasis on the   **89**
word. Attack on established church as temple money changers to be
driven out – New Testament – Christ's conversation and parables.

12   Enormous impact of production on advertising and use of newsprint
      designed to meet widest possible demands. Words of mythical and se-
      mantic character – tendency of printing to keep mythical element in
      check but also to crystallize its position. Periods of dominance of oral
      tradition apt to mean increase in mythical impact, i.e. myths driven out
      by laws, or by crystallization in writing, i.e. in Greece, but revived in
      inquisition with limited printing and during radio period with return of
      rhetoric and oratory, i.e. growth of mythical state.

13   Cassirer's account of difficulty of reading German with invention of
      Nazi words – these deliberately invented to give mythical emphasis –
      also social credit or new developments. Religions toned down in part by
      resorting to print – becoming sober with shift from preaching to oral
      tradition – organization of institutions and the like check fanatical out-
      breaks with logic of printing.

14   Printing necessitates great men – great writers – booming of circulation
      and books written about great figures – military designed to sell. Sys-
      tematic building up of imperfect competition – creation of monopoly
      as basis of advertising.

15   Purchase of *Albertan* by Aberhart's government to serve as check
      against attacks of other papers – inroads of radio on newspaper. Back-
      log of graduates from his school – influence as a teacher on large num-
      bers of students – also Bible Institute attracting religion. Significance of
      interrelation between printing or written and oral tradition – written
      disciplines oral tradition and loses control with sudden improvement of
      oral communication, i.e. radio and outburst of fascism and naziism and
      of small parties – Aberhart in Alberta, C.C.F. in Saskatchewan.

16   Significance of writing by hand persisting to invention of typewriter.
      Increased production of paper meant marked increase in demand for
      writing and for education – preparation for printing – consequent em-
      phasis on shorthand as device to save writing – similar to use of ligatures
      in copying. Limited copying in Germany and vernacular meant rise of
      printing – delay in France due to entrenched position of copyists and
      manuscripts and spread in Italy result of supplies of paper. Monasticism
      in England delayed education and printing emphasized vernacular – gap
      explained in part problems of Wycliffe and Henry VIII – destruction of
      monasteries. Shakespeare developed with restriction on printing and
      emphasis on vernacular in court. Stage declined after printing of Bible –

printed word. Importance of cathedrals or expression in architecture in checking spread of Bible and of university – in England cathedrals did not grow into universities – Roman law not taught – common law in London.

17   Blakiston Co. – interest in medical books taken over by Doubleday Doran in order to get a supply of paper for their books.

18   By-elections a means of keeping parliament close to public opinion and a powerful lever to move government policy.

19   Graham Wallas' belief that oral tradition very limited, i.e. group discussion and use of words to conceal thought. Oral tradition essential to thought, i.e. rural universities.

20   Italian economists shift to sociology – how far a result of Roman law background? Whereas Anglo-Saxon economists emphasize equilibrium and neglect sociology. Italian economists emphasize ruling class based on force and using persuasion to dominate subject class.

21   Increasing complexity of tariffs and restriction of markets in Canada means emphasis on possible exports with favourable outlet, i.e. newsprint or materials for opinion industries – this favours expansion of newsprint in Canada and stimulates advertising and industry within the United States. Canada forced to concentrate on production for exports to improve markets, i.e. newsprint and advertising.

22   'The fortune of a book depends upon the capacity of its readers.' (Terentianus Maurus)

23   Problem of writing for public – assumption of necessity of use of large number of words and condensation inevitable with demand for time but this checks dissemination. Mechanization of writing makes condensed writing extremely difficult because of limitation of possibilities of dissemination.

24   Kirkland argues case can be made for rebate system on railways – trial and error period until railways tested out possible refinements of rate structure – Delaware – small proprietary state – Wilmington centre of Duponts – latter becoming more powerful in Baltimore. How far small land states New Jersey, etc. become centres of capitalistic control – centralization of land followed by centralization of capital?

25   Washington becoming centre of those interested in power rather than profit – bureaucracy means hierarchy and power problem.

26   Power of monasticism based in part on Roman law of corporations -
      power strengthened throughout the Middle Ages.

27   Publishers have low view of knowledge of reviewers and place in their
      hands either by an elaborate jacket or detailed information the views
      which they expect the reviewer to accept.

NOTES

4   Note on Thorstein Veblen, *The Engineer and the Price System* (New York, 1921)
10   Note on V. Pareto, *The Mind and Society*, ed. A. Livingston, Vol. IV, 'The General
      Form of Society' (New York, 1935)
11   William 'Bible Bill' Aberhart was a fundamentalist preacher who led the world's
      first Social Credit government to power in Alberta in 1935.
13   Note on Ernst Cassirer, *The Myth of the State* (New Haven, 1946)
19   Graham Wallas, *Our Social Heritage*. See 3 / 5.
24   E.C. Kirkland (1894-1975) was an American economic historian whose best known
      work, *A History of American Economic Life*, was first published in 1932.

9

Probably 1946-7

1 Fall of Baghdad probably meant stimulus to paper making in Italy and Europe as supplies cut off.

2 Limited place of women in Moslem civilization meant harems and eunuchs and court intrigues – importance of force – part of imperial despotism – weakness of city state shown in artificial creation of capital centres such as Baghdad. Dangers of court life with changes in dynasties.

3 Puritanism – an outburst of church after destroying of monasticism and celibacy. Reform or non-conformist churches broke out in relation to Anglican church or following abolition of monasteries and paralleled monasticism in predominantly Roman Catholic churches.

4 Effects of centralized education as in Ontario to favour large city schools able to secure passing of matriculation students and to prejudice small schools with poor teachers. Fails to secure mobility in moving from out-lying areas to centre and thus to secure most efficient structure.

5 Influence of newspaper writing on speech – editors tend to speak a written language – see John Willison.

6 Monasticism deadly effect in attracting ablest people and in preventing reproduction – part of explanation of burst in Elizabethan England. Trade becomes a means of drawing off ablest people and securing reproduction.

7 Problem of Jews in abhorrence of celibacy and increasing to meet de-mands of church and state in finance largely excluded by church. Shift to force in crusades also opens way to draining of ablest groups to army and away from church and monasticism. Growth of law also attracted abler minds and produced unstable equilibrium.

8   Monopoly position of writing – inherent in skill and consequently per-
      petuates and strengthens position of writers. Oral tradition bound to
      written tradition notably in religion – this not evident in Greece.
      Preaching means linking of oral tradition to scriptures. Law not linked
      to written tradition facilitates independent development – common law –
      attracts abler people, but with Roman law jurist or writer becomes
      authority and possible split between written and oral tradition as in
      revolutions.

9   Russian literature – primitivism – restraint of elaborate ritual of church –
      vernacular literature came late and relative lack of abstractions makes
      for realism in great writers of 19th century. Late growth of printing
      facilitated great novels with emphasis on individual.

10   Malicious character of afternoon and evening paper partly result of
      more limited tradition than morning paper and concern with more
      sensational features incidental to large street sales. *Star* with long ac-
      count of bargaining to secure *Telegram* by *Globe and Mail* introducing
      [in its news stories] various malicious factors notably high price and
      possibility of Wright meeting it. Newspaper without ample check of
      price system indulges in violent attacks or sensationalism designed to
      increase circulation. News difficult to adapt to price system. Similarly
      in universities or hierarchies exceedingly difficult to use price system
      effectively as a moderating device. Promotions apt to become personal
      matters – difficulty and danger of relying on publication tests.

11   Monasticism emerged in opposition to absolutism of Egypt and became
      weapon against state in Europe.

12   Significance of mediums to administration – clay meant restricted,
      limited administration – suggests importance of force – constant decline
      and fall of empires and less suited than papyrus, the basis of administra-
      tion in Egypt and Rome. Greece joined papyrus and alphabet in rich
      literature but not suited to administration. Parchment – high value – de-
      centralized administration – paper – cheaper – meant influence of lang-
      uage on administration but ultimate tendency to bureaucratic growth.
      Paper the essence of bureaucratic administrations. Possibility of science
      in north – impossibility of admitting respect for animal life by Hindus
      because of difficulty of living – problem of climate compels emphasis
      on practical and opens way for science and machine industry. War im-
      plies device for constantly breaking down encroachments of social and
      political institutions on machine – implies friction between science and
      myth and religion – breaking through of machine industry.

13   Importance of succession duties to insurance – business firms (Crean) worth $400,000 with $150,000 succession duties compels emphasis on insurance – but insurance emphasis on savings and production must be offset by advertising and pressure on consumption.

14   Aquinas developed doctrine that natural law supreme over law of any state or community – how far basis for [Sir Edward] Coke and position of American colonies? Position of church made possible division of political states and led to rebellion. Encroached on position of emperor and state permitting rise of new states. Revolution first evident in Anglo-Saxon countries – England because of common law and power of oral tradition – spread to continent in France.

15   Necessity of writing and copying scriptures emphasized importance of authority in Middle Ages. Printing meant ease of reading and disregard of authority. Cambridge Platonists reflected revived interest in abstract with printing contrast with oral – preaching and emphasis on concrete. Civil war device for bringing able men to top – Milton in government and discharged wrote great poetry. Printing meant emphasis on logic of print and favoured encroachment of mathematics on language in development of prose – Hobbes – disappearance of scholastic language in Locke's prose – see Willey. Significance of scriptures to development of abstract ideas in areas unfamiliar with it and to retaining of fictional ideas in areas in which abstract emerged – Milton in 17th century. Scriptures offset nationalistic tendencies of literature – Homer, *Aeneid*, Italian epics, Milton but literature important also in checking nationalism, i.e. science favoured by oligarchic Royal Society and Charles II. Scriptures and copying lent themselves to commentaries and allegories – monastic mind played around limited field.

16   Periods of revolt with new developments in communication. Emergence of writing led to destruction of idols among Jews – also of idols by Mohammed in Mecca in 630. Bacon opposed ancient writing as having same place latter part of 16th century.

17   Difficulties of Arabs on sea – success of Byzantium probably drove Arabs to Spain. Flexibility of Christianity facilitated political change – Christianity essentially heretical – separation of west from east – crowning of Charlemagne – weakening of Byzantine in relation to Arabs by refusal to recognize heresy. Byzantine empire – Caesaropapism – Greek concept – control of church and state broken down by spread of communication in west – activity of papacy and empire – breakdown of Empire result of pressure from margin to south and west. Byzantine – upheld philosophy and law and military efficiency in contrast with Islam and west. Koran showed power of book to overcome tribal influ-

ence. Importance of monotheism to force. Significance of interest in meaning of words. Allegory – early Alexandria and 17th century accompanied meeting of Hebraic scriptures and Platonism. Role of Alexandria – papyrus rolls library imperial centre to prepare dogmas adapted to demands of various regions of Christianity. Nicene Creed, Monophysites, Constantinople versus Rome. Knowledge broke Christianity into malleable form suited to varied geographic and institutional demands and language – adapted to export. Division assumed divergence between Alexandria emphasis on dogma, Constantinople on force and civil administration and Rome on religious organization designed to control barbarians. Greek flexibility evident in position of Trinity in itself an adaptation of Christianity to paganism – discussion over Trinity left gaps open and compelled appeals to reason to repair them. Facilitated division into Protestantism and sects or facilitating adaptability to language and mechanization in printing, paper, and so on. Capitalism and commercialism in printing meant constant drive toward division.

18   Reception of Roman law in Germany and reaction of historical school under Savigny had influence on historical school of economics beginning with Roscher – classical school built up in England – historical school around edges in Germany – socialist school in France. Tendency of law to become concerned with statute and juristic science to work on code hampers relations of law to life.

19   Church helped break empire or destroy eastern empire in 800 and fall of eastern empire meant struggle with west. German emperor brought justification of papacy leading to Gregory VII. Weight of Roman empire broke power of king in Germany and meant elective principle – conflict and continuation of feudalism in contrast with unity of England and France or paralleled by unity of England and France. Church implied a weak Germany and a strong France – reformation compelled emphasis on centalized state in Germany – absolute church followed by absolute state.

20   Problem of Rome under papacy and Empire – centre of nationalism – opposition to papacy. Papal infallibility with Italian nationalism.

21   Efficient civil administration of Byzantine empire promoted growth of ecclesiastical system but importance of administration to church in west in destroying reverence for words of Middle Ages – basis of science. Monopoly position of Bible in printing weakened position of classics and favoured growth of science. Printing industry cracked work of medieval copyists in separating classical and Hebraic strands of scholastic philosophy. Puritans opposed alien elements in interpreting scriptures and attacked Aristotle – sympathetic to science. Belief in scriptures

led to break in efforts to merge classics and scriptures - science emerged with break between Hebrew and classic tradition.

22 Climate of opinion - in early 17th century belief in decay of nature and man attacked by Bacon. England on fringe could produce Bacon as continent dominated by monastic ideal. Suspicion of philosophy built on reverence towards words and demand for interest in things in 17th century - rise of science.

23 Increasing efficiency of language as it reaches to lower strata and consequently vernacular tends to replace learned and machinery becomes adapted to marginal or fringe areas - tendency toward English as progressively efficient and adaptable.

24 Spread of printing industry involved rise of science and in turn authoritarian character of science and extension to radicalism. Bacon's separation of science and religion enabled Puritans to take active interest in science - just as worship of Bible facilitated growth of science. Attack on authority in reformation linked to attack on Aristotle in science. Monasticism gave first great emphasis on division of labour - based on sex.

NOTES

5   Possibly note on J.S. Willison, *Reminiscences, Personal and Political* (c. 1919)
10 W.H. Wright (1876-1951) was a Canadian mine operator who together with George McCullagh purchased the Toronto *Globe* and the *Mail & Empire*, which were amalgamated in 1937 to form the *Globe and Mail.*
13 J.G. Crean (b. 1910) was a friend of Innis and President of Robert Crean and Co. Ltd.
15 See Basil Willey, *The Seventeenth Century Background* (London, 1934)

10

possibly 1946-7

1   Growth of towns favoured cathedrals and weakened rural monasteries.
Cathedrals became more important as schools and drew on wealth of
towns for large Gothic buildings – these became centres of universities
and new types of libraries.

2   Enormous significance of conquest of Sicily by Normans – meant a
court to which scholars in Arabic, Latin, and Greek could resort – became basis of penetration of Greek – protection from fanaticism of
church, beginnings of bureaucracy – secular type of state favoured learning – softened Mohammedan and Christian. Also recaptured Spain
meant contact between European scholars and Mohammedans.

3   Strong oral tradition and importance of dialectic in Greek philosophy
in contrast with written and revealed truth of Roman law and Hebrew
scriptures. Augustine developed position of revealed truth in scriptures.

4   Problem of democratic tradition – infinite squabbling and flattening of
individual differences – exhaustion particularly in academic centres
incidental to working out problems. Problem of knowledge and inability to reach a common point of view due to insistence on content and
what to teach – implications to university policy.

5   Shift from oral to written tradition – poetry to prose – class, i.e. aristocracy of feudalism to city state with dependence on justice and written law – paradoxical clash between growth of individual and growth of
laws – death of Socrates – escape of Plato in philosophy of state following his death. Crash of state through neglect of individual – rise of natural law – absorption in Roman republic and empire – writing implies
conservatism. Civilization loses freshness but at its peak in period of
shift from oral to written tradition or from poetry to prose or written
law. Implications to Christianity of parchment – collapse of old civilization – new basis – Scriptures – authority – pouring of energy into Latin –
enormous drain on civilization.

6   Bursting out of vernacular in Shakespeare, Caxton - English vernacular -
    similar to Dante - aristocracy of renaissance when oral tradition blos-
    somed on stage at expense of writing - place of monarchy and courts.
    Elizabethan - Puritan revolution - Milton - prose democratic in 17th
    century - printing press versus stage. Restrictions produce aberrations -
    Shakespeare - Milton. Significance of single books and authors - implies
    restraint on all other activity. Great book religions - Bible, i.e. Old Tes-
    tament a terrifying volume - not suited to reading by adolescents.

7   City state versus feudalism - writing, law, education - no longer possible
    to depend on traditions of feudalism - danger of emphasis on rhetoric
    and prose - oratory - how to manage people - education of leaders
    rather than people - grammar, rhetoric, dialectic - later mathematics
    added. Problem of recapturing Greek concept of training the mind and
    state. Latin and mathematics - language in senior matriculation. Prob-
    lem of bourgeois penetration - calculation.

8   Sixteenth century restriction on printing in France but encouragement
    of paper and sale of paper part of mercantilist policy meant revolt of
    countries purchasing paper and using it in manufacture of books. Hol-
    land and Germany had full advantage of printing restrictions in France
    - in use of French paper - ease of transport - disequilibrium in know-
    ledge - intense activity in Holland offset and followed restrictions in
    France.

9   Scholarship particularly since printing industry largely concerned with
    logic of print - equilibrium economics a reflection of spread of print
    and mathematics and necessity of cultural life operating within logical
    framework - reflected particularly in scholarly studies. Significance to
    England that universities not located in London where law predomin-
    ated - consequently latter responsive to trade and not in cathedrals -
    consequently grew up as possible centres of movements in Oxford.

10 Franciscans - established in period when cathedrals important in towns
    in Europe and monasteries *important* in rural areas in England - reflec-
    tion of lag in economic development. Arts tradition and division or
    specialization strong in England - law and medicine. Universities in
    Scotland associated with towns and trade - Adam Smith in Glasgow -
    use of English in lectures - Scotland absorbed Roman law, Calvinism.
    Glasgow university based on Bologna students' university.

11

Late 1946 and early 1947

1   Monopoly problem of knowledge - to an important extent based on
    mediums of communication - control over papyrus with Rome cutting
    in of parchment and religion with monopoly control in Middle Ages -
    emphasis on copying and sacred writings - cutting in of paper from
    trade and state. Changes in media of enormous significance to civiliza-
    tion as having profound implications to religion, learning, and intellec-
    tual capacity and training. Plato's Idea in a sense expressed in monopoly
    of knowledge - Aristotle came much closer to materialism in scientific
    approach - vernaculars reflect monopolistic competition. Problem of
    organization of education and mental capacity within national boun-
    daries - weak position of bilingual countries.

2   Shifting of teaching materials - Homer, Virgil, Greek literature to Bible -
    ecclesiastical state. Renaissance a return to Greece but influence killed
    off by printing of Bible as weapon against church. Break-up of Roman
    empire as political unit - enabled taking up of organization by church -
    absorption of Plato's philosophy in opposition to state - attempt to
    amalgamate Greek and Hebrew tradition. Old Testament a further indi-
    cation of effect of collapse of state - grinding of Jews between Oriental
    empires. Spiritual retreat of wrecked political systems. New Testament
    a product of Greek mind. Emphasized humility in relation to state. But
    church attempted to adapt Old Testament - Greek and Hebrew tradi-
    tion flew apart. Puritanism seized on examples of Old Testament -
    revolt against princes. Poison of old systems took on new virulence.
    Bible became weapon of revolt. Printing favoured spread of Erasmus to
    Luther, Calvin, Tyndale, in England. Restraint on printing in England
    in 16th century, rise of nationalism, Tudors.

3   Redemptionist Father McCardy age 50 - born Boston, stationed Anna-
    polis - had been in Virgin Isles - Porto Rico. Said he had several drinks
    in him but had never been drunk - sin comes from abuse or excess. In
    Porto Rico great wealth and great poverty - five masses on Sundays but
    five dollar collections - sent $450 monthly by U.S. order - paid $50 per

month for bus - supported 11 nuns. Priests drink, play cards, mild swearing, good mixers. Had never touched a woman - some priests thought marriage would help priests in country districts - regard themselves as a queer lot as result of celibate lives. Told story of woman who left church and married Protestant divorcee in Standard Oil - McCardy got her back into church and for 18 years they had lived as brother and sister. Women told priest he was meant for her and he said if he had married he would have preferred her to any other woman but that he was a priest. Tremendous emphasis on heaven - asked woman in case husband was dying to send for him and he would try to get him into heaven - advised her to stay by husband although not married in eyes of church. Great concern with sex in church. Catholic boys scalawags - Protestant boys preferred by Catholic girls as more mannerly, priest thinks a result of confession. Priest without marrying has greater 'apostolic freedom' to visit poor and sick, i.e. epidemic. Thinks well-meaning sincere Protestant clergy will get to heaven. Tremendous pressure toward celibacy of Hildebrand implied supervision of sex relations of people. Very great difficulty in enforcing celibacy contributed to problems of church.

4   September 9, 1946. Talked to [possibly James Douglas] Woods, grandson of Sir James - with Gordon MacKay and Co. - maintain contact with wholesalers in U.S., i.e. national distributors. Suggests that prices in Canada largely fixed by one company, Eaton's, through their catalogue - prices are measured against this throughout Canada. Eaton's expanded rapidly and now consolidating - Simpson's in process of expansion. Chain stores of Eaton's easiest competitors of MacKay's as they sell goods moving more slowly - MacKay's concerned with upper and middle class. Price control largely successful because of small number of department stores.

5   American unions fail to separate policy-making and policy-executing as in England. Problem in England of rigid adherence to rules - tying up vessel overnight for sake of putting on small amount of coal. Use of cigarettes in Holland as basis of currency. In U.S. emphasis on jurisdiction because of resistance to Knights of Labor - in England no problem of jurisdiction. In U.S. competition between unions for members - does not exist in England. Consequent difficulty of political movement in U.S. as compared with England and interest in strikes and manoeuvres to maintain the strength of the organization. Drain on resources with competition of unions for labour.

6   January 4, 1947. G.V.F. [G.V. Ferguson] on *Free Press* - operating on small deficit to 1917 or from 1900 - claim Dafoe had limited influence except at special crisis - Dafoe backed into Progressive movement rather

than started - probably had influence in Byng controversy in emphasizing constitutional question and thus playing down customs scandal. May have had influence in conscription issue in 1944 - Dexter sounded out Ottawa people and put articles in on things about to happen thus capitalizing apparent influence and prestige. Paper finds it necessary to blow up editor to immense proportions - *Free Press* beginning with Dexter - Dafoe assumed tremendous importance - Chancellor and so on. Dafoe may have saved C.N.R. with intensity of attacks on Bennett. King apparently told some one secretly that he suddenly found army had got out of control on conscription issue. So Lloyd George claimed Irish out of hand because of refusal of army to continue in Ireland.

7 [Stanley] Morison agreed to help *Times* when they showed determination by taking period out after heading - *New York Times* still continues use of period after word.

8 Television involves enormous outlay and black and white suddenly rendered obsolete with invention of true technicolor but problem of getting funds to develop program - unsatisfactory for ordinary events as crude and boring - necessary to make careful plans for attractive appeal - apparently production of film, photography, etc., not more than enough to handle eighteen hours a week and necessary to build up production to technical level. Enormous capital expenditure followed by problem of developing market and obsolescence with new technical development - even more powerful organizations unable to finance development. Significance to densely populated areas as these alone at present significant for limited range of television.

9 Gadsby - power of writing sharp phrases; Falconer - a burnisher of platitudes. Sharp writing characteristic of period to end of war - tends to disappear with large-scale business of newspaper.

10 Sombart emphasis on rationality as basis of late capitalism - a reflection of spread of price system and mathematics. Scholarship - concern with records of civilization - a breaking down of powers of vitality - occasional bursting out of flames - renaissance. Apt to be linked to intensification of aristocracy and courts - Charlemagne. Economic prosperity of Italian cities and interest in manuscripts.

11 Marxian class struggle - exploited vs. exploiters partly struggle between written and oral tradition - problem of law and state from standpoint of Roman law and necessity of withering of state. Agitation essentially an appeal to more vital oral tradition against written law but oral tradition in Marx crystallizes in written tradition and communist state. Contrast with classical tradition reflecting the logical demands of writing.

12   Learmonth, December 23, 1946. Large catch of white fox but prices
        down presumably because of Russian exports to U.S. White fox becomes
        less plentiful and blue fox more plentiful as movement proceeds to
        northern Arctic Islands. Complains missionaries use syllabic with Indians
        and Eskimo which prevents them learning English and shuts them off
        from outside world. Banks Island - greatest abundance of animal life
        and wealth of Eskimo in north. No whales in narrow region of Western
        Arctic as ice freezes over, but plenty of seals. C.N.R. Toronto to Winni-
        peg 48 hours reduced to 36 hours with Long Lac cut off. C.P.R. com-
        pelled increase of schedule to 38 hours to even competition. But C.P.R.
        advantage Fort William to Winnipeg as C.N.R. a local train.

13   Enormous significance of contact of language with culture without sub-
        mergence implies escape from subtle aspects of more developed culture
        and facilitates use of philosophy and science in contrast with religion -
        Greek and Mycenean, Latin and Etruscan.

14   V. Gordon Childe - archeologist point of view emphasizes bronze as
        centre of oriental Empire development - iron age typical of Graeco-
        Roman civilization with greater emphasis on democracy - metal inter-
        pretation of history - drain of gold and increasing slavery weakened
        Roman empire. Archaeologists lean on Marxist approach, i.e. impor-
        tance of technology.

15   Wilson - language responsible for time concept but written language
        brings time-space concept. Influence of written language on oral tradi-
        tion. Parchment implies greater emphasis on permanence. Science after
        renaissance and reformation - importance of mathematics particularly
        when applied to technology - limited application in Roman period but
        wide application after printing. Writing emphasizes logic especially with
        alphabet, whereas oral tradition emphasizes memory.

16   History does nothing else but repeat itself with dominance of type of
        thought. Monopoly control over thought and over media implies that
        nature copies art as nature seen through stigmatic spectacles. Abund-
        ance of media supports trade and assumes trade particularly in commod-
        ities which can be transported easily and on a large scale. Dominance of
        book paralleled Christianity - rise of newspaper meant shift to material-
        ism and impact on other media - difficulties of selling agnostic literature
        so long as publishing linked up to Christian literature. Book expensive
        and must reflect demands of institutions or inherent in Christian organ-
        ization. Wide sale of Paine and Priestley probably with possibilities of
        pamphlet. Church undermined in France by information - encyclopedia -
        demand of court for satire - Voltaire.

17   Rationality spreads with training - not necessarily with increase in
      communication - religion implies retraction of media of communica-
      tion - breaking down of religious control - linking of rationality, com-
      munication, and force. Collapse of Greek state with weakening of reli-
      gion - Roman Catholic Church attempt to dissociate religion or make
      it superior to political state. Return to problem of Greek state - driving
      out irrationality and religion, especially fanaticism.

18   Middle class reflected spread of money economy in Greece. Poetry un-
      translatable and buttress to court and hierarchy. Printing reaching lower
      levels and stirs up muddier sections of population and makes them
      more generally known - continued obsession with crime - continuing
      to legislative and social reform - result of successive exposure of lower
      levels. Increased communication brings division and class struggle. Ora-
      tory like tragedy and drama has purgative effect - became important
      with decline of stage. But rhetoric means influence by one individual
      whereas poetics collective. Print compels system of logic - provides
      framework demanding consistency of sort. Attempts to avoid print in
      political rumours and roorbacks, reluctance to set down in writing -
      business retreating to dinners, conversation, evasion of written word.
      Marxist links science to humanity - effect of impact of science on hu-
      manities also in philosophy - Whitehead, Russell, etc. Communism a
      continuation of Hegel and limitations of philosophy in the 20th cen-
      tury - continuation of romanticism and influence of printing. Commer-
      cial drive of printing emphasizes appeal to lowest common denominator
      and checks other books - overhead costs and mechanization - mathe-
      matics a type of language making heavy demands and limiting commun-
      ication.

19   Thomas Mann argues that it is necessary to have a large body of work in
      order to survive - points to interest of publisher in building up prestige
      of writer in order to widen market - search for bestsellers stimulated by
      demand for wide market for paper and implies escape from high costs
      of printing. Printers union increases costs and favours concentration by
      publisher on a single book - this weakens position of large number of
      writers unable to secure access to supplies of paper. Manuscripts rejected
      because of danger of dissipating publishers' energies over too many
      books - this in case of excellent work. Book has special prestige value -
      education largely built around element of prestige of book.

20   Problem of universities in overcoming effect of mechanization. Com-
      munism - conflict of science and humanities - mysticism.

21   Influence from east - Byzantium - monasticism. Cluny reforms - Hilde-
      brand a son of Cluny applied Cluny principles of monasticism to pap-
      acy. Rise and spread of Roman law increasing power of emperor.

22   Papyrus lack of durability and deterioration facilitating change in revisions - parchment durable and with little possibility of revision.

23   Significance of difficulty of efficient translation from Greek to Latin and of penetration of Greek ideas into Latin culture - had effect of opening up new horizons.

24   Use of Gallup poll as a check against propagandists - pressure of groups in Congress on separate issues checked against general information provided by poll - makes for greater stability and consistency.

25   Immense significance of injecting intelligence into hierarchy, i.e. social sciences - General Osborne influence in getting social sciences in American Army as contrasted with British - fact that nearly all army people from New York State.

26   Problem of success of Roman Empire - belief that emperor represented will of people and became divine after death. Marcus Aurelius broke tradition in appointing son and created difficulty. Emphasis on family - *patria potestas* - in Rome entry in Punic wars meant military problems. Civil war wiped out large number of family leaders and strengthened position for Emperor. Caesar conquered Gaul as means of securing a line against barbarians - line extended by Augustus. Decline of *patria potestas* - spread of Roman law - citizens and Roman civilization became a parade. Marcus Aurelius - loss of contact with appointing of Commodus son and losses in war. Breakup of empire left powerful influences in Roman law, Roman church which continued in west - sufficient power to dominate west at various periods - breaking out of emperor worship in France. Contrast with Byzantine - power of monotheism so great that church kept under control - caesaropapism but in west emperor became divine after death and church able to take lead. Russia absorbed idea of third Rome - took over Hellenistic conceptions of religion contrasting with power of law in west. Germany under Kaiser and Hitler continued as barbarians a conflict with Roman tradition of law. Continued clash of Greek religion with Roman law.

27   Otterville, July, 1946. Effects of W.P.T.B. [Wartime Prices and Trade Board] in holding down prices of consumers goods and increasing savings shown in sharp increase in price of houses and demand for new houses. Buying of old jewelry, second-hand furniture and so on with a view to remaking and selling an indication of the scarcity of goods and the abundance of money. Steady disappearance of houses in the country with increase in use of farm machinery - larger farms and pull to towns and cities. Change in attitude of banks - previously collecting funds and sending to city - new type of manager actively interested in

pushing loans and supporting enterprisers - private lenders now assisted
by banker whereas previously carried most of burden of local industry.

28   Importance of religion to ventures - belief that nothing can fail with
divine help and consequent activity. Dad moving old house to build new
in Otterville at over 80 years of age.

29   Simplified alphabet widened base for screening process and accentuated
rise of ability in Greece.

30   Burning of heretics meant beginning of period of eternal fire.

31   Impact of Babylonian astronomy on religion - rise of astrology, belief
in fate of universe recognition of universal law.

32   Enormous significance of printed word as a factor in mobility - particularly from rural to urban areas - knowledge of printed word as device
for promotion implies belief in printed word and emphasis on vital significance of learning - strength of church in attracting from relatively
non-literate to literate - over-emphasis on literate leads to breakdown
and lack of contact with city proletariat - significance of Marx. Learned
class and upper class limited to rural areas.

33   Profound importance of collapse of Roman political structure with emphasis on force and inability to resist horse used by barbarians - insec-
urity as to present led to emphasis on future - absence of media suited
to wide circulation in papyrus and emphasis in papyrus on Greece and
Egypt - cults and philosophy - parchment gave durable media in which
scriptures could be circulated - rise of single authority in church with
collapse of state and suitability of parchment to it.

34   Effect of format of book and belief in its greater impressiveness - blow-
ing up of articles into books - Adler, *How to Read a Book* [London and
New York, 1940] - 8 pages of lectures blown up to size of book - nec-
essities of distribution - retailers reluctant to handle pamphlet. English
preference for hard board bindings neglects importance of libraries -
places of luxury - difficulty of introducing paper covers and cheap
books - Penguin. Significance of publishing to law - monopoly control
of firms - West - lawyers compelled to buy continuous reports of cases -
lawyers pay $40 a week for publications - abridgements, indexes. How
far H.W. Wilson Index Co. a monopoly factor? Also medical books.
Importance of printed word in developing law cases - rise of precedents -
concentration on precedents and printed word hampers possibility of
creative thought in legal development. Reluctance of bookstores to
handle pamphlets in contrast with books - unsuited to second hand

trade. Development of aids to reading - pagination, title page, etc. in 15th century. Importance of lighting - limitations of candle, reading aloud - decline in reading aloud with increase in reading material and verbosity - also electric lights and large number of lights. With limited reading facilities greater dependence on writing - production of diaries, etc.

35 Christianity assisted Roman law in breaking down patriarchal family - defied power of family with emphasis on monasticism and celibacy and strengthened individualism. Puritanism as opposed to economic motive - refusal to grow tobacco or to sell spirituous liquor. Sacred position of Bible in Catholic Church intensified attitude of Protestants as chief medium. Greek - oral to written, poetry to prose and philosophy. Plato attempted to abolish poetry and rhetoric in favour of philosophy and prose. Written and printed tradition further from reality - moulding of civilization. Basis of Greece and Rome because of inability to conserve energies for purpose of discovering closer relationship between ideas and technology. Intense rigidity of machine in production - products turned out in the same fashion consequently competition between countries intense as between same product made by same type of machine. Hand products for style and human consumption - taste and art makes for flexibility and greater possibility of trade.

36 Lack of worship of Bible in France facilitated development of other literature - church occupied attention of Europe to disadvantage of state and opened way to spread of capitalism. Church an important administrative organization. Attempts of church to combine old and new testaments destined to break down - break between Hebraism and Hellenism.

37 Dislike of business and professional hierarchies shown in large-scale interest in clubs which emphasize an even footing but also admit of another type of administrative hierarchy. Decline of price system shown with importance of patronage - Roman Catholic Church securing bronze for small plaque during war.

38 Radio suggests levelling influence - powerful effect of country on city - advertisers appealing to country compelled to tone broadcasts to listeners.

39 How far puritanical revolution in England a printers' revolution, i.e. King James version following Shakespeare and bringing impact of Bible? Flexibility of period of written language and possibility of vernacular to get out of line compared with rigidity of print and newspaper bringing whole to uniformity but with chief drive from character of technical equipment or capitalism - perhaps more rigid than a writing caste.

40   Riley wrote poems for newspapers 70's - on lecture platform with Nye in 80's - wide sale of books in 90's.

41   Significance of writing as a screening device - a clumsy IQ test particularly with large number of characters - probably meant search for ablest children and attracted ability to administration. Query how far force an effective test of ability - survival - character of discipline and leadership?

42   August 2, 1946. Hydro-electric power - board to determine appointments and promotions - each promotion which disregards seniority subject to constant discussion and questioning - little interest among people in an industry who became largely night watchmen or firemen active in an emergency [and] have little other interests. Problem of large administrative bodies - determining criteria of appointments from standpoint of efficiency and morals. Popular appointments may mean emphasis on political activity. Advantage of large number of industries or organizations - constant interest in efficiency and attention to capacities of individuals. Difficulties in universities of deciding on merit as basis of promotion. Mobility involves enormous outlay of energy to appraise capacity.

43   *Readers Digest* thrives on verbosity of books and periodicals - ability to squeeze out verbiage.

44   Roman law created person in contrast with group and gave rise to problem of free will - this important in understanding theological problem of Augustine and Christianity.

45   Universities escaping from book tradition by emphasizing enormous buildings. Tendency of denominations to centre around universities - religious organizations always attempting to seize strategic points of education - Dominicans - St Thomas always poisoning education at the source.

46   Problem of Marxism - explanation of appearance of *Capital* - Caudwell claims a result of growth of evolutionary sciences concerned with time and adjustment to classificatory subjects (mathematics) leads to dialectic. Marxist interpretation of communism. On the other hand apt to take on character of miracle, i.e. event at appointed time. Tragedy appears with shift from religion and myth to bourgeois secularization or shift from oral tradition to written as in Greece and as in England under Elizabeth.

47   Problem of family in Roman empire with emergence of individual's place in law evident in accounts of sex and immorality. Religion in Christianity gave tremendous importance to sex - notably in emphasis

on celibacy and in opposition to divorce - attempt to restore family in face of law and trends toward individualism.

48 Pareto (Italian background) training in engineering and in science - approached social sciences from mathematical point of view. Crowding of students in mathematics leading to pressure from natural sciences on social sciences and drive on latter in terms of training. Pantaleoni - influenced Pareto toward mathematical economics - turned to Walras and found concept of economic equilibrium. Use of mathematics in price system compels individuals to think in terms of mathematics and consequently makes study of economics and mathematics more effective - becomes cultural with cultural bias of mathematical character and difficult to appraise culture in any other terms. Impact of logic of printing or of prose and difficulty of appraising culture in any other terms - mathematics becomes more important in cumulative fashion.

49 Kimball Young - grandson of Brigham Young - Mormon ritual apparently based on Masonic - always wearing long drawers with square and compass on chest - masonic ritual also follows trend of life of Christ. Was this result of publishing masonic ritual by Morgan?

50 Conflict between Russia and China in marginal area - nomad of steppe versus forest in Russia and versus agriculture in China. Ebb and flow probably prevented written language and kept oral tradition active - conqueror absorbing conquered language and rigidity of written language not evident.

51 Common law with emphasis on common politics or parliament as court meant restriction on religion. Made break with Rome easier with monarchy emphasizing law - strengthened position of science as contrasted with power of church on continent and hampering of science - emphasis on miracles - Church of England - Byzantine in character - king as head of church.

52 Thou shalt not press down the crown of Bretton Woods. Problem of international political adjustment - advertising - Social Credit - New Zealand, etc. Great areas - staple-producing areas breeding places of hot air currents.

NOTES

5 Possibly Note on W. Moore, *Industrial Relations and the Social Order* (New York, 1946)
6 A.V. Dexter (1896-1961) was an associate of Ferguson on the Winnipeg *Free Press*.

9   Sir Robert Falconer (1867-1943) was president of the University of Toronto from 1907 to 1932. Henry Franklin Gadsby was a newspaper reporter, contemporary to Falconer.

14   See V.G. Childe, *What Happened in History* (New York, 1942)

15   Wilson not identified

19   Possibly note on Thomas Mann, *Essays of Three Decades* (New York, 1947)

25   E.L. Osborne (1889-1973) was an American army officer and management consultant.

40   J.W. Riley (1849-1916) a popular poet, and E.W. Nye (1850-96), a humorist, lectured together in 1886.

46   Caudwell not identified

48   Maffeo Pantaleoni (1857-1924) taught economics from 1901 at the University of Rome.

12

possibly 1947

1   Railways limited to 2% grade - Pales [illegible] move to Upland after
    1851 dynamo radio. Hydro 90% efficiency, coal and steam 12%. Elec-
    tricity and alloys.

2   Factors making for timelessness, i.e. [Thomas] Hardy going outside
    time or going behind Christianity and history at the time of the break-
    ing of nations - poets able to go beyond time element.

3   Command of trade routes explains superiority of Egypt over Hittites,
    also superiority of Athens over Sparta. Tendency of cities to overcome
    basic civilization - Alexandria, Byzantium, Rome, New York - large
    growth of cities eats up civilization - inability to prevent overexpansion
    of cities - exhaustion of populations, agricultural resources. Emphasis
    on consumers goods in capitalistic society reflected in architecture and
    city planning - arranged that populations of city have quick access to
    department stores or shopping centres - makes city in plan of streets
    and architecture primarily concerned with outlets for consumers goods.
    Contrast with Russia - producers goods and less concerned with plan-
    ning in terms of retail trade - the basis of Veblen's dichotomy - engin-
    eer, i.e. Russia, and producers goods, and price system, i.e. Anglo-Saxon
    countries concerned with producers goods.

4   Over-emphasis on commerce and finance reflected in skyscrapers and
    architecture and encroachment on universities, publishing and printing
    histories of banks and other institutions - importance of indirect adver-
    tising. Brewers published Leacock's history of Canada - distortion of
    learning. Emphasis of commerce and finance on architecture, literature,
    and universities carried to excess but paralleling excess of concern of
    church with cathedrals and rise of scholasticism. Universities systemati-
    cally register effects of ground swells or affected by major waves in
    disturbances of civilization. Excess of religion paralleled by excess of
    commerce and finance. With emphasis on commerce words inadequate
    and resort had to architecture - building of skyscrapers. Banks with

solid pretentious-looking structures – the cathedrals of commerce – suggestion that book did not destroy architecture but commercial task so
heavy that architecture called in to help books. Architecture built
around selling – the store window – the chief centre of interest of the
architect. Constant pressure in advertising – architecture, etc. of consumers goods on population.

5   Henry Adams – following Balfour suggests significance of discovery of
radium – destroying illusions about 1900 – breaks down Darwinism.
But about this period press gets out of control.

6   Defeat of Austria 1866 – needle gun at Sadowa – smokeless powder at
Spandau. English Education Act 1870. Defeat of France 1870, Europe
lost a mistress and gained a master. German tariff 1878-9 emphasizing
industrialism. German expression of interest in colonies, following Bismarck's renunciation Bismarck dropped. English frightened into arms of
America toward end of century. German pressure on West Indies result
of sugar subsidy leading to Spanish American War, to difficulties of
French fishing – agreement handing over French shore. South African
war encouraged German army. Canada pulled in by Great Britain to re-
dress loss of prestige. France abolished clerical schools to facilitate linking with Great Britain (Combes). Reciprocity treaty intended to show
Imperial strength. Russian influence on French and American foreign
policy. War recovery – Northcliffe propaganda defeated Germany and
led Germans to concentrate on mass propaganda.

7   Good serial necessary to run from May through summer – maintains
sales. Serials overlap and poorer serials bring sharp drop in circulation.
Boom in book-publishing – new readers – cutting off of other expenditures – gas, etc. New book club – Simon and Schuster and Sears Roebuck – books selected by Gallup poll people – 75 people send in reports.
Sole selection by Book of the Month Club – $40,000 to author and
$40,000 to publisher to advertise book. Pocket books bring in new
readers. People buy large quantities of book of month outside club.
Sixty authors a year get $8[000] to $50,000 extra which they would
not have otherwise.

8   Monopoly of writing – Dickens exploiting monopoly of writing – turned
out material endlessly – Scott, Ainsworth, etc. Martineau's biography.

9   Significance of Greece – power with first extensive development of
literature – left stamp on all later literature. Conservative tradition of
printing in continuing classics and restricting new possibilities.

10 Significance of language as device for distributing ability – difficulties of
English weeds out less able or poorer memories. Mathematics becomes

more effective as language worn down. Cultural significance of learning –
to create freedom and bring ability through classes, i.e. church, socialism movement. Printing brought rise of new languages and decline of
Latin and in turn of sophistries of schoolmen and made room for Bacon
and Locke or for new ideas.

11   Planting of material to be pirated – prestige of publishing in England –
W.C. Bryant. Close relations with England. Monopoly – large profits –
importance of name – Trollope, Thackeray. Authors and magazines –
Dickens, Ainsworth.

12   *Readers Digest* contributed to marked increase in prices – *Saturday
Evening Post* prices increased from $500 to $2000. *Readers Digest* pays
$5000. Five book clubs of major importance – opposed by publishers
at first but three partly owned by Doubleday Doran – found sales enormously increased. Thirty-nine cent Woolworth novels raised to 49 cents
and greatly increased sales – then increased to 69 cents – no effect on
general market. Lid off magazines market – unprecedented demand –
ceiling on advertising – poor editors coming on market – serials dropped
and novels included whole or in two parts. Costain regards serials as
most important – good serials.

13   Admiral Mahan very influential on Germany – followed by Kaiser and
contributed to division between army and navy, and exhaustion. Significance of a book influencing naval and military strategy – danger of
believing in book. How far Russia saved by limited possibility of reading books? Germany suffered from belief in books rather than distrust-
ing them, MacKinder's book [*Britain and the British Seas* (1904)] had
similar influence after first world war on Germany. Pretentious character of books and lack of scepticism absorbed by Germany but scepticism or competition prevents belief in a single thesis. Importance of
scepticism and flexibility. Bible and Lutheranism. Problem of adaptation of technical force to cultural factors, i.e. language – technique of
force determines extent of control but cultural factor, i.e. language,
able to resist – problem of developing cultural machinery to adapt culture to force in terms of geographic area. Probable that geographic factor replaces kinship or tribal as it implies power and military technique.
Cultural factors, weakening military or offset by military. Difficulty of
large imperial militaristic structure based on effectiveness of attack increased by strength of cultural factors reinforced by military tactics
emphasizing defence – equilibrium between cultural factors and force
and attempt to work out coordination of divisive cultural factors with
world order.

14 [Auguste] Comte an illustration of French interest in system and unity, i.e. of work of scholastics in making language flexible.

15 Factors making for rationalism in society - particularly reasoning of law, spread of mathematics, role of great books, but each with limitations - even philosophers and theologians or organization of irrationality. Party organization.

16 Local newspapers - rely on advertising to secure local correspondents - regular copy supplied by those interested in advertising themselves - tap writing intelligence or rather literacy of whole community - enlisting their enthusiasm and support. Weekly newspaper becomes great coordinating factor for literacy - writing and reading public.

17 Implications of machine industry shown in pressure on trade and necessity of moving goods - imposed terrific load on communication or language with which to have goods placed on market - language tends to be exhausted with demands or to be particularly adapted to movement of goods rather than to former political or religious purposes.

18 Very great value of art shown in high pay of executives and scarcity of artistic interest following commercialism and industrialism.

19 Jews - toughness of religion strengthened growth of commerce and contributed to civilization in spite of fanaticism.

20 Walter's policy - absorbing of class papers - advertising - concentration on news.

21 Problem of English language - lack of precision following borrowing from outside, i.e. use of French in documents giving greater purity and precision. Significance of communication in determining competition. Demand and production of paper favours theories favourable to production of paper - Adam Smith but monopoly, i.e. religion, etc. checks expansion of paper production and economic wealth. Limitation of language in China prevented healthy growth of public opinion and led to crashes.

22 Emphasis on contract in law a further indication of spread of individualism and importance of price system. Legal institution like religious institution slowly adapted to technological change - particularly division of labour - checks communication by development of wills and corporation. Greediest of legal categories.

23   Inevitable tendency of religion and cultivation of virtues to bring wealth and conflict with poverty - latter leading to prophets and outbreak of evangelicalism - break from large organization and tendency of large organizations to link with wealth. Importance of elasticity to meet dilemma particularly in periods of depression - task to some extent taken over by labour unions, socialism, etc.

24   English language makes for greater flexibility - common law, parliamentary constitutions, trade.

25   Tendency of church to link with nationalism and consequently with military hierarchy at expense of proletariat.

26   Significance of necessity of constant change in advertising - rapid increase in sales comes during upward swing of campaign and falls off when name of product well known and familiar. Constant necessity of introducing new devices - new brands of cigarettes, new models - advertising must take on character of news.

27   Tremendous significance of impact of renaissance on England - shown in destruction of monasteries in freeing education in contrast with restraint in Catholic countries. Abolition of monasteries improved education and abolition of celibacy of clergy brought new life to nation reflected in grandeur of age of Elizabeth. Monasticism a powerful factor restricting Europe and abolition gave England a tremendous advantage.

28   Significance of rhetoric in securing unanimity of action - tendency to blur rational elements and particularly dangerous in wide class distinction between educated and non-educated.

29   Principle of concession in religion as to business and trade as well as science. Religion a sort of brake on business excess but may become a sort of fuel when adapted to business and a support of business organization. Religious organization a brake on fanaticism and forming background for more stable development. Rhetoric developed by church - particularly Protestant preaching by which compromises more easily made - sort of lubricant by which adjustments made in religion and in politics - also in law. Religious organizations as a check on the excesses of the price system and the price system as a check on religious organization. Religious organization with types of hierarchy attempt to remove asperities of price system and, in being weakened, admit of growth of business hierarchies tempered by religion - philanthropic measures, etc. Religion checks spread of ideas by communication through hierarchy of learning, etc.; universities, etc. restraint on competitive element.

1   Note on L. Mumford's *Technics and Civilization*. See also 6 / 31; 15 / 53.

3   Reference to T. Veblen, *The Engineer and the Price System* (New York, 1921)

4   Leacock's *Canada, The Foundations of Its Future* was published in 1941 under the auspices of Seagram's.

5   Note on Henry Adams, *The Education of Henry Adams* (Boston and New York, 1918)

6   J.L.E. Combes (1835-1921) was a French politician, premier from 1902 to 1905. He followed a strong anti-clerifical policy.

8   Possibly reference to either Harriet Martineau, *Autobiography*, ed. M. Weston (London, 1877), or J.C. Nevil, *Harriet Martineau* (London, 1943)

12   Costain not identified

13   A.T. Mahan's *The Influence of Sea Power upon History, 1660-1783* (London, 1890) was an influential argument for the strategic importance of sea power.

20   John Walter (1776-1847), a son of the founder of the London *Times*, developed it from a partisan sheet to an important newspaper.

13

1947

1   Effect of repeal referendum legislation in western states claimed to be
     very satisfactory on measures - namely discussion on merits appears to
     lead to a balanced conclusion and general agreement. On the other hand
     voting on persons for legislature and office claimed to be unsatisfactory
     and resulting in election of undesirable officials.

2   Problem of economists appearing as witnesses and making concessions
     in written briefs regarded by lawyers in charge of case as making over-
     tures to enemy and latter press for case to appeal to judge or to avoid
     support to opposition. Case method in Harvard neglects problem of
     flexibility. Decisions in the main must be made in the interests of flexi-
     bility or to facilitate retreat in case of difficulty - management favours
     efficiency but directors insist on safety or on flexibility and safety or
     capacity to retreat. Economists acting as arbitrators or judges become
     annoyed at lawyers' tactics in presenting briefs and favour appearance
     of concessions as an indication of truth.

3   Arlington cemetery - tomb and buildings to unknown soldier. 'Here lies
     an American soldier known only to God' - building up of militaristic
     cult cutting across religious lines. Decline in political sensitivity in U.S. -
     partly a result of effects of two wars evident in difficulties in assuming
     imperial problems - reliance on force, i.e. Marshall as secretary of state.
     Social scientists unable to see implications of political problems - work-
     ing for branches of air force or navy or army. Possible result of revolu-
     tionary tradition - trend toward totalitarian state in U.S. and in Russia -
     disappearance of diplomatic tradition of 19th century - appeasement
     the new word - little appreciation of importance of concessions.

4   Roman empire concentrated on law as force became more important -
     Anglo-Saxon law does not permit reliance on force and leads to division
     of empire.

5   July 1, 1947. Nova Scotia - tremendous amount of work on land removing stones and stumps to make adaptable to machinery. Flying Nova Scotian flag. White pine appears in middle of New Brunswick and to south.

6   Apollonic versus Dionysiac interpretation reflect written, authoritative versus oral tradition. Political arguments based on economic facts distort in relation to various points of view. Dionysiac in contrast with insistence of economists on a sticking to mathematics or appeal to Apollonic tradition.

7   A good host and the worst possible guest. Why is he so nasty? I have never shown him any favours.

8   Politicians expert in the art of diverting attention - W.L. Mackenzie King in Byng controversy obscured customs scandal [1926]. Developed provincial problem to offset interest in external affairs.

9   Struggle between religion and law - former builds up system of securing justice in hereafter and law attempts to secure justice on earth - as law succeeds religion apt to be weakened. Libraries part of power of religion - Sumerian literature centred in Babylon, later in Assyria (Nineveh) and in Alexandria - culture or knowledge an instrument of power.

14

possibly 1947

1   Interest in astronomy led priestly schools of Assyria and Babylonia to
develop deities to correspond to increasing number of stars - influence
of science on religion. Liver - large blood supply - used by Babylonians
for divining, i.e. relation to life. Priests able to adapt religion to demands
of force - force made religion malleable - had impact on laws - gods
reduced to order and tendency to reduce laws dependent on gods to
order - force meant uniformity of laws and emphasis on conciliation -
secular interest (Hammurabi). How far cruelty a result of necessity of
influencing opinion and possibly exaggerated? Importance of assembly
in Greece to oral tradition. How far absence of codes of law in Egypt a
result of papyrus and its significance to administration?

2   Monasticism spreading from Egypt in protest against absolutism made
encroachments on family or *pater potestas* of Europe though this had
been weakened by Roman law. Restriction of learning to monasteries
favoured outburst of oral tradition in universities and finally breaking
through in reformation. Monopoly of monasticism and church gave tremendous significance to coming of Greek and classics in renaissance -
attempts to dam back Greek influence in St Thomas Aquinas, etc.
failed with migration of manuscripts and printing or emphasis on Hebrew and scriptures and puritanism as against church and cathedral.

3   Problem of choice of subjects on which publishers concentrate - hero
worship - military figures and political figures or documents. Scholarship given definite slant by existing written material. Church seized on
written documents.

4   Competition between written works - scriptures of Jews and Christians -
later reinforced by Aristotle in Aquinas, Cicero. Rhetoric held sway
with decline in influence of Roman law in west until latter revived in
Bologna and spread through Europe. Printing brought renewal of place
of scriptures, Bible in countries which became Protestant or countries
in which Roman law weak. With strong Roman law, i.e. France, power

of state broke that of church - Philip the Fair vs. Boniface. Law spread
with influence of lawyers to check church. Battle between clergy and
law - latter supported by force to keep religion in check.

5   Problem of heredity - English admitting women to throne provide
     greater possibilities for expansion of government whereas French here-
     dity in male line strengthened power of dynasty. German empire system
     of election made for flexibility but difficulty of continuity. Roman em-
     perors unable to establish dynasty because of power of Senate and fam-
     ily not given place of dominant importance. On the other hand women
     on throne assumes a solidly entrenched dynasty with no fear of difficul-
     ties. Celibacy in church helped to cut power of family and prevent
     dynasties. Electoral system in Spain led to success of Mohammedans
     and division of latter to success of Charles Martel - importance of here-
     dity in male line seen in Charlemagne and Carolingian empire.

6   Problem of reason - whenever topic of discussion turns to reason ration-
     ality endangered - reason a concept constantly subject to exploitation.
     Stoics thought of reason and natural law in relation to equality. Again
     Aquinas used Aristotle and emphasized place of reason. Problem of edu-
     cation similar to reason - attempt to exploit points of strategy such as
     reason and education. Most difficult to refute subtlety of attacks on
     rationality. Religion constantly concerned with heading off philosophy
     and attempting to crystallize it in dogma, i.e. Dominicans - St Thomas
     Aquinas with Aristotle, Jesuits in Counter-Reformation.

7   Mackinder - closed sea, i.e. Egyptian kings, Crete, Greece in east, Rome -
     Mediterranean a closed sea - encroachment from Turks and Moham-
     medans turned Mediterranean from closed sea to moat for Europe. At-
     tack from hinterland on sea - control of coast meant control of sea.

8   Pressure of technology on scholarship - Eastman Kodak developed films
     and put pressure on libraries and other groups to use microfilm. Diffi-
     culty of scholars in resisting technological advance.

9   Business cycles - communication contracts and expands in efficiency -
     particularly with psychological effects of advertising during periods of
     boom - impossibility of effective diagnosis or of securing diagnosis but
     demands of business men to hear and read what they want to read
     rather than to present objective appraisal. Writers anxious to meet de-
     mands of business men and to tell them what they want to hear and
     read. Creation of belief in business cycle by studies of business cycle
     leads to action on part of business men designed to respond to business
     cycle. Role of economist in relation to business cycle.

10   Western civilization a struggle between patriarchal system and religion -
      religious emphasis on celibacy an attempt to break down patriarchal
      system - defeat of religion in Greece possibly result of strength of patri-
      archal system - Minerva's owl. Rome broke patriarchal system - revived
      in Middle Ages.

11   News - essentially concerns happenings in the past and serves as infor-
      mation as to happenings in future. Improved communication hastens
      information and facilitates action after information recorded, i.e. stock
      exchange. Constant search of past for guidance of action in future -
      possibility of steadying news with increased emphasis on immediate
      through interpretation, editorial policy, and the like. Inevitable that
      sustained studies of past tend to diverge from immediate demands of
      present. Gap tends to widen with improved communication - lag in rela-
      tion between demand for immediate news and sustained studies.

12   Rise of photography after last war (1918) killed illustrations in maga-
      zines and compelled them to be literary - possibly had effect of requir-
      ing clearer writing or more journalistic writing. Photography took edge
      off delights of travelling.

13   Printing seized on store of manuscripts and fastened them on the future.
      Scriptures given new sanctity with printing - previously could not be
      taken seriously and church organization more important. Law and be-
      lief by lawyers in efficacy and omniscience - great planners of society
      and monopoly on it. Claim by Pollock that lawyers lost British Empire.
      Enormous size of Bible meant emphasis on theological books, sales to
      church and defence of church - overemphasis on authority restricted
      market led to turn to new products - reformation a shift from single
      large buyer to large number of small buyers - from folio to small vol-
      umes and pamphlets.

14   Significance of architecture - restriction of parchment emphasized need
      of expression especially with prosperity in buildings. These in turn fav-
      oured oral expression in cathedral schools and universities and rise of
      scholasticism - emphasis on large books - St Thomas Aquinas *Summae* -
      cathedrals of thought. In this printing destroyed possibilities of archi-
      tecture as expression except with wearing down of words by advertising
      and rise of skyscrapers to reinforce words. Use of language or vernacular
      as basis of force in development of state of absolute character of Hegel.
      But force transcends language and necessity of appeal to ideology cut-
      ting across language. Law still important as against history or romanti-
      cism. Printing means destruction of hierarchical values, reliance on force,
      and mobilization of vernacular as of force. Romanticism of 19th cen-
      tury - breakdown of rule of law - appeal to nationalism and history.

Political myth revived when printing first developed - also compulsory education and rise of historicism and nationalism. Printing weakened initiative - opened way to totalitarian state.

NOTES

7   Note on Sir H.J. Mackinder, *Democratic Ideals and Reality: A Study in the Politics of Reconstruction* (New York, 1919).
13   The Pollock to whom Innis refers is probably one of the distinguished legal family which was prominent in England in the nineteenth and early twentieth centuries.

15

probably 1947-8

1   Public opinion agitated because of pressure of price system against
     monopoly - trust busting campaigns - newspapers concerned with direct
     consumers and advertisers. Effect of spread of communication on politi-
     cal theory and on economic theory - development of newspapers means
     destruction of monopolies of price information - equilibrium theory,
     i.e. Marshall, paralleling increasing influence of press in spread of infor-
     mation. Keynesian analysis a further step weakening monopoly of
     money or of giving states greater power over monopoly. Pressure of
     newspapers on consumers' goods - policies in campaigns or crusades
     designed to strengthen the position of consumers.

2   Price of sheet Baltimore $5 a ream or about 1¢ a sheet in 1827 and 3/4¢
     for sheet a third larger in 1832. Papers increased size of sheets rather
     than change prices to consumers - increased demand for composition -
     limited circulation - high price - gave advantage to penny press. Balti-
     more *Sun* and *Public Ledger* gained immediate favour by attacking
     banks. Increased literacy - public school system - new types of readers
     concerned with events rather than ideas and increased communication
     to give wider knowledge of events. Railroads enormously reduced time
     1827-1837. Use of express to handle Harrison's message March 4, 1841
     by *Sun* and *Public Ledger* strengthened position with exchanges to
     south - led to cooperation in expresses across Nova Scotia 1845 - sug-
     gests the significance of emphasizing facts in spread of communication.

3   Decline of parliament result of Irish question - obstructionist tactics -
     outbreak of bitterness - Carson in Ulster with support of army able to
     defy parliament - suggesting army had gained control. Ochs on *Times*
     emphasized news coverage to offset tendency of other papers to slant
     news in relation to different constituencies. Nearness of written to oral
     tradition checks authority of written tradition.

4   Newspapers against electing presidents by caucus – ended 1832. Hearst
     demand election of U.S. senators by direct vote 1911, i.e. creation of
     situation creating greater demand for newspapers. Greeley probably
     gained support of labour in general attitude for Republican party –
     source of embarrassment to other papers. Difference in time of Europe
     and America gave afternoon papers almost monopoly of war news. De-
     partment stores followed increase in availability of advertising space.
     Greeley – 'remember that ... the tax payers take many more papers than
     the tax consumers,' April 3, 1860 – consequent interest in keeping
     down taxes.

5   Nationalism in Canada exploited by publishers – series of Glasgow –
     sold by subscription – books article of furniture – Champlain society –
     Canada and its provinces – pulp and paper school. Necessity of relying
     on criticism of U.S. and England but latter apt to tone of snobbery and
     colonialism. Few escape into artistic freedom except in appeal to Eng-
     lish language, i.e. Stephen Leacock. Art a means of escape but checked
     by nationalism and parochialism – bigotry of church. Humorists more
     apt to have universal approval – Mark Twain, Stephen Leacock.

6   Significance of revolution in politics is preparation for revolution in
     economics – preparing people for discipline of machine – communism
     in Russia, fascism in Italy a device for compelling undisciplined people
     to accept discipline of machine – probable that revolutions have much
     of element of preparing for discipline – printing industry a part of dis-
     ciplining process – includes disciplining of language and literature.

7   Use of images in western church opened way for block printing and
     stimulated printing with special emphasis on Bible and paper-image wor-
     ship of print characteristic of western civilization – developed [out] of
     belief in abstract and growth of philosophy – belief in idea of Plato
     basis of west but this succumbed with rise of vernacular and emphasis
     on language and incommunicability – worship of print broke up western
     civilization into nationalism and adaptation of technology to militarism
     harnessed to nationalism – belief in material civilization – communica-
     tion not sufficiently powerful to overcome vested interests.

8   Rise of political reform movements in relation to staple producing areas –
     currents of hot air float upward from areas of sharp fluctuations – pres-
     sure through votes within area.

9   Closed systems result of written tradition, i.e. Spengler – Toynbee.
     Totalitarian states – belief in power of written word of government.

10   Enormous significance of music - Gregorian chant conflict with north leading to cathedrals and polyphony - German music protected by Hohenstaufens broke with church - basic to understanding of Luther and Protestantism. Concentration of effort implied in oral tradition in music until notation scheme devised.

11   W.A. White - used large returns of stories sold in national magazines to build up small paper in Emporia - suggests drive of advertising on national scale on advertising on local scale.

12   Abolition of pass system and introduction of primary destroyed power of railroads.

13   Impact of newspaper shown in 20th century in spreading out of empire - development of staple production. Use of religion in advertising - joining of Roman Catholic Church - Claire Booth Luce means of attracting Irish Catholic interest in press. Use of negroes on radio to attract negro market. Use of Irish to attract Irish market. Religion exploited by advertising groups.

14   Oral tradition reflected in religion - spread of Christianity filled gap between city state and empire and in west restricted growth of nationalism. Rise of vernacular and attempt of church through preaching orders to maintain contact, i.e. oral tradition in church organization became less efficient - unable to check growth of heresy and consequently Inquisition followed or to check growth of writing and political attacks of lawyers or of printing - obsession with letter - worship of graven image of printed word evident in protestantism. Printed word assumed learning and new type of priesthood - national churches - Anglican, Lutheran. But oral tradition in preaching persisted, notably in Methodism. Science in antiquity handicapped by poetry or philosophy. Have--nots - vernacular, oral tradition in contrast with haves - written tradition.

15   Limitations of writing in Babylonia and Egypt meant emphasis on sculpture and images but idea of monotheism developed by priestly class taken over by fringe areas and incorporated in priesthood with sacred book - *Avesta*, Jewish Scriptures, Sibylline texts, Koran, Bible of Protestantism. Worship of printed text took place of images - Greek philosophy - Plato checked theocracy. Deism a return to monotheism (18th century). Christianity spread to west where books not entrenched as in east.

16   Pareto - problem of elite and constant overthrow residues - suggests impact of written and oral traditions. Logical versus non-logical. Men of elite vs. force.

17   History - product of west in terms of linear progress of time. Contrast
     with China. Use of centuries - fingers and toes - distortion of history.

18   Weber - Calvinism regarded business success as a sign of grace. Success
     became linked to capitalism. Bureaucracy - an ideal type of capitalism -
     Germany - army - bureaucracy - also law - in England law did not pro-
     tect economically weak and facilitated growth of capitalism.

19   See Pareto on Roman religion and rites.

20   Diminishing returns in use of mathematics leads to monopoly and oli-
     gopoly. Intense problem of strategy with large numbers of competitors
     creates demand for simplicity and for monopoly and duopoly. Problem
     of how much a firm can afford to spend on mathematicians. Douglas
     presidential address suggests very little influence of monopoly - assumes
     competition with monopolies. Concentration on aggregates probably
     dangerous in limiting interest in reform - obscuring of problems under-
     estimates and averages.

21   Decline in power of politician after last war evident in success of Keynes'
     Economic Consequences and in political failure of Versailles evident in
     later collapse - economist in newspaper more powerful than politician -
     illustrating extent to which papers ceased to be influenced by politicians.
     Parliamentary government allows opposition to exploit oral tradition
     and eventually to overthrow government tending to be obsessed with
     written tradition over long period.

22   Campbell of Edmonton *Bulletin* making $22,000 a year through arrange-
     ment with Edmonton *Journal* over strike problems. Campbell formerly
     in Vancouver paid $40,000 by Vancouver *Province* as result of threat to
     abandon agreement over subscription rate.

23   Journalism in Nova Scotia in 1847 election reached low point in vitu-
     peration with filthy verses hurled between Baptists and Roman Catholics.

24   Pervasive influence of advertising - writers of one media place articles in
     another media and secure advertising for former as well as for latter -
     writing becomes a device for advertising advertising.

25   Limited medium for writing accompanied by emphasis on architecture
     and sculpture - images - Pyramids Egypt - Babylonian and Assyrian em-
     pires and Persian. In turn Rome but Greece emphasized resistance to
     Oriental cultures in restraint in sculpture and architecture. Parchment -
     Gothic cathedral; paper - skyscrapers. How far culture at maturity with
     architecture? Enormous economic power necessary for vast architectural
     projects.

26   How far lawyers emphasize vernacular in assisting empire and national
       state against Latin and papacy? As gap widens between Latin and ver-
       nacular possible that lawyers step into breach. In custom law in north-
       ern France and England necessary for lawyers to remain close to custom
       or vernacular. Repression of English with Norman court probably em-
       phasized its position in vernacular and saved it from imposition of other
       languages - made it easier to learn with less emphasis on learned lang-
       uages or learned style as in Germany - more adaptable to trade. Oral
       tradition in France - universities - richness of language and precision.
       Escape from drains of dual language - Latin and vernacular and empha-
       sis on vernacular made for rich development of literature.

27   Texas the great single market for textbooks in the United States as stu-
       dents supplied free with books by state. Texas apt to set standards for
       books sold in other states.

28   Trade publications put out in large numbers partly for prestige purposes
       and partly to cut down overhead. Run by single individual or editor and
       assistants - every five under a supervisor. So long as paper pays small
       part of overhead taken on.

29   Problem of accounting in large business and for government inspection -
       designing of system to show losses at proper places.

30   Cocktail lounges and retailers of beer make large profit on foam - sell
       150 glass keg to make up to 200 glasses.

31   Koran memorized by large numbers and consequently a tremendous
       pressure exists to prevent any changes. This in turn is reflected in cus-
       toms of people. In India music in oral tradition. Combination of oral
       and written apparently makes for rigidity and conservatism. Oral alone
       slowly adapts itself. See Milner's comment on empires in Shotwell's
       diary [February 10, 1919].

32   Spread of writing and parchment in Christian church utilized by Con-
       stantine to support empire. Church became more efficient channel of
       public opinion with parchment - spreading out of monasteries - limita-
       tions of courts. Theodosius in Byzantine empire developed contractual-
       ism - agreements to take place of unified bureaucracy. Church used
       councils as basis of democratic government in west. State use of repre-
       sentative government in estates or parliament. Clash between written
       and oral tradition that between Greece and Asia - influence of religions
       from Asia - with restrictions of science and literature in courts of ab-
       solute monarchs. Pouring out of religions led to force. Alexandrian em-
       pire - effect on India - rise of Buddhism. Power of Brahmins and impact
       of Buddhism on China and Confucianism - rise of printing and paper -

spread to west. Mohammedanism and Europe. Mohammedans - Jews opposed sculpture or representations to check influence of other religions.

33   Enormous power of history illustrating cultural influence - Mussolini repeating Rome - inability as result of cultural prestige to develop understanding of developments. Military leaders caught in trend and unable to see objectively.

34   Communism a device for saving capitalism as reformation saved church. Clash between oral tradition of Russia and written tradition. Protest against cash relationships and supporting social relations or oral tradition, i.e. communism.

35   Oral tradition after Augustus lost vitality in religion and codification of law. Growth of writing and loss of creative power after Horace and Virgil. Shock of discovery of oral tradition due to prestige of written tradition after Renaissance (i.e. discovery of sagas, etc.). Beginnings of German literature indicate appeal to oral tradition, i.e. sagas of Homer and Pindar rather than written literature. Biblical literalism mother of heresy - killed living spirit of vernacular and allegory. Lack of faith in France and Italy meant lack of heresy. Mrs Murphy's hand. Power of Bunyan in relation to oral tradition in preaching.

36   American frontier - soft - consequently individualistic; Russian - hard and consequently requiring centralized control of state.

37   Conditions of survival of empire - disequilibrium with overemphasis on knowledge or monopoly of communications and neglect of economic factors or training of military - problem of handling religion or opinion - breakdown with attack from military and technological advance outside.

38   Effect of accent on break up of Empire - oral tradition and attempt to enforce superiority by emphasis on accent led to revolt - variety of accents in England led to insistence on recognition of position and to toleration.

39   Indian music - strong influence of seasons. Claim war in west due to use of music at wrong time. Close attention to detail in music - probably reflecting influence in magic and need for exact attention to rules.

40   Absence of copyright meant emphasis on speed of manufacturing - printing books from England rapidly and building of technical plant with neglect of native writing. Probably explains difficulties of Harpers after copyright act - had neglected American writing. Importance of

families perhaps even greater in books than newspapers. Importance of religion as a background to publishing. Question as to how far book destroyed Byzantine Empire, i.e. in attack on images - iconoclasm. Also destroyed church in printing of Bible.

41   Destruction of states in modern warfare - overrunning of Czechoslovakia - Germany and allies, then Russia - development of underground movements inevitable, France, etc.

42   [U.S. Supreme Court Justice Oliver W.] Holmes favoured policy of recognizing importance of legislature and reflected influence of public opinion. American judges resent legislative interference - apt to oppose legislation and defeat its intentions.

43   *Evening Post* with long tradition exploded into *Nation, Saturday Review of Literature* and tabloid. Price of books rose after 1900 while that of magazines declined. F.D.R. [Roosevelt] brought cost of mailing books into line with magazines.

44   [G. Herbert] Mead - social mind - product of environment reflected back through communication to individual. Language making society possible.

45   [Maurice] Dobb - charge of abstraction of economics in algebraic symbols implies neglect of commodity values or labour theory of value.

46   Friars of Middle Ages held a position of special privilege by attacking political injustice and serving as outlet for public opinion of lower classes.

47   Soap opera - bogus emotional conflicts without thought.

48   New York newspaper critics extremely conservative - regarded as last word and comments fatal to drama and to leftist tendencies.

49   Possible influence of rental libraries on production of long books - this involves keeping book for greater length of time and paying rental - query as to importance of rental library sales to publishers?

50   Attack on corruption of church - result of pressure of writing and law on church organization. Criticism against church led to counter-attack - organizing of papacy and further attack following printing. Locke's psychology - emphasizing *tabula rasa* dealt a blow to the doctrine of original sin.

51   Close union of learning and belief characterizes Oriental religions.

52   Oral tradition - problem of date and calendar or history. Implications
      to philosophy of time and to literature. Emphasis on architecture, i.e.
      Egypt, Rome. Written tradition facilitates reckoning in terms of years
      and gives time as device for discussion of history.

53   Significance of glass - microscope, telescope - widened universe to
      infinity (Mumford).

54   Dutch - use of wind power - outburst of art - painting, etc. (turbines
      and civilization).

55   Coal - pollution of air - no recognition of rights in light and air - dis-
      covery of rights with electricity - prohibition of coal trains in large cities.

56   Configuration of cultural growth - applied to Kroeber, i.e. one of three
      or four studies on civilization appearing in 20th century.

57   Bacon attacked universities as centres of magisterial learning of contin-
      ent and favoured new institution emphasizing science - reflected inter-
      est of London in practical affairs whereas universities distant from
      London remained centres of ecclesiastical tradition.

58   Francis Wiese 62,000 words sold to *Women's Home Companion* and cut
      to 42,000 to make two instalments, published in book form in 62,000
      but English market requires 82,000 words and blown up to that amount.

59   Growth of emphasis on national status partly a reflection of increased
      importance of advertising - similarly provincial autonomy Alberta,
      Saskatchewan.

60   American Economic Association largely concerned with law - most pro-
      grammes on questions of laws or specific acts - decline of interest in
      universal laws.

61   G.L. Dickinson - wanted relinking of life and poetry - importance of
      poetry.

62   Brooks Adams - centralization - civilization; decentralization - barbar-
      ism. U.S. favoured decentralization, then centralization and imperialism.

63   Sacred character of writing - Bible and Koran - difficult basis for em-
      pire - weakness of law but building up of learning - emphasis of Islam
      on Greek. With collapse of civilization possible for learning to be taken
      over by conquerors - Spain and Frederick II - also Byzantium. Mono-
      theism emphasizes prestige based on learning - Baghdad - Constantin-
      ople but weakness from military point of view. Sacred character of

ancient writing - Roman law - printing of Bible. Christianity - Jesus reflecting oral tradition in opposition to book - coming from rural areas. He spake as one with authority. Roman empire - adoption of Latin in Roumania and elsewhere important in holding empire together - Christianity and national conversion created literature and separate linguistic development.

64 Significance of department stores and advertising pressing on factors making for newspaper circulation and emphasis on type of opinion affected by it - lack of continuity. Commercialism an unstable factor with consequent danger of war.

65 Persia - influence on Arabs stimulated splendour of Baghdad which emphasized concern of Constantinople with scholarship and lessened prospects of union under papacy. Pincer-like movement via Spain and via Constantinople - impact of paper. Parchment as limited meant emphasis on hierarchy in church which probably meant hierarchy in state. Rome solved problem of family (Maine) but Semites failed, i.e. Mohammedan problem of succession and medieval civilization wrestled with it over long period - solved by church with celibacy. Power of vernacular in England and Germany probably explained growth of common law in England and development of printing and reformation in Germany. 'Getting at the facts' a reflection of the power of mathematics and neglects getting at the problem. Problem of change in velocity of time - difficulty of those operating at one time or tempo suddenly placed in a new tempo - probably a factor in business cycle. Importance of wiping out differences between space and time as both categories of communication. Religion becomes powerful in conflict between two cultures or between force and law, i.e. Roman Catholic Church in Europe in opposition to barbarians - Palestine - use of book makes for rigidity.

66 Use of mountains for advertising purposes - naming of Rockies by C.P.R.

67 Weeklies - *Colliers* - able to get interpretative stories with background in contrast to spot news of newspapers. Writers proceed from reputation with background stories to write best sellers - crowding of news on weeklies and on books - weakening position of other books.

68 Sharp edges of religion cut across national boundaries - role of Jews in defeat of Hitler - role of Roman Catholic Church in defeating loyalists in Spain.

69 Constant depreciation - new books drive out old books - publishers concerned with depreciation in publishing new books but also concerned with monopolies in building up their lines. How far printing essentially

based on controversy perhaps centring around price system and philosophical books became byproduct of excess capacity in quiet periods –
Descartes in Holland centre of printing industry for Holland? Printing
meant mechanical reproduction of images – consequent deterioration in
value and closer adjustment to goods – advertising.

70 Role of women – Irene – reflecting attitude of Macedonia but led to
excuse in which Pope crowned Charlemagne in 800 and to excuse in
which east returned to iconoclasm. Patriarchalism helped to separate
east from west. Salic law preventing election of women in Europe possibly contributed to disappearance of monarchies – whereas recognition
in England probably favoured continuance of monarchy. Parchment –
enormous importance of codex in transfer of books and founding new
libraries in contrast with papyrus. Monotheism meant scattered and
rather uniform resources. Economy of writing on parchment – abbrevi-
ations and suspensions and problem of highly skilled craft in writing
and reading. Contraction of knowledge.

71 Stefannson claimed sale of enormous numbers of *Forever Amber* weakened Macmillans as in ration period very little paper was left for other
publications and list neglected. Montgomery Ward apparently sold
Herbert Spencer and works by radical authors in contrast with Sears
Roebuck.

72 Oral tradition among Eskimo – speaker starts story then interrupted by
someone who says uncle had different version – long dispute and if
speaker shown wrong must start at first again and continue along
divided route – telling of story requiring all winter.

73 Impasse of journalism – effective journalists those most subject to emotional instability. Circulation dependent on commercial instability.

74 Influence of church – images – in west – outbreak of crusades – growth
of political and economic power. Political organization strengthened by
Roman law and spread of Norsemen from north – reliance on force.

75 Writing essentially mechanical in contrast with speech. Thucydides –
prose undermining state built on oral tradition. Christians against Jewish
law and spread without fear of opposing law in Roman empire.

76 Extent to which Tories forced to join labour in position on English
press. Oastler felt compelled to write for illegal unstamped press because
no other avenue opened to working men.

77 Pressure of courts on legislation - enormous numbers of employer-employee suits cluttered courts until Workmen's Compensation came along and removed it. Periodic use of courts as pressure gauge leading to statutes - tax problems godsend for lawyers.

78 Music - emphasis on special advantages - foreign music, special church music, teaching. Concentration on magazine *Etude* gave Presser Philadelphia control over large publishing business at expense of Boston. Magazine effective in reaching purchaser.

79 Aristotle return to life - temporal. Militarism developed on edge of Greek culture - Macedonia.

NOTES

11 Note on W.A. White, *The Autobiography of W.A. White* (New York, 1946)
19 See Vilfredo Pareto, *The Mind and Society* (New York, 1935)
20 P.H. Douglas delivered the presidential address to the American Economics Association on 29 December, 1947. It was published in the *American Economics Review*, March 1948.
31 For Shotwell, see 5 / 41.
35 Mrs Murphy not identified.
44 Note on G.H. Mead, *Mind, Self and Society* (Chicago, 1934)
45 Note on M. Dobb, *Political Economy and Capitalism* (London, 1937)
53 Note on L. Mumford, *Technics and Civilization*. See 12 / 1
56 Reference to A.L. Kroeber, *Configurations of Cultural Growth* (Berkeley, 1944)
58 Francis Wiese not identified.
61 Dickinson (1862-1932) was a British humanist, historian, and philosopher.
62 Note on Brooks Adams, *The Law of Civilization and Decay* (New York, 1943)
65 Reference to H.J.S. Maine, *Ancient Law* (London, 1906).
71 This is possibly Vilhjamur Stefannson (1879-1961), the renowned Arctic explorer.
76 Richard Oastler (1789-1861) was a British industrial reformer.

16

Innis travelled to England and France in 1948 to deliver the Beit lectures at Oxford, which were subsequently published as *Empire and Communications*. This section, and the next, contain travel notes made during the trip.

1 Break between vernacular and learned language a rough indication of the bias incidental to communication mediums. Panic in England over navy budgets in 1909 and later behind reciprocity agitation in Canada.

2 Art a buttress for talent against wealth.

3 Pulitzer had excellent editorial page because of blindness - editorials read to him.

4 Common law countries tend to have lawyers as legislators - consequently journalists excluded whereas Roman law countries have large numbers of journalists as legislators.

5 Morning press of great advantage in politics in U.S. - Democrats in Cleveland had evening paper - resorted to morning papers in election years 1852, 1872, 1880. Improvements in telegraph gradually weakened advantage of morning papers in news. Editors kept in line by threat of establishing new papers, i.e. short-lived rivals of Democratic *Plain Dealer* when editor too independent of party. Incorporation with increasing demands for press equipment and capital. Corporate system facilitated use of ambush for control - buying up of shares until majority acquired.

6 Science concerned with inanimate material enormously favoured by writing and power of making results permanent and accessible - economics gains because of concern with inanimate material - question as to limitations of sociology or subjects less concerned with inanimate material. Tendency of science to apply type of measurements of space to time, i.e. astronomy, and destroy concept of time in myth or religion.

7 Libraries appeal to 10 per cent of adult education in U.S., possibly one half of number of adults using books.

8   Problem of appeals or movements – objective to secure newspaper space by creating news or advertising but failing through competition from other movements and inability to strike roots.

9   Rogers on insurance (August, 1948) claims insurance companies tending to get away from straight life protection and introducing capital saving element but at high cost. Straight life protection very much cheaper but companies prefer to sell other policies – Occidental able to undercut during periods of difficulty when protection alone demanded by selling straight life. August, 1948 – severe drought – all signs fail in a drought. Ford's popularity largely result of quick service on cars as compared with other makes – emphasis on sales organization and repairs. Department stores – basis of success of price control in Canada. Economics of peace or what people do not want rather than what they want – insurance, health, armaments.

10   Scarcity of paper or high price of paper means emphasis on single book to secure largest possible sales and greatest possible economies, i.e. effect of war and quotas – narrowing of lists.

11   Oral tradition – Greek and Teutonic Homeric ages – absorption of military age semi-civilized peoples from more highly cultivated peoples – tribal bonds breaking down – oral tradition form of resistance against highly cultured – characteristic of Europe. Flourished in Greece but largely overcome in Teutons by Christianity but persisted in German superiority complex and in north. German intervention under emperors in Italy accentuated feudalism in weakening powers of central authority and gave France opportunity to become centralized. English advantage in small change and closing of gap between cost and price, i.e. avoidance of flat rate on buses. Bicycles used in large numbers – unused capacity on roads. Problem of accent in English schools – handicap to reform in education. Those with poor accent unwilling to send children to school with those with good accent and *vice versa*. Oral tradition a powerful influence on English life – middle classes and education – private and public schools.

12   New Light movement supported opposition to international organization and imperial organization. Opposed unlimited centralization with emphasis on individual. Breaking out of oral tradition in protests against written, i.e. rich oral tradition in Thoreau and England. Emerson's protests against books in Phi Beta Kappa address. Heroes always appear on fringes of cultural development – heroic age, i.e. Lenin.

13   Printers in Chicago concentrate on commercial printing – time-tables, etc., and consequent high cost of printing leads books to be published in New York.

14 Dependence on votes - arithmetic as a solvent to political and social
rigidity.

15 Maintenance of dollar at par with U.S. shuts Canada out of empire markets - with lower price sterling and U.S. able to undercut Canadian producers in other markets, i.e. Cook on quinine and chemical products.

16 Tombstones and cemeteries a continuation of reverence for relics and relic worship. ·

17 Interest in modern history at Cambridge overshadows other subjects as does interest in law in Paris. Tendency for best man to be attracted to Paris and for provincial universities to be weakened and in turn for students to go from provinces to Paris.

18 Paper industry built up in relation to city with supply of rags. Parchment produced over wide area in France and sent to Paris - probably explains differentiation between magissier and parcheminier - rise of guilds among latter. City type of culture ending with Paris - absorbed monarchy - Fontainebleau - luxury industries centring around Paris - Gobelin tapestries, Sèvres pottery, Essones paper, local crafts.

19 Work of Charlemagne in conquests turned Scandinavians toward England. Parchment - small limited governmental areas - division, warfare, disturbed government - loss of leaders in war.

20 General antagonism to Americans in France - capitalized by communists - object to France being made an American colony.

21 Oral tradition important in appraising theatres - books - sale dependent on conversation. All advertising successful by making people talk about goods.

22 Problem of scholarship - French insist on high standards of knowledge of language in severe examinations - able to take work in mathematics where this does not arise. Difficulty of creating understanding through scholarships - English students in Paris almost all in modern languages. French-Canadian students bothered with widely different accents - avoid too much contact with French in Paris.

23 Babylonian empires - importance of religion - priests - introduction of force brought constant disturbance - particularly influence of technology. Empire concept - Egypt, Assyrian, Hittite, Persian apparently triumphant over religion but culture persisted. Greek - empire - also Roman empire influenced by same concept but religion reasserted itself. Clay - problem of writing, schools, education.

24 [It is important to] ask allowance for bias toward written tradition to strengthen conclusions regarding oral tradition.

25 Time and space concept essential basis of law - i.e. Timasheff force and religion.

26 Rise of merchants able to evade implications - usury from 1100 to 1600 - paper probably supported business activities which overcame restrictions of church as to usury.

27 Oral tradition - Gay, Bullock - individual doing very little writing but exercising a profound influence over students - stimulating them in teaching.

28 Problem of church maintaining connection with oral tradition - rise of revival meetings and conversion to bring people into church and to subject them to more advanced teaching - neglect of language problem responsible for Inquisition and introduction of more humane method of preaching. Church littered with institutions designed to bridge the widening gap between the written and the oral tradition. Preaching an effective means of keeping church close to oral tradition.

29 Sacred character of writing once capital has become involved, i.e. copyright protection once material has been printed restricts possible dissemination. Brahmanism - oral tradition - limits on writing checked possibility of capitalism - Buddhism linked with Mohammedanism and writing.

30 Conversion of orgies and demand for excitement into a factor for the movement of trade - news to secure circulation for the sale of goods by advertising.

31 Claim George Drew received information from Victor Sifton while in government leading to Hong Kong investigation and that Drew held Sifton double-crossed him in the *Free Press*. Heard French-Canadians - Madame Garneau attacking clerical control of education in Montreal - reporting Gilson as saying University would never flourish under clerical control.

32 Economic history largely a study of accounting - following logic of accounts reflected in history of firms. Athens - publishing of accounts on stone - public finance.

33 Introduction of fast press by Pulitzer on [New York] *World* broke power of Republican party - swings in political power with new developments - radio, etc. Significance of drama - freshness of oral tradition - Greeks, Shakespeare.

34   Instability of regions with religions and learned languages. Monopoly of
      Brahmanism led to pouring in of Buddhism and writing and defeat of
      latter had implication to China. Re-established Brahmanism and Sans-
      krit created monopoly again favourable to spread of Islam. Emphasis in
      India on Brahmanism and Sanskrit and defeat of Buddhism with empha-
      sis on writing followed by migration of Buddhism to China and by col-
      lapse of influence of Seleucids in India. Consequent vacuum open to
      inroads of Mohammedans particularly with supply of paper as a medium
      and with Arabic alphabet – rapid and large-scale extension result of
      monopoly of Brahmanism and relative simplicity of alphabet. Antagon-
      ism of Mohammedanism to image meant discouraging of print until
      very late date and emphasis on writing, concentration on Koran and on
      great feats of memory. Mohammedanism flourished with writing and
      paper.

35   Enclosure movement apparently never succeeded in France as contrasted
      with England and consequently probably never became as efficient in
      agriculture. Paris with favourable climate suited to highly specialized
      street markets – stamp sales at specified area in Champs d'Elysees – bird
      and seed sales on Ile on Sunday mornings. Problem of diet – France –
      fried foods – also typical of countries with olive oil and this necessarily
      linked with dependence on wine. England greater variety of boiled foods
      and dependence on beer – variety of religions meant variety of drinks
      and hence a more varied trade – tea and coffee. France tends to be
      coffee.

36   Scottish universities more influenced by Bologna than English – Univer-
      sity of Glasgow constitution follows that of Bologna – basis of student
      election of rector who becomes chairman of court in Glasgow though
      seldom taking chair. Explains election of rector at Queen's in Scottish-
      Italian tradition. University of Glasgow founded by pope.

37   Lord Cobham – Hagley Hall – reflects profound influence of France –
      Fontainebleau through Charles II – setting up of tapestry factories re-
      sult of French example.

38   Manx continue ceremony of reading laws in English and in Manx before
      becoming effective – probably continuous with Iceland and reflecting
      position of oral tradition – Scandinavian oral tradition probably with
      William the Conqueror in Normandy, i.e. jury system and brought to
      England or merged with English oral tradition. Strong oral tradition evi-
      dent in common law in contrast with written tradition of Roman law.
      Oral tradition flexible and adaptable to demands – French revolution –
      Rousseau's general will – a protest against inflexibility of written Roman
      law tradition – United States written law – constitution protest against
      rigidity of oral tradition or of oral combined with written tradition –
      newspaper tends to keep written tradition linked to oral tradition.

Politicians' problem of keeping close to oral tradition or of not losing touch. Problem of government or common law that of keeping in touch with oral tradition - thereby encroaches on position of religion. Problem of international agreements - written but combining strong oral traditions and consequently ill adapted to changes over long periods. 'Breast' law - that held in the breast of the deemsters (judges) and in oral tradition.

39   Universities in British Empire apt to overemphasize power and political influence and to overlook outstanding significance of France or to make it difficult to appreciate position of France - important to develop philosophy of western culture. Danger of reading national statistics and concentrating on these statistics which show pre-eminence in various lines and to emphasize the largest or those increasing most rapidly.

40   Typically English position that Churchill should suggest [1940] union of France and England - emphasis on importance of political organization and neglect of sharp differences between cultural development of France and of common law countries. As important to be British as not to be parochial.

41   Centralization of King following Bennett - strengthening of civil service weakened Liberal party in provinces - left road open to provincial autonomy parties. Federal party weakened by neglect of provincial organization.

42   Religion a means of avoiding acceptance of opinion from someone else. Consequently broken by force. Oral tradition - role in maintenance of classes - placing of individuals by accent.

43   Canada changed from nation to colony to nation - King found Canada a nation and left it a colony in relation to U.S. - particularly a result of radio - statistics tend to take the heart out of mathematics.

44   Common law countries emphasize politics whereas Roman law countries favour cultural development. Occupation of France meant disappearance of politics but French cultural life survived. Occupation endured partly to save beauty of Paris.

45   In France food extremely precious and consequently cooked with great care - in England food a mass production question and little attention to cooking - perhaps explains limited success of rationing in France. Warm climate - eating and drinking outdoors more favourable to discussion in France - in contrast with inconstant weather in England. Inde-

pendent ownership of land in England involves depletion of capital – rental and lease meant landlord provided capital in buildings and fences and tenant livestock and crops – capital supply larger. In many cases farms only equal value of buildings. Enormous importance of stone tradition in England, France – monuments, old churches – in contrast with U.S. – but even here skyscrapers – stone tradition in pyramids – Stonehenge – architecture and sculpture – also painting. Intense individualism and self-confidence of French – also true of England and old culture generally.

46 Absence of word 'conscience money' in French – also of word 'pickpocket'. Inflation, etc. advantage of country as against town – makes it difficult for town people to secure food and compels country people to eat their own food – country people formerly intent on money sold everything – with money worth little kept food themselves. Rents frozen in Paris since before war of great assistance with inflation. Problem of inflation and devaluation in relationship between prices – Metro at 5 francs as compared with enormous increases in taxis. Insistence on equality – passengers stopped from entering platform when train in station to prevent crowding – tickets available at bus stands giving numbers and avoiding necessity of standing in line. Lack of conscience toward state – probably result of dominance of Paris and tradition of administration in Roman law – Anglo-Saxon countries – common law – state part of customs and traditions – absence of a revolutionary tradition.

47 England (1948) contrast between efficiency of controls – relative limitations of black market as compared with France – French less adaptable to control – black market apparently on larger scale – controls even in England making honest men do illegal acts on a large scale – comparable to prohibition in the United States. Rise in prices in England due to limited goods – production for export leaving less available. Difficulty of introducing policies making for equality when economy directed on large scale to production of luxuries, i.e. agriculture – intensive specialization – subsidizing of sugar beets – raising of cherries – highly expensive fruit and of hops and materials used in production of beer. Restraints off agricultural products directs energy toward luxury – notably products demanding large quantity of labour. Extremely difficult to turn to production of goods of greater necessity.

48 France behind Italy in Renaissance and England behind France – influence of U.S. on England – architectural styles appearing in England about five or ten years after U.S. Film strips brought to England long after use in U.S. Straight roads in England left by Romans in contrast with crooked roads of English as conquerors – Romans could take land and build straight roads. Tremendous significance of absence of Roman

rule in Ireland, i.e. monastic organization - probable base of split from Great Britain. Isle of Man Christianized from Ireland, then overrun by Norse and Christianized from England but deep strain of paganism, i.e. in three-legged symbol. Law not written down until compulsion of Stanley, Earl of Derby probably in 1417. Oral tradition continued until late date - resistance to feudalism and ultimate establishment of odalism - strong Scandinavian influence in law of Isle of Man.

49 Monarchy never acquired prestige in England as in Paris partly because of power of city of London in struggle against Crown. How far link between journalist and politician in France makes latter sensitive to public opinion - certainly very much alive as to possibilities of influencing public opinion? Enormous significance of use of paper before printing for archives of government - state, provincial, municipal - parchment apparently more useful to church.

50 Future of Europe largely dependent on France with possible support from England - possibility of evading strangulation by Anglo-Saxon barbarism - especially North America - and by communism. Threat of mass production of North America to French culture and taste - advantage Paris left largely intact possibly improved by removal of iron statues by Germans. London and Paris again by metro and tube but London population declined and carrying charges higher on tube than on metro. France gained by occupation in sense that culture stressed when state lost - preservation of culture or of Paris more important than political state - constitutions can be made and remade.

51 Culture survives ideologies - equality - liberty - fraternity, i.e. in preparation of food and taste - limitations on rationing. Food easily rationed in England considering what it is. Restrictions on rent in Paris emphasizes expenditures on food - also clothing with emphasis on style. Advantage of large number of parties in giving more adequate reflection to views of divergent groups - parties less apt to be tyrannical - each with newspaper less apt to be dominated by advertising. Disastrous effect of common law in making politics part of law and emphasizing position of state - especially in North America or United States. With Roman law culture had an opportunity to expand, but with common law energies absorbed in politics.

52 Priest monopoly - law, writing result of protest against oral tradition weakened power of religion - facilitated spread of eastern religions. Writing proceeded with lawyers but separate from state and left Senate or Assembly and oral tradition controlled by force or concerned with army. Little chance of writing influencing public opinion other than as rhetoric - borrowed from Greece. Emphasis on force meant growth of

empire - central offices. Oral tradition in law facilitated invention - contract, etc. - persisting to end of republic. Written tradition implied rigidity. Oral tradition disappeared with Empire - control with writing -
and power of civilization to break through family. Written law to offset
dangers of monopolies of oral tradition, i.e. demands for written constitution of U.S. a protest against monopoly of judges or of parliament over
oral tradition. Also control of parliament over monarch in William and
Mary - compelled oral tradition to be put in writing - succession duty.

53 Fay stories about Marshall - Meredith visiting him warned to stay only
12 to 12.20 started conversation - hope I am not interrupting - answer-
ed you have spoiled my morning but that is all right. Spoke of teaching
12 hours. As a human being it is my duty to wish you well; as an economist, I have no further interest in you. Two women coached by Mrs
Marshall stood highest in Tripos. Marshall said this will ruin the reputation of the Tripos. Mrs Marshall - 'Alfred does not approve of us.' Constant fight between Robertson, Pigou who claim Keynes differed little
from them but was wrong. Cannan on Keynes-Robertson controversy
like two Roman orators disputing over the entrails of a goose. Copyright
on modern plays leads to a great emphasis on Shakespeare's plays by
colleges in Oxford - even to plays which are very little known - Shaw
compelled to compete with old plays.

54 Problem of sex in church - rigid emphasis on celibacy leads to com-
plaints against clergy interfering with wives and women through confes-
sions and to anti-clericalism. Rigid opposition to divorce leads to 'af-
faires' typical of French life. Protestant countries compelled to develop
divorce laws. Homosexualism a reflection of individualism in France
(Gide) - also important probably to literature and philosophy in Greece.

55 Numerous detailed regulations on paper result of ease of deception as to
quality and importance of standardization for wider markets. Inspection incidental to mercantilism and exports of paper.

56 Tendency of printing on pre-existing culture - spreading out - critics
looking at past see their own reflection - history of criticism a succession of mirrors showing smaller and smaller fragments - Edmund Wilson,
Chesterton and others on Dickens. Emancipation of slaves - votes for
negroes in U.S. followed by votes for whites in England.

57 Laissez-faire tends not to leave records whereas planning and state intervention characterized by records - spread of socialism - spread of written tradition - at expense of oral tradition. Adam Smith emphasizing
method of operation or oral tradition and socialism written tradition.
Laissez-faire was planned - planning was not.

58   October, 1948 Gras - history of Standard Oil - three quarters of a mil-
        lion - company concerned with large-scale advertising in several volumes
        to offset weakness of other types of advertising - similar to architecture.
        Problem of large-scale whitewashing and securing information. No white-
        wash, no information. Influence of Myron Taylor, U.S. Steel, on papacy
        in securing statement against communism - church as ever exposed to
        influence of power or capitalism. Use of Canadians to sweeten capital-
        ism - Victor Ross improving public relations - Mackenzie King industrial
        relations and Gras in large-scale advertising. Standard Oil New Jersey -
        board of directors all paid - and spend all time - men trained for special
        work - technical experts kept out.

59   Homan argues influence of Marshall - oral in England - through books
        in U.S. - consequently difference between developments.

60   Writing compels monotheism - also enables law to break up family into
        individuals - Rome.

61   Importance of alphabet and language to machine industry - basis of
        large-scale literary advertising and trade. Appeals most directly to largest
        number.

62   Linking of Christianity to politics under Constantine followed by large-
        scale adoption of Christianity by rulers and in turn by subjects - basis of
        savagery peculiar to Christianity - unable to assimilate savage barbaric
        elements in effective fashion - inquisition, crusades - destruction of life
        in 30 years war.

63   Use of advertising agencies in political campaigns also arranging details
        of conventions gives power to those controlling funds and able to pay
        for campaigns at expense of local political interest.

64   Council of Churches Amsterdam emphasizes continuity in time and or-
        ganization suited to continuity - opposed to Congregational or Baptist -
        aggregative type as lacking continuity.

65   Irwin Maclean's magazine - trained on newspaper - seizes on elements
        neglected by newspaper and yet commanding public interest - giving
        George Drew hint about Hong Kong and writing it up for him. Gallup
        poll difficulties accentuated by sales to newspapers and opposition of
        latter regarded as advantage to politician - unable to meet problems cre-
        ated by radio. Cumulative bias of Gallup polls - difficulty of getting
        near voters - reluctant to give views. The Gallup poll the new factor
        not recognized by the Gallup poll.

66 Graham Wallas became too concerned with act of thought and neglected spontaneity. Fruit of tree of knowledge means neglect of spontaneity – reading about sex – self-conscious elements leads to divorce – story of Garden of Eden. Monopoly of mechanized press – cutting under Marxism appeal to proletariat – fringe areas and classes – communism – nationalization.

67 Production based on consistent irrationality – possible to predict only because of bias or habit – consequent intensification of irrationality.

68 Problems of power in part arise in areas not amenable to the influence of the price system, i.e. newspaper editors struggling with proprietors' interest in power means jealousy of proprietors and editor not paid sufficiently to enable him to resist or paid too much.

69 Byzantine empire compelled similar arrangement in empire of Charlemagne, i.e. linking of church and state but in west Teutonic system of inheritance defeated empire and contributed to feudalism and power of church. Church attempted to dominate state through emphasis on parchment but state gained influence through paper.

70 Economic position of family – importance of corporation as means of offsetting limitations of continual family control.

71 Significance of Roman religion in emphasizing specific hours or days as expression of *fatum* in development of Roman law – emergence of single acts as in contract – Christianity – birth of Christ a specific act – Augustine reflected concept of time.

72 Problem of cost of law – if over cheap everyone can use it – mere introduction of suit an attack on character – high cost checks abuses but favours exploitation by lawyers.

73 Pressure of western papers and control from West – Stone. Illinois Press association – protest of *Sun* – U.P. Battle with A.P. leading to collapse of U.P. Burden of N.Y. A.P. contributed to difficulties of N.Y. *Times* – *World* under Pulitzer joined Illinois A.P. and prevented Hearst securing A.P. – latter compelled to build up own service – contributed to his emphasis on local crusades and to his interest in politics. Link of A.P. with Reuters probably facilitated banning of Hearst papers by European governments and to his anti-English attitude – led to his piracy of A.P. news and to suit before Supreme Court banning piracy 1919. Routine of A.P. in morning papers gave advantage to Scripps in U.P. for evening papers – led to emphasis on new technique – telephone, radio, etc. Restrictions

on Hearst contributed to emphasis on pictures and features and magazines. Limitation in Hearst in foreign news involved emphasis on local news and crusades. Monopoly of news held by papers in A.P. compelled development of chains by those not included, i.e. Scripps, Hearst.

74   Standing army – source of strength of bureaucracy – Moscow.

75   Printing industry sucks everything out of the past, i.e. Romantic movement in Germany – particularly after long period of stagnation – pumps up material from the bottom.

76   Price system penetrating to success of bourgeoisie – then to proletariat.

77   Aristophanes apparently first to have play written before performance – place of comedies suggested people no longer able to follow play as dealing with new material with which they are not familiar and necessitating a preliminary description.

78   Law in continent in charge of a segregated profession and in common law countries placed at heart of affairs. Journalists in France stepped into role of lawyers in England.

79   Effect of colour photography on contents of magazines – *National Geographic* emphasizing women's dresses and flowers susceptible to colour photography.

80   Significance of *Prometheus Bound* in Freudian interpretation – man bound and at constant mercy of women.

NOTES

5   Note on A.H. Shaw, *The Plain Dealer: One Hundred Years in Cleveland* (New York, 1942)

12   Emerson's Phi Beta Kappa address was delivered on 31 August, 1837.

15   Possible reference to A.C. Cook, *Financing Exports and Imports* (New York, 1923)

18   A parchemier is someone who prepares and sells parchment.

25   Note on N.S. Timasheff, *An Introduction to the Sociology of Law* (Cambridge, 1939)

27   Edwin Francis Gay (1867-1946) and Theodore Bullock (1889-1953) were American professors of economics.

31   George Drew was Premier of Ontario from 1943 to 1948. Sifton became the publisher of the Winnipeg *Free Press* in 1944.

40   Odalism was a system of freehold property rights.

53   C.R. Fay had been a senior colleague of Innis at Toronto until he left to rejoin Cambridge University in 1930. Alfred Marshall (1842-1924) was a founder of the neo-classical school of economics. A.C. Pigou (1877-1959) was Marshall's successor

to Cambridge University's chair of political economy. Edwin Cannan (1861-1935)
taught economics at the London School of Economics.

58   Myron Taylor (1874-1959), an American lawyer and industrialist, was the official
representative of Presidents Roosevelt and Truman to the Pope. Ross (1878-1934)
was a Canadian financial journalist who joined the Standard Oil Company in 1917.
N.S.B. Gras was professor of business history at Harvard.

59   P.T. Homan (1893-1969), an American economist, was author of *Contemporary
Economic Thought* (1928).

73   Note on Melville E. Stone, *Fifty Years a Journalist* (Garden City, 1921)

17

This section includes travel notes from England and France. Note 21, 'Why do we attend to the things to which we attend?' formed the focus, according to Innis in his preface, for the essays collected in *The Bias of Communication* (1951).

1   Oral tradition explanation of 'ahistorical' character of Greek civilization. Possible article on trade and communication Phoenicians, Carthage, Italian cities, etc.

2   J.G. Bennett interest in cable and building up news for *Herald* from Europe. Pulitzer concentrated on building to advertise *World.*

3   Importance of external problem to national cohesion - Irish problem solved and Liberal party disappeared. French problem with disappearance of Alsace-Lorraine difficulty.

4   [Chapter II, 'A Digression on Legal English'] Reading list - chapter on legal digression. No such word as 'discourage' in legislation - impossibility of using certain words in legislation.

5   Problem of psychological differences in attitude of various provinces to dollar - Nova Scotia high value and B.C. lower value - varying attitude toward government subventions.

6   English use of words in law loose but not as loose as American. French language - logic makes loose language impossible.

7   Inns of court - oral teaching - disputations survived threat of civil law and after middle of century with printing of books common law safe.

8   Emphasis of early empires on capitals as means of emphasizing fusion of politics and religion continued to Constantinople - revived in federal governments - Washington, Ottawa, Canberra.

9   Contrast between law in Quebec and Anglo-Saxon provinces – former
     divided between lawyers and notaries – latter academic course includes
     notarial code and former on procedure. Lawyers have possibly 90% of
     business in form of litigation and notaries handled other business in
     Quebec, whereas possibly 90% outside courts or in forms other than
     litigation in Anglo-Saxon provinces. Business of courts declining in
     both regions and lawyers settling cases out of court or in forms of busi-
     ness other than concerning courts. Advice to lawyers to use the lang-
     uage of the individual they are defending to create a sympathetic reac-
     tion – limited vocabulary of lawyers. Significance of war in releasing
     energy and breaking down conservative convention especially in techno-
     logical advance, i.e. aviation, economies or effective use of prospect of
     economies. Extensive concern of lawyers with economic subjects ac-
     companied by numerous fallacious arguments protecting vested interests –
     meaningless averages and statistics put forward by lawyers.

10   How far Christianity a religion of persecution as compared to others –
     Mohammedan, Buddhism, etc? Dangers of Palestine – taking Jewish en-
     thusiasm from western civilization and making for greater friction.

11   Kaffir – based on Arabic word meaning people without the book.
     Respect of Mohammedans for people with book.

12   Tragedy of U.S. – opposition to government ownership and demands
     for technology, i.e. aviation, for government support compels emphasis
     on militarism.

13   Limited vocabulary of lawyers – emphasis on restricted number of well-
     used words.

14   Brown on Venetian publishing – suggested book trade and friction with
     Roman censorship in 17th century enabled Sarpi to work out principle
     separating more precisely position of church and state. Book trade con-
     tributing to rationalism in Venice and outside.

15   Struggle over common law rights of author in 18th century. London
     booksellers favoured by English courts in favouring rights in perpetuity –
     attacked by Scottish courts as supporting London monopoly at ex-
     pense of Scottish printers. Difference between laws of England and
     Scotland important in securing legislation restricting monopolies.
     Possibility of politicians exploiting religion – stand on religious questions
     had enormous possibilities for advertising, i.e. Gladstone, Morley.
     Herbert Stone – publisher in Chicago, son of newspaper man – repub-
     lished material appearing in newspapers – i.e. George Ade – significance
     of newspaper to Chicago.

16   England, 1948. High prices, scarcity of goods because of exports - diffi-
      culty of getting into American market - search for dollars - effects of
      American tariff. Annoyance with Americans - strong pro-Arab senti-
      ment not anti-Semitic. Crowded travel - spending on railways and
      resorts - Isle of Man experience - unable to travel elsewhere. Prices
      high - tobacco a little more expensive than silver. Attitude toward gov-
      ernment - revolutionary but England always in revolution. Feeling of
      fairness toward increased miners' wages - stories of soldiering. Interest
      in welfare of children. Devastation greater than expected - London -
      Liverpool - increased costs of transportation. Affection for Mr Churchill
      but distrust of his judgment - feeling that he should have retired.
      France devastation - Boulogne.

17   Difficult for Anglo-Saxon to understand French - have something which
      we do not have and we have something they do not have - understand-
      ing impossible - Anglo-Saxon compromise seems hypocrisy to French.
      Common law versus Roman law. No other country has made such con-
      tributions as France to west. French revolution still active. Interest in
      artistic culture contrast with Anglo-Saxon obsession with politics. Paris
      intact compared to London. Some of statues melted down by Germans -
      standing bases more striking than statues - [Max] Beerbohm proposal
      for veiling days [i.e. days on which statues would be veiled].

18   Food - taste - individualistic - rationing possible in England because
      English poor cooks - black market in France because French insist on
      good cooking. England one sauce and a hundred religions - France one
      religion and a hundred sauces.

19   Emphasis on politics in early American press a result of dominance of
      literary by English writers - made press more fundamentally political.
      Consequent emphasis on politics and news and technology in U.S. Re-
      gional character of press explained effectiveness of radio on regional
      level - i.e. Aberhart, Huey Long.

20   Education - 'the art which teaches man to be deceived by the written
      word' ([Harold] Laski).

21   'Why do we attend to the things to which we attend?' (Ten Broeke)

22   Freedom of press - U.S. - restriction England - concentration on and
      expansion of technology in U.S. - overwhelming influence on English
      journalism in latter part of 19th century - undermining position of
      writers in England built up outside *Times* monopoly in early part of
      19th century. Printing of American [illegible] on *Sun* (1833) in features
      developed in England. Demands for rags in U.S. from Europe supplied
      partly with rags released by newspaper monopoly in England.

23   Problem of economics emphasizing division of labour - also division of
      knowledge - fragmentation in contrast with Comte's concern with
      universalist approach. How far economics destroys art?

24   Fall of Constantinople 1453 followed by attempts of Rome to recap-
      ture position, i.e. building of St Peters, Vatican library, work of Michel-
      angelo - emphasis on St Peters and drain on funds through sale of indul-
      gences led to revival of concept of dualism in England - Henry VIII -
      and in Germany to reformation - interest in scriptures in Hebrew and
      Greek and emergence of sacred word in uniform German - Germany.

25   With [Arnold] Toynbee and histories of civilization - the factory sys-
      tem developed in learning and scholarship.

26   How far space, time problem reflected by interests of landlords (time)
      in England as opposed to interests of manufacturers and friction assist-
      ing in development of parliamentary constitutions?

27   Great editor an artist whose medium is the work of other men
      ([Hippolyte] Taine).

28   Difficulties of advertising books because of inability to emphasize repe-
      tition as in general advertising offset in part by publisher's anxiety to
      have authors - limited repetitive advertising - probably explains great
      emphasis on title. Emphasis on salty literature an indication of encroach-
      ment of printing on oral tradition, i.e. Rabelais (Boccaccio, Chaucer) -
      also tendency of books in 20th century to emphasize sex - attempt of
      printers to escape their own traditions.

29   Dangers of doing good - gives people a sense of power and a fanatical
      belief that they use power for good - support of Christianity to bureau-
      cracy.

30   Were long novels of Dickens result of small type, i.e. newspapers and
      stamp taxes?

31   Danger of newspapers - writers in U.S. to secure direct sense of contact
      - [Theodore] Dreiser, Hemingway, Edmund Wilson, Stanley Pennell,
      Stephen Crane - but without sense of style - Perkins of Scribners for-
      merly of *New York Times* concerned with books reflecting contact
      with life.

32   Was writing sacred because of necessity of relying on supernatural to
      introduce it against prejudice in favour of oral tradition - among Jews
      Moses introduced it under God's order?

33   Emphasis on education with oral tradition – chiefly memory – Charle-
      magne court regarded as successor of Theodoric – influence on building,
      statue – painting – latter influenced by Irish and Anglo-Saxon. Initial
      particularly developed independently in north – under Ottos – Byzan-
      tine influence in illumination – greater evidence of independence from
      Irish and Anglo-Saxon.

34   'If a man love the labour of any trade, apart from any question of suc-
      cess or fame, the gods have called him' (R.L. Stevenson).

35   Secretary of Navy to H.L. Satterlee former assistant secretary of the
      Navy, 'Mr. Secretary, you are a Republican. My party has the responsi-
      bility of this war. I know your record but I can't use you anywhere.'
      (p. 350)

36   Copyright act made available American fiction to meet demands of
      Curtis who discovered that fiction scattered through pages compelled
      people to turn pages and read advertising material at side. Large circula-
      tions based on advertising – length of articles determined by needs of
      magazine. Second basis of large circulation in fashion patterns – *Delin-
      eator* (Butterick Co.) circulation 500,000 by 1900. Women always the
      backbone of magazine business – women most popular and highest paid
      contributors woman's magazines largest circulations. Writers to live
      must concentrate on magazines. Textbooks in public schools train
      youth to read magazines. Quasi-sanctity of written word evident in
      people who resent misstatements of authors.

37   Property like incest holds the family together.

38   Significance of time to economic theory, i.e. contributions of father
      and son or family to development of theory. Walras (father and son),
      Clark (father and son).

39   Simmel – sociology of entertainment – study of sociability.

40   Problem of electricity and time – rapid communication in conflict with
      relative slowness of earth's turning around sun. Time zones cut down
      with radio but differences in night hours of different periods – tendency
      for local news to become less important.

41   War weakens emphasis on theoretical speculation and overemphasizes
      practical problems – little room for genius.

42   [Frank] Knight – uncertainty becomes risk when organizes as in insur-
      ance and made into cost – uncertainty not suited to risk – field of entre-
      preneur rather than manager.

2   Bennett (1841-1918) was proprietor of the New York *Herald.*

4   Note on Sir Ernest Gower, *Plain Words* (London, 1948)

14   Note on H.R.F. Brown, *The Venetian Printing Press* (London, 1891). Fra Paolo
       Sarpi (1552-1623) was a Venetian theologian and scientist who quarrelled with the
       Pope over clerical immunities.

21   Broeke taught Innis philosophy during his undergraduate studies at McMaster
       University.

35   Note on Arthur Train, *My Day in Court* (New York, 1939)

39   Possibly reference to G. Simmell, *Grundlagen der Soziologie* (Leipzig, 1917)

18

In 1949 Innis undertook his most important governmental responsibility, as a member of the Royal Commission on Transportation. This section includes notes made when he flew to Newfoundland with the Commission in September.

1   Complaint that Liberals dominate parliament and judiciary - 93 per cent of judges in Ontario members of Liberal party - all of the Supreme Court. Cost of running election - Rodney Adamson of West York claimed about $13,000 necessary or about 75 cents a vote.

2   English reputation for coolness and understatement held to be result of Wellington and his opposition to emotionalism of Nelson. High designs.

3   The longer the life of the assets on a railway the greater the tendency to bunching of retirements, i.e. on railways - bunching of retirements emphasizes reserve accounting - significance to financial problems of railways.

4   Secret of political success in Canada - that of keeping Scottish Presbyterians and French Canadians in the same party - importance of oral tradition in keeping alive party technique. Covert with story of petition in Department of Munitions and Supply threatening to resign if conscription not accepted - Henry Borden finally persuaded of inadvisability and petition destroyed. Law is anything 'boldly asserted and plausibly maintained.' MacPherson apparently promised position on bench after accepting position as debt administrator - Bennett alleged to have gone back on promise and appointed Gordon - immediately on appointment of latter MacPherson resigned as debt administrator.

5   Autobiography largely unknown in east - Gandhi's attempt to write one possibly result of western influence. *Young India* Naviajivan to support Gandhi's interests - refused to take advertisements. Bombay *Chronicle* suspended by government. Influence of Ruskin *Unto This Last* [1862]. Use of English language in Congress meetings probably offset effects of dialects.

6   Footnote - parliament and printing - control of printing on speaking - footnote.

7   Problem of dynastic problem - Charlemagne. Power of religion in solv-
    ing problems of family and of dynasties but this effectively achieved by
    Roman law.

8   English escaped direct influence of classics but scholarship after Bentley
    separated from literature and latter in 18th century influence by Latin -
    Greek reinforced interest in vernacular, i.e. Wordsworth and 19th cen-
    tury. Development of anti-classical sentiment - competition of other
    subjects in schools - consequent lack of sense of form - impact of sci-
    ence - civilization in literature and sense of form broken down with
    machine industry. Plowing of profits back into newspaper industry as
    general practice probably accentuated development of technique and
    expansion of large papers. Problem of capital equipment in engraving -
    gift books in U.S. - early 19th century used plates again and again -
    publication - monotony killed sales and artistic expression.

9   Gandhi - training in English common law and effective use in South
    Africa in defence of rights of individuals - tactics worked out in South
    Africa applied to India - common law basis of British Empire implies
    emphasis on local customs and hence facilitates gradual breaking away
    rather than rebellion - exceptions in Ireland and United States.

10 Influence of Haultain regarded as important in higher tone of Saskat-
    chewan controversy and in contrast with Manitoba and low level of
    political life. Greenway charged with being in bed with hotel chamber-
    maid but Joe Martin as attorney general diverted attention by playing
    up school question.

11 Radio enabled political leaders in assemblies to appeal directly to public
    and have them exercise pressure on opponents in assemblies - thus pass-
    ing necessary legislation - Al Smith in 1924.

12 Amazing limitations of publisher's memoirs - acquaintances with fam-
    ous people - possible threat to insubordinate writers, little interest in
    actual business on which they might make contribution but a belief in
    their capacity to write - also means of advertising firm similar to insti-
    tutional advertising - books celebrating 100th anniversaries.

13 Germany continued as part of Roman empire with prestige and ambi-
    tion of Roman empire.

14 [Mackenzie] King refused to appoint Fee as archivist because he was
    about 60 years of age and gave as reasons fear that on retirement a Con-
    servative government would be in power and would have access to pap-
    ers in the possession of the Archives. Lanctot apparently bought Simcoe
    papers for $5,000 and sold them for $15,000 to R.S. McLaughlin who
    presented them to the University of Toronto. Valuable duplicates in

Archives sold by exchange arrangement through Duchesne and led to suggestions that Lanctot received funds from this source.

15 Significance of late development of artistic interest in posters in the United States with excellence in lithographic technique - artistic interest of publishing firms using posters for magazines - adaptability of posters to any size - facilitated use by magazines. Impossibility of reaching peace in war 1914-18 with power of press in various countries and concern with division.

16 Lawyers accustomed to speaking for record develop remarkable diction for reading purposes - possibly at expense of speaking.

17 American influence in journalism - MacGahan stirring up interest in Turkish atrocities in Bulgaria - driving out of Turk from Europe.

18 Text books used on large scale throws research into hands of relatively small number and dissemination in hands of text book writers who make revision in terms of work done by researchers. Systematic damping down of intellectual work on part of teachers by importance of texts.

19 Importance of cable rates to news - high rates kept Franco out of war - subsidized news strengthened position of Australia. Incredible belief of journalists of their power, i.e. MacNair Wilson on Lord Northcliffe - changing whole character of England from Germany to France. Tendency of periodicals to have work done by paid staff - decline of amateur writing and manuscripts sent to periodicals - large professional staff.

20 How far effects of export of bullion to India contributed to development of interest in trade contrary to mercantilism - reconciling advantage of bullion exports with mercantilism?

21 Adam Smith - great advantage in being on fringe of Roman law and of common law and able to emphasize deductive and inductive approaches - Christian Science attacked liaison between pain and religion. Pareto - elite theory met demands of Italian nationalism for protest against French egalitarianism - similarly German and Italian fascism opposed to French.

22 'Never call a man righteous until you have read his will.' Capacity of legal training to enable lawyers to seize on central problem in shortest possible time - Lloyd George - effectiveness in politics.

23 Political parties evidence of continuation of oral tradition.

24 Lewd books a device for securing revenue in spite of difficulties of publishers under Walpole - in addition to publishing compilations, i.e. Curll.

25   American capital supporting English publishers. Harrap began with
     agency of D.C. Heath - emphasizing educational texts.

26   Chester Walters claimed Ilsley wrecked provincial conference on Rowell-
     Sirois report [on Dominion-Provincial Relations, 1940] by his rigidity.

27   Problems of rationality of price system evident in Y.W.C.A. - half paid
     staff and half voluntary - latter become extremely difficult to deal with
     because contributions voluntary and dismissal difficult.

28   Mongols with invention of spur developed military strength to destroy
     monopoly of knowledge in China in east and among Moslems in Khwar-
     azm [a province of ancient Persia] - merchants assisted Genghis Khan in
     order to secure order for trade - reliance of trade on force to overcome
     monopoly of knowledge and defeat its inequities.

29   Mathew Carey as publisher became interested in protection for Ameri-
     can books after 1816 and pamphlets by him and his son H.C. Carey had
     an important effect in undermining position of Adam Smith and free
     trade. Publisher protected his own work and secured market for his own
     writing.

30   Problems of artistic development - hotels - emphasizing names or sizes
     of pictures to prevent theft rather than concern with artistic interest.
     Women wearing uniform through inability to meet demands of artistic
     appearance - uniforms - standardized dress - problem of art and mass
     production.

31   Common law absorbing elements of civil law through increase in stat-
     utes - harshness of common law with new developments such as auto-
     mobiles leads to recognition of civil law in statutes. Civil law came into
     common law also through international law and admiralty law.

32   Oral tradition - effectiveness under conditions in which minority can
     become majority - rise of bureaucracies and civil service gradually weak-
     en conditions favourable to oral tradition - R.K. Merton's division of
     influential people in towns - local, oral - cosmopolitan, written, profes-
     sions.

33   Interest of church in women's dresses - bathing beaches - overlooks
     general unattractive character of bare limbs and trunks in great numbers.

34   Freedom of press developed with idea of importance of property and
     rights in printing, i.e. Locke, Defoe, etc. Importance of accurate news
     for stock exchange - South Sea Bubble result of inaccurate news.

35   Importance of learning to religion, i.e. Richard Bentley, Master of Trinity College, as scholar able to dominate appointments in church. How far dualism in religion results of conquest in which gods of conquered religion displaced and become devils to religion of conquerors? Mysticism with lack of anthropomorphism and need for interpretation of inadequate deity, i.e. animal - vagueness leads to emphasis on the word, logos, i.e. is this incidental to a writing civilization in contrast with Greek oral tradition.

36   Northcliffe - *Answers* - printing plant added newspapers - developed large-scale printing competitive with Cassells exploited American salesmanship. Methods of Encyclopedia Brittanica in cooperation with *Times* - enormous sale of Harmsworth encyclopedia - development of Children's encyclopedia - carried to U.S. *Book of Knowledge* - concern with facts - printing industry emphasizing large-scale production of information - influence on publishers - Macmillans - Walls collection of short stories, etc.

37   Thesis that wheat from U.S. and Canada destroyed English agriculture and competed with Russian, contributing to revolution and to protectionism of Germany giving agrarians influence on legislation - also led to tarriffs in France.

38   Weakness of newspapers in Germany probably accentuated power of propagandist organizations. Bitterness of agrarians in Germany against England - opposed English liberalism cosmopolitan trade unionism - philosophy of industrialized state.

39   Architecture reflects weakness of writing, i.e. pyramids, Trajan's column, Gothic cathedrals, skyscrapers.

40   Jews helped to make Christianity tolerable and to check fanaticism.

41   Talkies destroyed comedy - characterization of silent film - former unable to develop comedy - see *Life*, September 5, 1949. Actors and journalists have similar interests in exhibitionism - Dickens.

42   In U.S. anti-Masons linked with federalism opposed Jackson and Van Buren - success of Whigs - Blair formerly Jackson's supporter a founder of Republican party. Difficulties with south complicated problem of party.

43   Sept. 29, 1949. Smallwood - editor of *Fishermen's Advocate*, Coaker's paper, secured interview with Miller editor of [N.Y.] *Times* (life written by Bond (nephew?) of Sir Robert Bond) - Smallwood worked on

Halifax *Herald*, Boston *Herald* and *New York Times* - letter of recommendation from Miller. Worked in London probably with Labour party. Continued tradition of opposition of outports to St John's - confederation becomes outport policy against St John's. Smallwood - wide experience newspaper - author of *Book of Newfoundland*, broadcasting as 'Barrelman' - significant that journalist exploiting new techniques of communication responsible for profound changes in constitutional machinery - offsets conservatism of law and trade. Explains significance of technological changes in common law countries with conservative legal profession. Capitalized on significance of book, newspaper and radio. *Cod Fisheries* quoted extensively in debates of convention and used in broadcasts of Smallwood - Marxist approach appealed to Smallwood, i.e. linking of economics to politics.

44   Sept. 30, 1949. Bishop Falls - Groundwood - slush pumped eleven miles to Grand Falls - taken over from Albert Reed Co. in 1920 by Anglo-Newfoundland Development Co. Grand Falls - Northcliffe's summer residence - strong influence of company (600 tons newsprint daily) keeps religious schools in check - advantage of capitalism in stopping waste of religion - Corner Brook - up to 1,000 tons of newsprint.

45   Problem of Supreme Court - reluctance of lawyers to give up fees and live in Ottawa - result that provincial courts very strong compared to Ottawa. Orders in council numerous in war as means of circumventing red tape of civil service commission - individual appointed under order in council.

46   Botwood [Newfoundland] declined in importance during war as shift developed from sea planes to land planes and building of landing strips. Use of oil to replace coal by [Anglo-Newfoundland Development Company] - large numbers threatened with unemployment. Confederation partly result of pressure of Orangemen frightened of Catholic aggression. Small number of Catholics elected in Smallwood's party.

47   Non-commercial literary periodicals probably flourish in depression periods - small pamphlets, i.e. Stone and Kimball, Chap Book and others in nineties, also in '30's (Robert Cantwell, *New Republic*, July 25, 1934). Problem of overcoming dominance of New York illustrated in difficulties of Stone and Kimball. Book-selling, book publishing, book printing became separate trades after about 1850. Suggests effects of newspaper and fringe areas in breaking down standardization in publishing. Stone, son of Melville Stone.

48   French empire supported by church - with failure church continued to support British empire in Canada.

49 Newfoundland entered Confederation partly as result of influence of radio – Smallwood financed by Crosbie in publishing books about Newfoundland and in broadcasting about Newfoundland over long period became thoroughly familiar with Newfoundland audience and able to appeal to it in asking support of Confederation. Labour government in England sent out representatives from labour disliked by those accustomed to old aristocracy. Evidence of unsuitability of democracy to empire.

50 Influence of religious organization on language – restricting obscenity and blasphemy and driving them into oral tradition. Problem of oral tradition supported by radio weakening printed tradition, i.e. explanation of failure of polls – lack of contact between oral and printed. Limitation of propaganda in Germany and Italy – control over mechanism failed to imply control over oral tradition.

51 Church control over time – feast days – Saints – Gregorian Calendar.

52 Problem of tendency toward stereotype of formality and periodic breaks through to oral tradition, i.e. McClure and Munsey – personal writing and enormous circulation at expense of monthlies. Northcliffe at expense of older English journalism. Photography magazines at expense of written magazines. Importance of advertising to times probably led it to favour general advertising interests, i.e. support of Reform Bill, opposition to Corn Laws in 1839.

53 Writing enabled Greeks to leave a powerful stamp on all later communities.

54 Gregory VII – Vicar of St Peter; Innocent, the Vicar of Christ – probably led to interest in Virgin Mary on intercession. Fortescue – sensible cooperation between men of good will – oral tradition of common law. Sudden development of printing meant reformation never linked up with ancient traditions of German medieval liberty and the promise they contained of the capacity to self-government. Support of tyrannicide by Jesuits (Mariana) comparable to that of anarchists – drove terror into minds of political or economic rulers. Power of scribe in written tradition in contrast with mechanic and technology of north in oral tradition. Christianity emphasized oral tradition in early stages probably with strongly entrenched written tradition of Jews.

55 Significance of radio to interest in confederation – disastrous effects of commission government in stifling political activity and leadership. Walsh in return for promise to appoint Smallwood as premier appointed lieutenant-governor and given chief justiceship. Outerbridge suggested he would not call Smallwood and not made lieutenant-governor to follow Walsh until Smallwood became premier.

Newspapers monopoly position in party organization and financial in-   **159**
dependence enhances difficulties of control and leads to attempt to set
up rival paper to keep paper in line. Influence of newspaper owners at
point in which party compelled to attempt a new paper – established
paper brought into line by threats. Oral tradition of party in conflict
with written tradition of papers latter with greater demand for consistency.

NOTES

5   M.K. Gandhi's *Young India* was published in London between 1924 and 1928.

8   Note on J.A.K. Thomson, *The Classical Background of English Literature*
    (London, 1940)

10 Sir Frederick Haultain (1857-1942) was premier of the North West Territories, and
    afterwards of Saskatchewan. He was chief justice of Saskatchewan from 1912 to
    1937. Thomas Greenway (1838-1900) was premier of Manitoba from 1888 until
    his death.

11 A.E. Smith (1873-1944) was governor of New York State and a Democratic candi-
    date for the Presidency in 1928.

14 Norman Fee was appointed Assistant Dominion Archivist in 1945; he was born in
    1889. Gustave Lanctot was Dominion Archivist from 1937 until 1948. R.S.
    McLaughlin was a distinguished Canadian businessman.

15 Note on Walter Millis, *Road to War, America 1914-17* (Boston, 1935)

17 P.J. MacGahan (1888-1922) was an American journalist and a presidential press
    aide in the 1930s and 1940s.

19 Note on R. MacNair Wilson, *Lord Northcliffe: A Study* (London, 1927)

24 Edmund Curll (1675-1747) was a bookseller notorious for his obscene publications.

26 J.L. Ilsley was appointed federal Minister of Finance in July 1940. Walters had
    been the Province of Ontario's representative at the Rowell-Sirois Commission's
    hearings.

29 Mathew Carey (1760-1839) was an Irish-born publisher and economist who fled to
    America in 1784. His son, H.C. Carey (1793-1879), also an economist and publisher,
    was his leading disciple in economics.

32 Note on W.L. Schramm, ed., *Communication in Modern Society* (Urbana, Ill.,
    1948)

36 Note on Sir John Alexander Hammerton, *Books and Myself* (London, 1944).

52 S.S. McClure (1857-1949) was editor and publisher of *McClure's Magazine* founded
    in 1893. F.A. Munsey (1854-1925) was a dominant figure in newspaper and maga-
    zine consolidation.

19

probably 1949

1   Significance of oral tradition shown in place of Maritimes in Canada – intensive training facilitates adaptability of college presidents from Maritimes to larger universities of which scholars have been more concerned with oral tradition.

2   Dominance of family groups in American cities – constant shifting of population to urban centres offset by place of old established families – evident in large cemeteries and monuments – probably kept up by older families – checks déraciné elements of life.

3   Oral tradition in economics – [Alfred] Marshall's delay in printing and emphasis on monopoly of teaching rather than publishing. Keynes on the other hand emphasizing publication.

4   Effects of revolution – disappearance of pluperfect subjunctive with aristocracy in French revolution.

5   Sociology of learning – oppressed groups as Jews emphasizing learning as device for penetrating class structure or emphasizing arts generally literature, etc. involves constant disturbance on part of highly specialized class – Marx, Heine – Marx attempted to penetrate class structure by emphasizing class struggle.

6   Oral tradition – university, overthrow of monasticism by printing revolution – Chinese – limited alphabet – writing class restricts growth of law and accentuates religion – personal law. Extent of Roman empire emphasized written tradition of law – ownership and possession not sharply separated in England as in Roman law led to attempts to find out what law was. How far writing at basis of class structure and consequently permitting organization of force? China unable to develop class structure suited to force.

Troeltsch's neglect of importance of law and overemphasis on religion
in suggesting explanation of revolution. Fratriarchal vs. patriarchal interpretation. Former emphasis on oral and latter on written and oral? Extension of communication accompanied by religious interest - Buddhism -
Protestantism - fanaticism until checked by law and force. Literature
significant in bridging gap between written and oral tradition - centre
of interest in freedom. Buddhism spread from margin - vernacular more
adaptable to change. Technology and science, i.e. revolution in force
linked with vernacular and favouring improvement in communication
which breaks down monopoly of knowledge. English colonies crossing
water taught law - taught philosophy - tough in mixture of oral and
written tradition - Augustan England - coffee house oral and written
Addison, Steele, etc. - printing an instrument to be used not worshipped.
Parliament kept printing from being dominant.

8 Destruction of civilization probably means destruction of writers' monopoly built up on religious basis.

9 Indo-European philology discredited in England because of H.S. Cham-
berlain, Stoddard and others (p. 164). Tenacity or oral tradition in areas
settled and occupied before introduction of writing, i.e. continuance of
language, place names, legends - in Germany, teutonic tradition continued particularly as it escaped Roman tradition – also in Scotland evident in Pictish church followed by suppression under Roman church
but return to Protestant in Reformation. With migration emphasis on
print, i.e., in New World - New England - importance of Bible - dependence on old world for books - printed tradition - also tenacious in
Ireland.

10 G.V.F. [G.V. Ferguson] argues that competition between newspapers
leads to malicious features - sensationalism - lowering of standards -
monopoly makes possible general improvement of standards. Canadian
press insists members have membership in relation to place of publication of paper - Roy Thompson advised newspapers to accept radio -
became Vice President and announced purchase Orillia paper to be
printed at Bowmanville (?) and shipped by truck to Orillia contrary to
rules of association. Complaint of newsprint producers that newspapers
do not charge sufficiently for advertising and hence opposed to increased
prices of newsprint.

11 Great significance of place names in oral tradition. Significance of
Aryan language - flexibility at basis of abstract ideas, i.e. growth of science, Hindus and Greeks, also two world religions Buddhism and

19

Zoroastrianism – Christianity linked to political division after Constantine reinforces national states. Aryans – western wing advance guard in Kassites about 1900 B.C. and reached Mittani before 1500 B.C. – east wing in India not much later. Technological migration preceded language, i.e. bronze age, megalithic monuments, iron age – partly determined by geography – valleys and mountains – spread Babylonia to Europe – bronze age – returned in iron age bringing Aryan language – beginnings of friction Persians and Greeks. Stages – pure food gathering, nomad pastoralism and agricultural life not tenable – in some cases pastoral nomadism followed sedentary agriculture – grave misgivings of anthropologists as to value of cephalic index alone as a test of race. Childe holds Peake wrong in assuming iron came from Koban or Caucasus Aryans (p. 123) – iron came to Koban from Asia Minor (124). Peasant communities Danubian basin – industry in relation to tin for Troy and amber for Greece and Crete – development of slashing sword – emergence of aristocracies of war, chieftanship, sovereignty beyond village. Oral tradition associated with demands of metallurgical advance for larger political units in war than village. Significance of language and mechanical development of transmission in adjustment of political boundaries and hence impact on trade. Prior to development of writing technological change probably concentrated on weapons, i.e. on metals – copper and bronze and iron – trade with light commodities – pottery with migrations – land trade – barter hand to hand – island production assumed definite organization of trade – use of stone instead of timber the essential mark of civilization, i.e. for defence purposes – and did this lead to writing? Phoenicians expanded trade after fall of Knossos and again after Dorians overran Greece. Problem of integrating or understanding earlier cultures by those steeped in influence of print, i.e. influence of nationalism – also in unfortunate effects of Vitruvius on architecture. Printing the art preservative of all the arts. Spear and sword triumphed over hammer or battle-axe – presumably latter stone – bronze assumed use of fire and knowledge of metallurgy. Stone important in defensive, new weapons in offensive. Bronze drove out trade in copper and stone flint even obsidian fairly quickly. Did necessity of organizing trade from islands or across water, i.e. in Mediterranean, lead to organization migrating to land – penetration inwards rather than outwards – basis of government in contrast with Teggart?

12   Full employment leading to exhaustion of resources – militarism used to maintain employment but attracting undue proportion of resources and involving consequent scarcity of consumers goods – attempt of Bevan to stress place of consumers goods.

13   Success of Bryce and de Tocqueville in interpreting U.S. reflects inability of self-analysis of complex unstable history. Did the struggle, i.e. Jackson over the Bank of the U.S., precipitate Mackenzie rebellion [1837] in Canada?

14   Problem of conditions of meaning in writing varying from more or less
        direct reflection to deliberate distortion, i.e. studies of documents –
        problem of historians – economists attempting to go direct to techno-
        logical facts, i.e. problem of reflecting significance of oral tradition.
        Charisma in oral tradition versus rational legal or written. Problem of
        placing people – importance of army or church hierarchy – or political
        hierarchy so that people may know where they belong.

15   Alexander Hamilton – illegitimate birth.

16   Sweden developed industrial revolution at a late date and hence nation-
        alization took place easily, i.e. a soft capitalism which facilitated rapid
        development of trade unionism and co-operation. Australia similar to
        Sweden – industrial revolution took place rapidly and created a soft
        capitalism which permitted the rapid development of trade unions and
        a labour government – nationalization of railways.

17   Nichol – owner of French papers in Eastern Townships – a Huguenot –
        illustrates importance of minority groups securing control of means of
        communication to resist pressure of majorities.

18   Problem of development of research in Canada linked to dominance of
        American organization – research concentrated in U.S. parent firms and
        checked in Canada – Australia less exposed to American influence.

19   Deification of rulers gave validity to *acta* after death – *lex* fave validity
        to *edictum* of praetors after end of year. Deification chiefly for political
        purposes – *aerarium* (treasury) brought under control of *fiscus* of em-
        perors after Augustus – linked soldiers direct to emperor.

20   Improved communication versus improved transportation – latter may
        facilitate movement of raw materials and finished products and special-
        ization but also migration of industrial machinery and skilled labour
        and hence leads to break up of large political organization based on eco-
        nomic organization, i.e. Roman empire (Walbank) and British empire –
        tariffs to hasten process. In Roman empire migration of industry to-
        wards periphery and bureaucratization at centre – constant expansion
        and increased taxation and rigidity – British empire migration of indus-
        try and withdrawal of political organization United States – raw mater-
        ial production increasingly outside – check of competition from manu-
        factured goods by tariff, i.e. technique eventually followed by England –
        also be exchange regulations. Problem of adaptability of political mach-
        inery to shifting economic centres of production incidental to techno-
        logical change especially in transportation – location of industry prob-
        lem – significance of coal as determinant – conflict with technological
        change in communications, i.e. nationalism based on vernaculars – radio,
        etc. with little relation to results of industrial revolution.

21   Significance of technological change - Q Celts bronze age driven back
      by P Celts in shift from bronze to iron - division of Celtic languages -
      weakening of Ireland in relation to England.

22   [Wesley C.] Mitchell's present mindedness contrasted with [J.A.]
      Schumpeter with European background - speculative long-run interest.

23   Monopoly of oral tradition - increasing complexity - use of writing to
      strengthen oral tradition and emphasis on minutiae - similar to printing
      in relation to Bible.

24   Significance of statistics - encroachment of mathematics on economy -
      escalator clauses [linking wage increases to price level increases] political
      arguments over costs of living and statistics giving evidence of finality.

25   Resort to oral tradition in labour disputes - escape from rigid elements
      of documents.

26   Decline of *patria potestas*, i.e. Victorian father, evident in politics, jour-
      nalism, and business - partly a result of the six shooter and change in
      character of business demanding continuity and elimination of depen-
      dence on a single individual - also use of committees.

27   Impact of west on east and importance of individuals facilitates possi-
      bility of assassination, i.e. of those under influence of west.

28   Resurgence of Mohammedanism under pressure from west - attempt to
      improve economy - [President Harry Truman's] point four programme
      [1949], etc. leads to emphasis on nationalism and independence. Amer-
      ican imperialism reflects dependence on Marx - belief in changing eco-
      nomics, i.e. betterment not followed by friendliness toward west but by
      increased bitterness.

29   Did Sargon of Akkad know of copper - Cyprus - and of tin and in turn
      of bronze - were Sumerians prospectors and traders (pp. 42-3)? Goods
      traded by hand - i.e., durable - or easily damaged and appearing over
      wide areas such as pottery suggest migrations. Trade in pottery points
      to high civilization (100). Break in pottery tradition - geometric prob-
      ably with Dorian invasion (105). Apparently swords developed from
      dirks made of bronze - mountain zone - and with discovery of iron, say
      1100 B.C., in plain zone became basis of Dorian invasion (121-5, 131).

30   Constantinople and Christianity reflected advancement of flexibility in
      place (movement of capital) and in time (religion for export). Rigid
      control of trade and consequent corruption. Companies organized to

handle shipments between Germany and Denmark - profitable character
of bribing officials - an increase of taxes on consumer.

31   Impressed by isolated character of Egyptian civilization - probable that
      tools developed in relation to demands of complex civilization not
      suited to less primitive civilization and hence borrowing restricted and
      centralization enhanced.

32   W.F. Storey, Chicago *Times* specially concerned with printing - display
      type for heads (p. 119). New reporter to F.H. Hall, city editor, *Chicago
      Tribune:* 'Hello Fred'; Mr Hall in an engaging tone: 'My dear fellow,
      pray don't be so formal: call me Freddie' (181-2). In libel suits, 'the
      purpose of delay is to worry and wear out the plaintiff' (232). Paris
      press, 1874, more concerned with writing than news (218). Fanatic
      character of editors - Storey, Chapin, Northcliffe, Bennett, Greeley.
      Telephone replacing speaking tubes. Wilkie's sketches reprinted in
      books. Great difficulty starting morning Democrat papers in north
      before civil war - Storey's experience. Storey as printer emphasized
      appearance.

33   Task of economic historians to test economic tools on a broad canvas
      and to indicate their limitations, i.e. within language groups, political
      boundaries and the like.

34   Migration of parliamentary party after restoration of Charles II to New
      England, i.e. gravestones in New Haven of refugees of Cromwellian par-
      ty - fermenting element leading to revolution in colonies.

35   Recent emergence of word adolescent - result of industrial revolution -
      emphasis on secondary schools. Proliferation of educational administra-
      tion, i.e. division of presidents and deans organization of universities
      (i.e., graduate schools) - devastating influence of administrative hier-
      archies. Impact on universities of medical schools with social health
      schemes - enormous expense of medical institutions. Menace of educa-
      tional organizations - attitude toward academic freedom - crystalliza-
      tion of opinion against freedom. Professional education dominating dis-
      cussion - details of income tax, government contracts - neglect of prob-
      lem of university tradition. Abhorrence of a vacuum and necessity of
      reports, annual and otherwise, to keep printers busy - individuals fearful
      of being alone. Threat of elementary and secondary schools to colleges
      and universities - demand for graduates of colleges to teach practical
      subjects or general education - emphasis on life.

36   Aristocratic elements in American life - impact of technology on demo-
      cratic ideology, i.e. disposal of atomic energy, bombs, etc. Virginia and

south with round head - cavalier tradition - ecclesiastical appointments of Church of England - part of aristocracy - opened way to spread of evangelical religions - Methodism and Baptists - after revolution - successor in episcopalian church became low church to offset others. With civil war aristocratic elements weakened - encroached on by hillbilly, i.e. poor whites secured freedom rather than negro. This involved savagery of lynching and attempts of southern aristocracy to maintain position - mental disintegration - Faulkner, Cauldwell. In New England aristocracy weakened by trust funds left for descendants - meeting of New England and Virginia aristocratic elements in Ohio. Constant battering of aristocratic element by emphasis on democracy and problem of building up new hierarchy of technology and militarism.

37   *Guardian* in [Prince Edward Island] secured arrangement with C.N.R. bus scheme favouring its position as a morning paper and weakening position of evening papers - thus leading to opposition of latter.

38   Attack of newspaper on trusts at period when threatened with newspaper trust, i.e. effect on Theodore Roosevelt trust-busting and securing support of newspapers. 'It is a sin for folks to waste their good time readin' lies' - attitude of puritanical Iowa to novels (p. 171). 'I lose readers whenever I publish anything but trash' - wanted articles on financial crisis 'to show to advertisers' - owner and publisher of popular magazine about 1910 (179). Impact of Henry George partly result of attack on land to advantage of capital - conversion element - Quick, Thom Johnson, G.B. Shaw. Birth control old American stock after 1840 (4-6). Teachers linked to law, journalism and textbooks - American Book Co. checking intense competition for contracts. Textbook lawyers - followed by Encyclopedias (315-9). J.S. Clarkson assistant postmaster general - 38,000 post offices - got nomination for Harrison against Blaine (220).

NOTES

7   Reference to Ernst Troeltsch, *The Social Teaching of the Christian Churches* (London, 1931)

9   Note on V. Gordon Childe, *The Aryans, A Study of Indo-European Origins* (London, 1926). See also 19 / 11.

11   Note on Childe, *The Aryans* (ibid.). Reference to Teggart is possibly to F.J. Teggart, *The Processes of History* (New Haven, 1918).

12   Nie Bevan (1897-1960) was a senior member of the British Labour party, holding cabinet office in the 1940s.

17   Jacob Nicol was a lawyer and businessman who served in the Quebec Liberal cabinet in the 1920s and 1930s.

19 Note on W.S. Ferguson, 'Legalized Absolutism en route from Greece to Rome,' *American Historical Review*, XVIII (1912), 29-47   **167**

20 Reference to Walbank's, *The Decline of the Roman Empire in the West* (Toronto, 1946)

21 Note on T.F. O'Rahilly, 'The Goidels and their Predecessors,' *The Proceedings of the British Academy*, XXI (1935), 323-72. See also 29 / 9.

29 Note on H.J.E. Peake, *The Bronze Age and the Celtic World* (London, 1922)

32 Note on F.B. Wilkie, *Personal Reminiscences of Thirty-Five Years of Journalism* (Chicago, 1891)

38 Note on J.H. Quick, *One Man's Life: An Autobiography* (Indianapolis, 1925)

20

possibly 1949

1   Prose a reflection of penetration of writing to lower levels or to conversation and influenced by poetry became rhetoric.

2   Nationalism and monetary management interest in manipulation of currencies on national basis a result of intensification of vernacular and concern with national approach - reflection of power of new journalism and radio at expense of universal approach. Nationalism and protectionism a reflection of influence of Germany. Development of national statistics also a reflection of nationalism and intensified vernacular. Language broken into national boundaries - U.S. - Commonwealth of Nations - Ireland.

3   [Vilhjalmur?] Stefansson - Arctic encyclopedia - estimated at 5 million words - illustration of constant turning over of words to meet demands of machine industry.

4   Geography emphasizing maps and charts subject to fatal tendency to make difficult matters look easy and consequently to continually emphasize information and neglect interpretation.

5   Problem of capturing imaginations with trimmings - probable that churches will swallow social sciences but this makes for greater similarity in churches - emphasis on social work and the like.

6   Role of women in emphasizing native language and compelling struggle with more artificial language - significance of women's education to vernacular and adaptability of language struggle of church with monasticism against women - this probably explains emphasis on confessional.

7   Every man his own telephone exchange - a centre of contact of several other contacts and marked to appear as telephone exchange.

Ochs on *Times* emphasized more coverage to offset tendency of other **169** papers to slant news in relation to different constituencies. Nearness of written to oral tradition checks authority of written tradition.

9   Alphabet meant relation to sounds in contrast to sight – latter characteristic of empire – former especially Greek civilization – return to sight with printing and to sounds with radio.

10   Polite essay in 18th century in periodicals largely excluded instalments of novel as too small in size. Expansion to Pacific after 1849 led to *Harpers Magazine* in New York and *Atlantic Monthly* in Boston. Satire possible with anonymous writing. Repression of printers under Charles I undoubtedly contributed to rebellion. Probably development of stationers as booksellers led to increase in number of printers to secure cheaper product and to output of seditious work leading to rebellion. Struggle between booksellers and printers – former favouring increase of latter and leading to seditious literature and repression. Monopolies under Elizabeth gave popular books to small number and such books increased in price by monopoly narrowed market for other printers – consequently other printers forced to pirate books and sold them in provinces and fairs. Stationers having effect of pressing books to lower levels and other areas. Repression of 1586 of printers followed by publishing of prohibited works supporting Puritan movement to offset official episcopacy. Rise of literary agent paralleled decline of three-decker novel and dominance of circulating libraries. Competition in book trade – emphasis on monopoly – few buyers, high prices opposed by principle of taking advantage of overhead costs – larger numbers, low prices. *Edinburgh Review* flourished as uninfluenced by booksellers and penetrated London market. Murray started *Quarterly Review* in competition with *Edinburgh Review* then went into poetry by securing Byron and drove Scott into novels – influence of publishers on writing. Publishing career apparently open to talents – possibilities of moving from various backgrounds into publishing. Significance of movements in permitting ability to rise and in reflecting ability. Auctions of books a device for overcoming rigidities of fixed price system and probably developed to offset tendencies toward fixed prices.

11   Power of Greek oral tradition bent alphabet into vowels and consonants.

12   Decline in typography in 16th century as restraining influence of manuscript declined and problems of modern book faced – particularly with use of copper plate engraving. Monopoly of type founding in Holland enabled Caslon and English to develop new types in 18th century. Baskerville – influence on French (Didot) and Europe.

13 Common law emphasis on trade implies neglect of imperial problems - dissolving of empires - British empire hence dependent to an important extent on Roman empire.

NOTES

8 A.S. Ochs (1858-1935) bought the New York *Times* in 1896.
12 Caslon, Baskerville, and Didot designed type faces.

21

1949 or 1950

1   Lord Randolph Churchill recommended 'constant attendance at the
    House, fluency when wanted rather than set speeches being the desider-
    atum. You will do well to "abuse your adversaries and then apologise.
    They like that." ' (p. 71). Dalziel controlled news agency, bought Dublin
    Daily Express. T.P. Gill became editor, Plunket and friends advisers (81).
    Paper came into hands of Lord Ardilaun, President of Royal Dublin
    Society - extreme unionist and bitter opponent of Plunkett (82). A.E.
    Russell, editor *Irish Homestead*, founded I.A.O.S. in 1896 (104). 'Anglo-
    Irish history is for Englishmen to remember, for Irishmen to forget.'
    'The more business in politics and the less politics in business, the better
    for both' (109). Political doctrinaire - 'One who regards politics as an
    exact science' (254).

2   Importance of bell - device in hands of church to control time - 'Angel-
    us' - control over time from earliest period of day.

3   Mackenzie King said to have remarked that French Canadians a protec-
    tion against British influence and against American influence. King ac-
    cording to Turgeon a synthetic rather than analytic thinker - works his
    way through in course of speech to conclusion - speeches in spite of
    circumlocutions full of meat for use of election campaigns. [R.B.]
    Bennett - extremely fluent but speeches have very little in them - spoke
    five hours on money.

4   Larger number of words in English than in French because of two
    sources of English language. Lack of classical novels for children in
    France as compared with England possibly makes English children reach
    maturity over long period than French children. Gap in France between
    child and adult-reading not bridged as in England.

5   Position of university as a destroyer of new ideas or as creator and des-
    troyer of ideas - new ideas being taught lose freshness and vitality. Uni-
    versity of Paris had restrictive effect on ideas - England escaped restric-
    tive effect through separation of universities from capital and division
    between universities.

6   Spelling matches possible with variety of words in English not possible with greater precision in relation to sounds in French.

7   Judge Turgeon claimed to be first to introduce liquor control in Saskatchewan and in Canada - followed experiment introduced in North Carolina.

8   Johnston found Laurier reluctant to set up Canadian representation in Washington while Bryce in office. Hibbert Tupper expressed very strong views against representation by British Embassy in letter to Sir J.A. Macdonald in year of 'A British subject I was born a British subject I will die.' Blaine as secretary of state told British Ambassador accompanied by Tupper 'I did not expect you to bring this fellow with you' and on one occasion refused to see British Ambassador accompanied by Hibbert Tupper. A general change came with visit of Laurier to McKinley after election as President and before inauguration and relations improved. Johnston protested to Borden in letter of neglect of Canadian interests - letter sent to Sir Cecil Spring-Rice and discussed with Johnston at Rideau Hall but Spring-Rice died at Rideau Hall. In 1913 Johnston sent to meeting on shipping lanes in London following *Titanic* disaster - British and Americans had resolutions regarding all shipping lanes with Portland as farthest north - Johnston threatened to withdraw delegation unless shifted north to Halifax - supported by Scandinavians and Germans - Johnston saw Buxton - resolution withdrawn. Johnston arranged with Phillipps of Secretary of State department to sign Halibut Treaty with Canada. Lapointe and Johnston went down and were disregarded by the British Embassy under Geddes.

9   Position of Roman law in support of position of divine rights - especially canon law - leading to civil war and to American Revolution - Divine right of parliament. Purging of Roman law elements - problem of Ireland and House of Lords - development of Commonwealth - India, Pakistan.

10 'Tout ce qui est exagéré est insignifiant' (Talleyrand).

11 End of Byzantine empire 1453 left Church in west in stronger position and probably accentuated intolerance which led to revolt of Protestantism.

12 Importance of communism as a western phenomenon in spreading over China - first impact of west through Marx first in Russia, then in China - Marx a forerunner of industrialism in other civilizations.

13   Best sellers and booming of star system among authors weakens interest
in foreign writing – English publishers in early 1900s refused to publish
translations of German because of interest in booming established English writers. Strong anti-Russian feeling in Germany supported by German professors forced out of Balkan Russian Universities in 80s.

14   Precision of French language admits of growth of code – lack of precision of English language emphasizes common law and possibility of use
of cases to determine meaning of words – 'as far as appropriate', 'just
and reasonable' – common law leads to breakup of empires – respect for
local tradition – rejection of government. How far appropriate for
world government? – limitations of English language for purposes of
world governments as contrasted with use of French for diplomatic
purposes. Need for veto with inadequate drafting of charter – problem
of a strong court.

15   T.S. Eliot argues duty of poet to prevent too rapid change in language.

16   V. Gordon Childe claims historians as members of small literate group
in class society affiliated with upper class and write history from that
point of view – but Childe an archaeologist impressed by technology –
possible interpretation of Marxism as arriving at point when technology
of printing permits writing history from lower class point of view but
further advance of technology of printing since Marx probably calls for
writing of history from standpoint of entertainment.

17   Importance of philosophy in weakening position of realism – dangers of
latter in Germany and attractiveness of realism to militarism.

18   Character of books influenced by furniture – claim that in England small
tables in drawing rooms led to decline of Christmas books after sixties.
Increased power of publisher weakens position of bookseller – commercialistic influence.

19   Tarte left Conservatives after MacGreevey scandal – compelling Langevin
to resign as minister of public works, organized Liberals leading to election of 1896 – became minister of Public Works under Laurier [1896-
1902] – a strong C.P.R. and protectionist man – took line of protection
when Laurier in England and compelled to resign by letters from Laurier
on same date that Tarte resigned by letter to Laurier. On resignation
took *La Patrie*, the Liberal paper, with him. P.C. Armstrong as public
relations man for Canadian Dairy Council claims to have played an active
role in defeat of Liberals in 1930.

20   'That narrow imagination which is admiringly called the practical mind'
        (George Eliot).

NOTES

1   Note on Margaret Digby, *Horace Plunkett: An Anglo-American Irishman* (Oxford,
        1949). J.H. Dalziel (1868-1935) was a Liberal politician and newspaper proprietor.
        I.A.O.S. was the Irish Agricultural Organization Society.
3   W.F.A. Turgeon (1877-1969) had been chief justice of Saskatchewan before he
        entered the diplomatic service in 1941. He was chairman of the Royal Commission
        on Transportation of which Innis was a member.
8   Alexander Johnston (1867-1951) was a member of parliament from 1900 to 1908,
        and later became a senior civil servant. Innis served with Johnston on the Nova
        Scotia Royal Commission in 1934. Hibbert Tupper, son of the former prime
        minister Sir Charles Tupper, was a leading figure in the Conservative Party in the
        early twentieth century.
13   Note on Sidney Whitman, *Things I Remember: the Recollections of a Political
        Writer in the Capitals of Europe* (London, 1916)
15   Note on T.S. Eliot, *Notes towards the Definition of Culture* (London, 1948)
16   Note on V.G. Childe, *History* (London, 1947)
19   Israel Tarte (1848-1907), editor and newspaper proprietor, was Laurier's Quebec
        lieutenant until he broke with Laurier in 1902.

22

1949 or 1950

1   Advantage of war to bureaucracy - importance of secrecy emphasized
and deprives opposition of information on whole range of foreign policy.
Story of Dewey dissuaded by army officials from campaigning on certain issues because of significance to defence, on both occasions on
which he ran for president. Importance of emphasizing war as an element in political strategy and consequent tendency to bureaucracy.
Marx destroyed importance of general will as developed by Rousseau in
suggesting influence of materialism in class struggle and emphasizing
dialectic. Alternative swings of communication from eye to ear and ear
to eye - weariness of one sense offset by dependence on other.

2   Significance of culture - religion offset by politics, i.e. tyrants in Athens,
scholars in Alexandria, Nineveh, Augustus. Religion tends to emphasize
ascetic and breaks with culture - Elizabeth - absolutism with Church of
England led to flowering of culture offsetting Catholicism but to demands of Puritans in Cromwell and Parliament.

3   Christianity meant freedom from superstition as basis of rational state -
law. Importance of Protestantism and asceticism to capitalism. Geographic costs of transportation in India and China checked capitalism.
Calvinism emphasis on good works led to rational economic ethic. Importance of sects to capitalism - Quakers, Mormons opposed to stimu-
lants - contrary to demand of rationalism - irrationalism essential to
capitalism (Weber). H.M. Robertson emphasizes systematic bookkeep-
ing responsible for capitalism but book-keeping a tool not the spirit.

4   Struggle between oral and written tradition - Greek versus Hebrew, New
vs. Old Testament. St Augustine, Aquinas written tradition against
Greek of Erasmus.

5   'I am sceptical about the value of 90% of press reports. Most of them
tend to say enough to be misleading and not enough to be in any sense
informative (in planning papers).' (E.H. Woodward) How far newspapers

and paper became frontier in development of trade - sales organization, price policy, etc. - lightness and ease of sale? Importance of politics, i.e. Kohlsaat in Chicago bought Chicago *Post* and *Mail* and changed policy Democrat to Republican - J.R. Walsh bought out by Kohlsatt purchased *Interocean* and changed name to *Chronicle* and policy Republican to Democratic - again lost circulation - old papers destroyed through political change and way paved for Hearst. McRae in '90s bought paper as low as $1.65 and for this reason supported development of 1 cent dailies of Scripps papers. Scripps-McRae papers exploited weakness of political city machines and gained publicity in early fights against corruption. Scripps-McRae papers exploited limitations of party organs attacking political machines - emphasized independence. Importance of staff in newspapers evident in purchase by McRae of Toledo and Columbus papers to enable faithful employees to become stockholders - consistent Scripps-McRae policy - expansion and purchase of newspapers to get young men financially interested. Advertising censor appointed 1903 vigorous attack on proprietary medicines and opening way for efficient foreign advertising. Newspapers gain or lose money rapidly and not understood by bankers and financiers - Scripps-McRae followed conservative policy. Hearst concerned in paper to entertain women, girls and children. McRae apparently looked over cities of 250,000 or more and saw possibilities of press able to turn out 36,000 48-page papers per hour - exploited inadequate knowledge of machinery. Americans use press as instruments of imperialism - device to attract settlers and secure occupation - in California, probably also in Oregon. Republican papers gained as result of Civil War in North particularly with outburst following Lincoln's assassination. Democrats retreated to city and state machines. How far press introduced sense of balance with corruption of Republican domination - Greeley, Independents, etc.?

6   Place of poetry in aristocratic society, i.e. use of prose by Shakespeare by members of lower classes. Probably also prevails in Greece - epic of monarchy and aristocracy. Problem in England of oral tradition and its importance in public schools and old universities - new types of students from lower classes securing academic standing by books and written tradition and consequently weakening atmosphere of old institutions.

7   Significance of vertical integration, i.e. paper industry and newspapers. Beach and the *Sun*. Opposition of newspapers to attempt of International to acquire control of newspapers to secure a steady outlet - appealing to public opinion to check tendency and using public opinion as means for securing competitive prices in newsprint. Drive of overhead in newsprint toward increased production possibly result of ability of newspapers to check integration from below and possibly this encourages vertical

integration from above - *Chicago Tribune.* Henry George fought attempts to control land in San Francisco and interest in threat of unearned income led to appeal on broader scale. Scripps League bought *Report* in San Francisco but failed because of hostility to pennies. Gold mining town accustomed to bits, hostile to nickels and very much opposed to pennies. Problem of monetary denomination - attempt of Scripps to exploit shift to lower denominations - also important to department stores to support cheap papers to get advertising. Perfecting press and wood pulp chiefly responsible for expansion of newspapers and reading habit. Sunday magazine 'an anthology, a repository of knowledge; a compendium of history and often history itself'. In nineties, syndicates gave authors tremendous advantage especially with international copyright - impact of magazine, especially Sunday newspaper on writing in U.S. Uncalendared paper and fast press checked development of pictures in newspapers. Larger heads, larger type and display, liberal leads, illustrations meant savings of linotype disappeared with need for larger number of compositors - cheap paper, rivalry, facility - preparing material for forms. Disregard of shorthand reporting meant American press developed facile writers who contributed to literature. Role of newspaper campaigns in planning of cities.

8   About 1322 Italian furniture became lighter as result of use of saw rather than of axe or instrument to cut wood into blocks.

9   Power of oral tradition reflected in Greek literature and in Cicero at point in which writing became dominant became protection in later periods - possibility of appealing to classics and maintaining contact with oral tradition. Cicero's dominance of Middle Ages, also Herodotus and Isocrates - overthrew written tradition of St Augustine, Thomas Aquinas, etc. except as they reflected Plato and Aristotle.

10   Persecution of Jews and baptized descendants (marrani) brought stagnation in Spain and economic prosperity to Holland as persecution of Huguenots in France brought rise of Prussia and limited economic possibilities of France. Cunningham held English economic life directly and uninterruptedly influenced by political events. McCulloch held bellicosity generated capitalism.

11   Dynastic arrangements powerful factor in determining states 14th to 19th centuries - Austria. Language more important as national factor after First World War.

12   Shifting economic balance along long river of Nile meant shift of religious power with change of temples - disruption of power of priests. Demands of Nile in centralization - pyramids and problems of central-

ization of long river. Spread of writing and feudalism of middle kingdom. Increased writing - feudalism then military state - priesthood as centre of ability - Thutmose III former Amon priest (1501 [B.C.]). Kingdom - pyramids - rise of religion - priests - Re with decentralizing bias. Feudalism - Hyksos - military plus priests - Amon centralization Ikhnaton - return to Re - empire 379. Priests of Amon - 18th dynasty - brought to an end after Ikhnaton followed by army Harmhab. Power of priesthood - decline of army and economic power.

13   Paper mills in France apparently as early as 1320. Freedom of the press. 'Singulièrement contribué à faciliter la réaction et par suite à rendre les grands revolutions à peu près impossibles; elle presente cet avantage immense qu'elle ne permet pas aux forces de s'accumuler d'une manière effrayante, et que la reaction se manifeste presque aussitôt après l'action, quelquefois même avant que l'action ait eu le temps de se propager.' (I, 290)

14   Silas Bent claims newspaper editors generally behind in responding to technological changes. Advertising emphasizes significance of goodwill and slowness in change to joint stock. Dominance of family.

15   Problem of money economy - enormous increase in distribution costs involving demand for paper - advertising exchange, etc. Accentuates growth of metropolitan economy emphasis on gold and mining and rise of neo-mercantilism. Tariff decline in importance. Problem of public finance - linked to feudalism so long as dependent on property tax. International interest handicapped by financial policy except in so far as private industry compelled to invest outside as result of demand for protection - international cartels, branch plants, etc. But emphasis on land or political boundaries a handicap - immigration, tariffs, etc. Concentration on military defence contrasted with naval defence.

16   Outstanding position of president in U.S. involves tremendous ambitions which apt to overreach themselves. Webster, Clay temporized with slavery and made it difficult to elect them. Buchanan weak and carried too far - temporizing involved policy of drift especially with strong central political influence of south. Evasion only came though election of Lincoln - fundamental free soil interest of Illinois. Enormous difficulties of centralization for northern army - ineffective leadership and loss of life as contrasted with Jackson and Lee in south. Problem of control over money - a central bank not possible in U.S. - federal reserve system.

3 Max Weber's *The Protestant Ethic and the Spirit of Capitalism* was first published in German in 1904 and in an English translation in 1930. Robertson's *Aspects of the Rise of Economic Individualism* was published in 1933. See also 5 / 57.

10 William Cunningham (1849-1919) wrote the first systematic economic history of Great Britain. J.R. McCulloch (1789-1864) was a pioneer of economic history.

11 Note on Robert Michels, *First Lectures in Political Sociology*, trans. A. de Grazia (Minneapolis, 1949)

13 Note on L.A.J. Quetelet, *Sur l'homme* (Paris, 1835)

14 Possibly note on Silas Bent, *Newspaper Crusaders: A Neglected Story* (New York, 1939)

16 Daniel Webster was a candidate for the presidency in 1836, as was Henry Clay in 1824, 1832 and 1844. James Buchanan was the Democratic president who preceded Lincoln.

23

1950

1   John Bright's address on second reading of Burial's Amendment bill in 1875 a rare instance of effect of oratory on legislation - also Macaulay's speech about the Mastership of the Rolls (p. 171).

2   Great pulpit eloquence of nonconformists of Queen Victoria's reign (pp. 209-10).

3   Without political or national unity Greeks evaded demands of space - emphasized time and sense of unity in games and festivals. Encroachment of space and outbreak of wars in 5th century and later. Romans recognized problem of space by facilitating emphasis on municipalities. *Symposia* (Plato and Xenophon), Plutarch's *Banquet of the Seven Wise Men* and Athenaeus' *Banquet of Learned Men* important in understanding of Greek life. Religious need and fulfilment of religious desire largely displaced sexuality - recognized by Catholic church in auricular confession, celibacy (p. 181). 'At that time nothing was sacred but the beautiful' (Schiller) - key to understanding of Greek mythology (183). Ancient poetry and plastic art a single hymn on almighty power of Aphrodite and Eros (198). Julian the Apostate in Ibsen's *Emperor and Galilean* 'against stupidity the gods themselves fight in vain' (Schiller).

4   Theory of money as basis of state - essential control of large power to avoid exploitation of private money - the rise of tyrants - absence of metallic money - Egypt, Babylonia, Assyria, monopoly of money acquired by empire and probably a basic factor of empire - division of sovereignty - feudal system and rights to cast money absorbed and maintained by state.

5   Success of papacy over council meant absolute pope as model of absolute king, i.e. Louis XIV - beginning of triumph of centralized bureaucracy.

6   Bureaucracy in orthodoxy of eastern church after 6th century and in eastern empire. Augustus found Rome brick - left it stone. Babylon brick. Egypt stone.

8   Luther in 1508-9 found clue Romans I: 17: 'The just shall live by faith.' In meeting Luther's demands papacy blundered: 'the result of the triumph of officials over statesmen - the papal court' (Creighton) - is supremacy of bureaucratic tradition. Benefit of clergy 'one of the worst evils of the later middle ages' (Maitland).

9   Nef points to effect of industrialization in bureaucracy.

10   Emergent event in the system of the past from which it emerged and in the new system into which it will be placed - emergent event in two systems the basis of [University of Chicago sociologist] G.H. Mead's most original conception 'sociality'. Mead's emphasis on present a reflection of pressure of immediate.

11   Re Parnell: 'There can be no argument about expediency from the point of view of politics when a moral question remains' (Cardinal Manning) (p. 53).

12   German 'sentences in which one sets sail like an admiral with sealed ordrs, not knowing where he is going till he is in mid-ocean' (Lowell).

13   'A child's vocabulary is almost wholly Saxon' (Spencer).

14   French verse - sharp words, suited to rhyme but not blank verse - unsuited to emotion as in Teutonic languages for poetry.

15   Printing in U.S. - journalism in 19th century - imports of novels from England, neglect of drama, and imports from France - particularly as latter subsidized in France.

16   How far did Jesuits reflect spread of book to Roman church and decline of emphasis on art?

17   Beginnings of amber trade to Jutland synchronized with early bronze age - possibly exported with tin from Bohemia and bronze imported - zenith of amber trade to Italy about 650 B.C. - decline a result of influence of Greeks - a cause of collapse of prehistoric civilizations of Sweden, Denmark, Germany. Fear of tyrants evident in Greece after Peisistratus and finally made impossible in Athens by paying jurymen - this also a cause of lack of knowledge of economics - Thucydides and Herodotus little interest in economic factors in war (p. 25). Fall of Lydia probably weakened Alcmaeonides and led to tyrants. Loss of Thrace and Paconian mines probably brought tyranny to an end.

18   'The hopeful theory that advance of international commerce would
      destroy national hatreds convinces all mankind that it is a brotherhood
      with common interests and therefore banish war, has turned out to be a
      total delusion. The competitions of commerce are more condusive to
      conflict than to brotherhood and peace' (Frederick Greenwood, 1892).
      Pen-knife - word derived from period in use of quills. Democracy 'a
      continually shifting aristocracy of money, impudence, animal energy
      and cunning.' Greenwood argued for succession to throne in female line
      to give stability to empire. 'All great men have the same religion' (Ben-
      jamin Disraeli, Earl of Beaconsfield). Greenwood an illustration of
      independence shown in resignations to the right in Conservative ranks
      in contraste with resignations to the left.

19   Root crops - turnips brought winter feeding and expansion of wool
      trade - more prosperity in architecture of Tudor England.

20   'Pay them well; where there is a Maecenas there will be a Horace and a
      Virgil also' (Martial). 'Complaints are made that we have no literature;
      this is the fault of the Minister of Interior' (Napoleon).

21   Authors have great advantage in periods of rapid expansion.

22   The cheque, 'that species of literature which has the supreme art of con-
      veying the most pleasure in the least space' (Lowell).

23   'There are virtues that one can practise only when one is rich' (Rivarol).

24   Cause of Manicheanism served that of Iran. Iranian spirit lived and lang-
      uage flourished in rich poetical literature as states more independent
      of Bagdad emerged.

25   Chosroes II introduced paper probably from China where monopoly
      held (p. 155).

26   Diet adjusted to problems of constipation - constipation theory of his-
      tory - richness of cooking and necessity of offsetting it with beverages -
      olives for oil grown with grapes for wine, i.e. Greece.

27   Universe divided in two - Ormuzd (good), Ahriman (bad).

28   Friars weakened bishops' authority through resort to exemption and
      injured church. Problem of space with removal of papacy to Avignon.
      'Where the Emperor is there is Rome' (Herodian). Spiritual Franciscans -
      vows of apostolic poverty - concentrating on time element - papacy in
      temporal power and space. How far did problem of transfer of funds

for papacy bring revolt, i.e. shipment of money injured trading interests -
drained money from commerce? (p. 117). Destruction of Constantinople possibly emphasized dangers of Roman dominance and strengthened nationalism or religion without a capital. Distinction between Catholic Church and Apostolic - former all believers - latter Pope and cardinals and can err - similar to basis of early Celtic church versus Rome.
Binns argues papacy fell because of weight placed on centre, i.e. ineffectiveness of bureaucracy in competition with developments of courts,
law, commerce. Problem of education in which clerks in government
were the products of monastic education - difficulty of achieving separation overcome with rise of law.

29   You cannot hope
     To bribe or twist
     Thank God, the
     British journalist

     But seeing what
     The man will do
     Unbribed, there's
     No occasion to.   Humbert Wolfe

30   Did problem of Bohemian tin and its export favour making of swords
     by Danubians on Hungarian plains - metals carried as manufactured
     products rather than as raw materials?

31   Clannishness of newspaper people a handicap in politics - Harding great-
     ly influenced by McLean of *Washington Post.*

32   'Modern languages tend to separate abstract thought.'

33   Schoolmen influenced by logic of writing, i.e. Aquinas neglected sci-
     ence - latter always partial to science but science itself endangered by
     writing - 'not the devil but St Thomas Aquinas the first Whig' (Acton).
     Aristotelian doctrine a basis of conciliar action. Monasticism - dualistic,
     sub-Christian renouncing of world. Monasticism extended Christianity
     beyond limits of Roman empire but involved a different type of Chris-
     tianity than that under Roman empire. Monasteries renounced world in
     remote spots - friars emerged in relation to urban demands. Rhyddrich
     first Christian sovereign to establish Christian church and to protect it
     as national church with capital at Dumbarton 573-601 (p. 201). Celts -
     Catholic organization based on St Martin at Tours, later on *Candida
     Casa;* avoided bishops, diocesans, and monarchic structure which
     brought linking of state to church or occasional conflicts between them
     or brought wealth and corruption - about 700 centres of Pictish church

Bangor, Glasgow, Candida Casa outside Pictish state - contrast Scottish state where religion or church a device for propaganda. Type of organization of Celt. Catholics facilitated keeping alive religious element in opposition to centralization of Rome and background of Reformation in Scotland, also of Scottish nationalism in Ulster as well as of Irish nationalism - created problem of division of Scottish church. Problem of Christianity that of overcoming traditions of early monasticism - under apostolic succession previous to increased supremacy of Rome - latter at basis of French Gallican church. Roman church favoured absolute kings and monarchic structure as device for Christianizing populations - opposed democratic election by clan system - interaction of church and state - appointment by cardinals to avoid power of absolute ruler, appointment by electors to avoid power of church. Church became absolute and monarchic as political structure became democratic. Santayana probably wrong in suggesting protestant as Teutonic - they are rather early Christian pre-Roman Church with organization better adapted to clan or primitive government organization. Roman church attempted to shoulder burden of empire at expense of church - Protestants continued Greek tradition - contrary to Santayana.

34 Problem of approach to unity, i.e. birthplaces and early growth in one centre assumes a particular attitude to other centres, i.e. G.V.F. [Ferguson] born in Nelson - attitude toward Winnipeg, Calgary and the like contrasted with attitude of Torontonian. Problem of school to break down variety of approaches or weaken element of space - *New Yorker's* view of U.S.

35 'There is no such thing as inevitable war. If war comes it will be from failure of human wisdom' (Bonar Law).

36 Criticism a sixth sense of Parisians - must express an opinion and a peremptory one quickly.

37 Sharp decline German book trade after first war result of depression of French currency and competition in Switzerland and of nationalism in Czechoslovakia, Poland, Latvia.

38 Significant influence of France in England, i.e. *Figaro* followed by *Figaro in London* (1832), *Charivari London* followed Paris *Charivari* - political editorial supported by large cut, i.e. importance of woodcuts. Importance of drama - all earlier literary members of *Punch* staff in Dramatic Author's Society. Dramatic authors got inspirations from à Beckett (p. 56). Wilkie Collins, determined to get low prices, transferred from Smith to Chatto & Windus, and prices reduced to 6/ - (p. 83). Smith publisher - great fortune from 'Apollinaris' - support to *Pall Mall*

Gazette also Dictionary National Biography - lost £70,000 on this (102). P.M.G. aimed at demand for paper before lunch rather than before breakfast (123). Part of training of minds from church to journalism following Darwin (also Newman) in *Saturday Review.* Morley Stephen, P.M.G. to bring thought and culture of reviews into daily journalism (129).

39 'In Queen Victoria's reign, honours were far rarer than in this century' (R.C.K. Ensor). Gladstone made Lawson (*Telegraph*) a baronet in 1892.

40 Probable that tyrants - Saite dynasty, Egypt and others - result of coinage and wealth and stimulated writing down of texts - was rule of tyrants linked to writing? Monopoly over money, i.e. Lydia probably made government and brought tyrant to throne.

41 Religion developed to spare men against their consciences.

42 Genealogy an important role in the oral tradition - significance of family and family connections.

43 Importance of negroes in U.S. to urbane living - contribution of the South in aristocratic life, i.e. negroes in domestic service, hotels, etc.

44 Problem of early Netherland painting - materialistic tradition compelled to make compromises, i.e. problem of perspective in relation to emphasis on religious topics.

45 Struggle over time or control of time, i.e. between northern church and Romans in determining date of Easter.

46 Oral tradition - Celtic clan organization replaced by Roman pro-consul in Britain, i.e. written tradition - clash between Roman central control in church with Pictish organization. Problem of dynasty - Picts clannish chiefs appointing king in contrast with emphasis on direct line from royal father - Picts escaped problem of regencies, i.e. effective government of oral traditions.

47 Curtis first to exploit advertising in magazines - magazines dominant in national advertising - hence planned on national scale - became danger of American propaganda for other countries. Economy and standardization not craftsmanship or art. Magazines, newspaper, radio - created public opinion they later influenced. James T. Fields, 1861, editor of *Atlantic*: 'I could double the merit of the articles in the *Atlantic Monthly* and halve my subscription list at the same time' (p. 247). 'Couldn't you write on the natural history of the diplomatic cuttle-fish of Schleswig-Holstein without forfeiting your ministerial equanimity?' (Lowell

to John Lothran Motley, minister to Austria 1864) (264). 'Most of the best literature now sees the light in the magazines, and most of the second-best appears first in book form' (W.D. Howells, 1902). Tendency for American magazines to be alike - *Readers Digest* a great leveller. Readers liking every article of periodicals indicates lack of variety in mood, writing and content - difficulties in launching new magazines, magazines becoming more like newspapers (286). Irving S. Cobb, similar to Mencken but without his bitterness - greater tolerance of southern tradition. Tremendous vigour of newspaper men - Drieser, also Nevins - in history.

48 Arch troublers of human race - superstitious fear of supernatural and self-conscious questioning about duty and destiny of man. Homeric morality dependent on honour and public opinion.

49 'The acme of art production has always been attained during political stages of autocracy or limited aristocracy, which precede the acme of well-being' (Hogarth).

50 Printing and obsession with detail - necessity of extensive courses in contrast with importance of general lectures. Printing divides a knowledge of the arts because of emphasis on details and specialization.

51 Influence of Egypt and concern with time probably evident in use of stone rather than wood and brick in Greece.

52 Hall of Initiation at Eleusis built probably after 550 B.C. towards close of Peisistratus's tyranny - perhaps first public building with a roof to preserve secrecy of mysteries. Did mystery religions demand closed buildings, i.e. encouraged by tyrants in opposition to Delphi? (p. 109). Introduction of cement as revolutionary material in Rome late second century B.C. contributed to divorce between function and decoration characteristic of Roman architecture. Greek architecture chiefly in temples. Dorian - followed by Ionian especially toward east and by Corinthian with Romans to west. Development of cement facilitated emphasis on secular buildings and made possible handling of interiors with great halls using arch, vault, dome.

53 Oral tradition - Sumerian probably written down with imposition of Akkadian language - writing a device for protecting religion, language, and law. Hence earliest writing powerfully influenced by oral tradition. Homeric poems. Old and New Testament written as protection - oral tradition extending in monasticism beyond Roman empire - Celtic Catholicism. Impact on later political organization writing - centralization of Rome - translation of scriptures Greek and Latin.

54 Chronology reckoned by genealogies. Domesday book, Magna Carta – written tradition – meticulous character.

55 Persistance of oral tradition written and unwritten – church services – Parliament and common law – drama, Greece and Shakespeare – oral tradition written down.

56 Fundamental problem of written constitutions – U.S., Roman law countries.

57 'All them foreign parts is pretty close together.'

58 Barrows, rough stone monuments definitely intended as focus of traditions – significance of stone and durability to time and lack of portability to space.

59 Knossos without walls of defence – dependent on navy. Use of place names and geology in archaeology – in types of stone. Possibly Homer's single mention of writing a result of hostility of minstrel to writing – also indicates disappearance of knowledge of writing in Aegean (p. 229). Cremation apparently accompanies iron age. Lack of interest in political and economic history Greeks explained wars with Troy on human basis – the rape of Helen.

NOTES

1   Note on James Milne, *The Memoirs of a Bookman* (London, 1934)
2   Note on W.Y. Fullerton, *C.H. Spurgeon: A Biography* (London, 1920)
3   Identified by Innis as by Ticht or Ficht
8   Note on M. Creighton, *A History of the Papacy during the period of the Reformation* (Boston, 1882)
9   Note on J.U. Nef, *War and Human Progress* (London, 1950)
11   Note on J. Milne, *A Window in Fleet Street* (London, 1931)
12   James Russell Lowell (1819-91) was an American author, educator, and diplomat.
17   Note on P.N. Ure, *The Origin of Tyranny* (Cambridge, 1922)
23   The Comte de Rivarol (1753-1801) was a French journalist and epigrammatist.
25   Note on C. Huart, *Ancient Persia* (London, 1927)
28   Note on L.E. Binns, *The History of the Decline and Fall of the Medieval Papacy* (London, 1934)
29   Wolfe (1886-1940) was a British poet and civil servant.
31   E.B. McLean succeeded his father as proprietor of the *Washington Post* and Cincinnati *Enquirer*.
32   Note on T.S. Eliot, *Dante* (London, 1929)
33   Note on A.B. Scott, *The Pictish Nation: its People and its Church* (Edinburgh and London, 1918)

38	Note on J.W. Robertson, *The Story of the Pall Mall Gazette, of its first editor Frederick Greenwood and of its founder George Murray Smith* (London, 1950)
39	Note on R.C.K. Ensor, *England 1870-1914* (Oxford, 1936)
40	Note on Ure, *Origin of Tyranny*. See 23 / 17.
46	Note on Scott, *The Pictish Nation*. See 23 / 33.
47	Note on J.P. Wood, *Magazines in the United States: Their Social and Economic Influence* (New York, 1949)
52	Note on D.S. Robertson, *A Handbook of Greek and Roman Architecture* (Cambridge, 1932)
59	Possibly note on a work by Cecil D. Burns.

24

1950

1   American reprinting of English annuals - i.e. Hood's comic annuals checked by difficulties in obtaining wood-cutters in 30s (p. 52).

2   'Close relation between technical virtuosity and the fullness of artistic development.' Thesis of Franz Boas.

3   Rise of middle class in 18th century and of market for writers - end of patronage - increased size of music halls, painters' expositions (p. 49). Musical science 'a social science devoted to the properties of a musical system or language belonging to a specific culture area and a certain stage of historical development' (Norman Cazden) (95).

4   Tolstoy's infection theory of art - aim to achieve social solidarity by promoting community of feeling. One man hands to others feelings he has lived through.

5   Oral versus written tradition reflected in religious versus legal tradition - spread of writing and printing leading to revolutions in religion - new religions based on writing or pretence of writing - Mormonism, Christian Science. Bible largely of oral origin an effective competitor with religions based on writing.

6   Plato - Being - Geometry; Aristotle - Becoming - Biology. Conflict between two in space and time. Plato displacing Aristotle at end of Middle Ages. Impact of concern with immortality in Egypt evident in realism of art to assist individual. Contrast with Greek - opposed to realism and to symbolism. Influence of death on art, i.e. realism. Greeks opposed to learning other languages. Drama as unique Greek creation - fusing lyric feeling and epic story of Athens - space and time. Absence of history in Indian literature - lack of concern with time.

7   Mencken as newspaper reporter attack on books as reviewer of *Smart Set* - essentially a journalist against book. Mencken leading attack on

'puritanism' from bottom. How far was this true of Moore in England? - probably compelled to make a direct attack. Banning of books in Boston - continuation of struggle between puritanism and monarchy - north and south. Each region intent on producing its own writers - boomed by local newspapers. 'My dissents are from ideas, not from decorums' (Mencken).

8   *Time*
Emergence of capitalism and overhead cost as church released control over time and seizure by entrepreneur, i.e. long hours in mines - also continuous operation with various shifts - using up of biological time or energy and necessity of pensions - necessity of state intervening to prevent abuse by technology and business. Control over time by religion, i.e. Jews, leads to type of internationalism - protests of Jews against Russian pogroms, enlisting of international sympathy implying international direction in terms of time - necessity for Jews emphasizing communication - press, radio, films - as device for protection. How far setting up of Palestine weakens international influence of Jews in reducing it to vote of a single small nation or strengthens it by compelling Jews to emphasize internationalism?

9   How far writing emphasizes universal - oral tradition and hierarchy, i.e. Christianity?

10   How far language a factor in class, i.e. dialects, etc.? How far Fascism and Bolshevism based on Sorel (p. 72)? Absolute developed in time, in circumstantial - proclaiming decadence of form of mind from Plato to Kant hallowing existence as conceived beyond change - the treason of the clerics (80). Neo-Thomism opposes cult of Being to that of Becoming but these particularist in their own way (81). A scholar who 'had read himself into ignorance'. 'Out of frequent and close conversation and much social intercourse a light is of a sudden kindled in the mind, as from a fire that leaps forth, which when once generated keeps itself alive' (Plato). Silliness of mind an acquisition of 19th century - belief that teachings drawn from past will come out of examination of the *facts* - desires which have been realized (95).

11   Only dead languages those in which nothing living written (Lowell).

12   'Peace is not the absence of war, but a virtue born from strength of soul' (Spinoza).

13   Christian accepts ideas of justice and charity only for the sake of his salvation.

14   'The passions have taught men reason' (Vauvenargues).

15   '1793 the bad paper year' - impressions of an old man to [Jules] Michelet.

16   'Politics are a science' - the superstition of science.

17   'Everyone cannot philosophize and that, for man, the essential thing is to choose a master' ([Jacques] Maritain).

18   Significance of writing to individualistic religions, i.e. Egypt, also Orphism.

19   How far education in schools an emphasis on ear - recitation - and more recent emphasis on eye? How far scientific work a question of concentrating on the eye rather than the ear and hence more individualistic?

20   'It is no doubt as unkind and as great a waste of time to give the public *what it doesn't want* in the way of art, literature or science as it is to degrade it below what it does actually want in order to make money out of it' (94). 'Let them study those arts whereby the opinions of the minority may be made to seem those of a majority' (Samuel Butler). 'If there was a city of good men, the contest would be not to be in the government, as at present it is to govern' (Plato). Facts - *Das Kapital* taken out of books or somebody else's pamphlet (Shaw). 'Tout le monde est malheureux dans le monde moderne' (Peguy). 'Property is theft' - a phrase stolen by Proudhon. Did French inheritance of Roman administrative capacity lead to revolt of Rousseau in interest of individual? 'Because an insular nation favoured by the commercial indolence of France has enriched itself by monopoly and maritime spoliation, behold all the old doctrines of philosophy disdained, commerce extolled as the only road to truth, to wisdom and to happiness, and the merchants become the pillars of the state' (Fournier).

21   Interest of Europe in problems of class and consequently in sociology in contrast with Great Britain - interest in economics.

22   Evolution probably result of sudden development of favourable conditions in early stages - rapid change possible at early stage and very difficult at later stage when it becomes crystallized, i.e. in case of man and change difficult to introduce other than by force. With increasing period of time possibility of sudden rapid adjustment of earlier periods disappeared - resources of world less abundant and available.

23   Time - Horizon projects.
       Time - perspectives of two (or three) economically variant companies at the present time in the different areas of their operations (*a*) the

companies: a crude oil producer, a department store, a machine builder, a railroad and (*b*) raw material supply, product planning, inventories, etc.

Changing time - perspectives of: all areas of a given company, a selected area in a given company, a selected area in several regionally diverse or vari-sized companies in the same industry; a trade association, a labour union, a provider of equipment for manufacturing or transportation, a management consultant. Statistical studies over forward orders of machine builders - or inventories or stand-by equipment.

Time as a measure of proper planning.

Time as a directive of thought.

Time as a measure of action.

24   Latin Church stood above and outside Orthodox empire - latter on level with state and people - closer to them than Latin Church but union with empire meant persecution though checked by political influence - contrast with absolutism of western church and inquisition. Explained difficulty of orthodox church with Roman church, also with Monophysites. How far was Henry VIII in Church of England influenced by policy? (XXV) Importance of eunuchs - could not become emperors or usurpers of Byzantine Empire and would not leave descendents.

25   Importance of Greek interest in character dominated by oral tradition - with rise of aliens around Piraeus, Cleon tends to succeed Pericles, i.e. extravagance, lack of balance contributes to defeat of Athens.

26   Lawyers trained to essential ruthlessness of political life - conventions and the like necessary to enable individuals to meet its demands. Much as military parades, etc. necessary to cover the sordid demands of war. Price system to some extent provides an escape from ruthless demands of politics. In France ruthlessness of journalists adapts them to government and politics.

27   Censorship primarily for advertising purposes - to demonstrate power of church or of group protesting against censorship - Mencken - advertising value of censorship chief reason for abolishing it.

28   Extent of free masonry among women perhaps a survival of matriarchate - interest in church - retreat of matriarchate to religion. Portrait painting of women largely disappeared and emphasis chiefly on men supported by boards, committees. Wealthy men less concerned with wives' portraits.

29   Function of newspaper to maintain mobility in adjustment of hierarchy - giving news about individual, i.e. health, achievements and enabling

others to adjust themselves or scoring successes enabling readers to
place individual in perspective. This offset to some extent by those
knowing how to use news - getting in limelight, choosing committees in
parliament with news value and getting information in that way. Also
use by members of *Hansard* and of *Congressional Record.* Newspaper
and magazine concerned primarily with mobility within a plutocracy.
Emphasis on commercialism implies neglect of interest in art or culture.

30   Enormous importance of commercialism in literature in U.S. partly result of reprinting English books without copyright - also of subscription
sales emphasized until dime novel emerged - consequently absorbed all
worst commercialistic elements of English books suited to wide sale in
U.S. Significant interest of Mark Twain in setting up his own publishing
firm. Commercialism of book had implications for drama, i.e. *Ben Hur*
in literature influenced drama. Role of Bible in Plymouth and activity
of separatists beyond range of Virginia - English government and Anglican Church - gave tremendous emphasis to book ([Brooks] Adams,
Emancipation of Massachusetts [Boston, 1887]) and restricted possible
development of drama and other arts - disastrous influence of Bible.
Anthony Hope, *Prisoner of Zenda* [Bristol, 1894], dramatized. Introduction of copyright destroyed cheap unauthorized editions - Kipling
sold widely in pirated editions before copyright and sales declined with
higher prices of authorized editions. Harold Bell Wright sold through
publisher - formerly a mail order bookseller - 1909-1934 publication
dates spaced to have new book appear as old one declined in popularity.
Movie exploited best sellers or influenced best sellers - Four Horsemen
1920, Valentino 1921.

31   Oral tradition - survival in obscenity and blasphemy. Epic of Greece
and of Teutons in oral tradition. Tragedy developing at periods of transition from oral to written. Greece and England. Importance of courts
in oral tradition - women and vernacular - Louis XIV, Charles II. Rhetoric, oratory reflecting early influence of writing on speech. Essay of
18th century part of oral tradition, i.e. Boswell's [*Life of*] *Johnson* -
disappeared with interest in study of literature. Courts, parliament,
church service continuation of oral tradition.

32   Overwhelming importance of manuscripts based on parchment and paper prior to printing - also paper production in relation to commerce
in Italy - migration of printing and issue of humanist books in Italy and
export to north - emphasis on classics - closeness of writing as handicraft to production of works in vernacular and in metre. With printing
press demands on literature and emphasis on rhyme. Attempt of [Ezra]
Pound and others - [T.S.] Eliot to recapture European tradition of
metre and writing but difficulty of maintaining level. Printing - mass

production - the Bible - consequent problem of other arts - painting, sculpture - lack of energy and influence of Protestantism - also of Catholicism.

33 Impact of radio on writing - literature and limited audience - emphasis on training - everlasting maw of radio programmes and demand for raw material - dredging of whole field of literature - topicality - necessity of repeating two or three times in contrast with writing in which reader turns back - emphasis on simplest words - inviting whole scheme of hierarchy - small numbers for literary development and large numbers for radio - consequent facility of journalists in radio. Necessity of turning up old stuff which may be suitable or made suitable for radio.

34 Oral tradition cheap - probably written down as paper became cheaper, i.e. influence on Mohammedanism or with printing - Protestantism.

35 Threat of Latin to English in 18th century. Also in Byzantine empire - decline of Latin - return of Greek - influence of Greek characters on Russian - adaptability of orthodox liturgy to Slavic vernaculars. Awful cost of German language strengthened by book. Does oral tradition emerge to strengthen aristocracy and monarchy, i.e. bards, minstrels - emphasis on time?

36 Significance of writing in enabling civilization to conquer and maintain conquest - Babylonia and Egypt but improved method of writing enabled Hebrews to establish own religion - also Greeks - maintaining tradition in Byzantine empire though subjected to invasions strengthened tenacity of Hebrews - introduction of writing and its sacred character - Rome and spread of Latin writing surviving barbarians - oral tradition - huns, mongols, norsemen brought under control by writing - conservatism of writing incidental to its sacred character. Oral tradition and Bible moulding later history of literature and providing vitality to literature sufficient to withstand effects of writing and printing. Possibility of using the conservative character of institutions as a basic factor in method in the social sciences, i.e. monopoly factor. How far Mohammedans brought time concepts (algebra) to Europe to offset dominance of space of Plato? European philosophy footnotes to Plato (Whitehead). Illumination - books - crafts highly developed and elaborated - importance of colour - expense of purple obtained from molluscs and use with gold - technical problem of handling gold leaf - influence of chemistry from Mohammedans - making available colours - 12th, 13th, 14th centuries. Book dominating cathedral - increase in use of substitutes for colour - tendency toward mass production - late Middle Ages. Importance of colour to period prior to written or printed tradition, i.e. purple toga - also gold.

38   Logic of print and writing and reading. Gesture - visible to eye - word - ear; writing return to eye but for long period eye supplementary to ear. Enormous importance of oral tradition in religion and literature.

39   *Space* - problem of space on the stage, i.e. unity of action a single problem at the same place (unity of space) and in 24 hours (unity of time), i.e. oral tradition and demands for balance of space and time (Racine).

40   Religion a reflection of social hierarchy, i.e. in Babylonia pantheon a reflection of social system - use of reflection as a mirage to interpret the underlying conditions. In feudal system arrangements of heavenly hierarchy a reflection of social system - extent to which mirage becomes a system of beliefs to hamper another type of society - and change of mirage.

41   'The art preservative of all arts' - motto on house of Laurent Koster at Haarlem.

42   'The invention of printing, and the easy power and extreme pleasure to vain persons of seeing themselves in print' (p. 43). 'Whatever material you choose to work with, your art is base if it does not bring out the distinctive qualities of that material' (Ruskin). 'The work of art at its best is beautiful in its very substance and, *per accidens*, as serviceable as an article of commerce' (Eric Gill).

43   Well boys the sky has just fallen in. Shall we make it a 'splash' or keep it down to a column? - nonchalant journalist. Importation of advertising ideas from U.S. to Canada especially T. Eaton Co. and from that firm to England by their advertising agent. Advertising writing becoming gateway for entrance to journalism. In turn advertising used to advance prestige of advertiser by turning to politics and used to win political campaigns - revolutionary implications to politics. If there is a fire in London and £100,000 worth of goods are destroyed, it is worth two lines. But if there is a fire in which a fireman rescues a kitten at the risk of his life then it's a top. Importance of specialization to point of danger - problem of proper superficiality in increasing complexity of subjects requires specialization but journalist in danger of losing all round ability. Oral tradition and limited demands on energies of population facilitated development of diversity of arts - sculpture, painting, architecture.

44   Influence of writing in Italy and in antiquity permitted turning of energy to painting, sculpture, and architecture in Renaissance or return

to standards developed in oral tradition with its impact on early writing in Greece.

45   Widely disseminated system of communication – writing and printing makes it possible for individual to develop belief in individual and hence to give energetic drive to society in contrast with limited system, i.e. pyramids, which limits possibilities of belief in individual and emphasizes belief in society.

NOTES

1   Note on Leslie A. Marchand, ed., *The Letters of Thomas Hood* (New Brunswick, N.J., 1945)

2   Boas (1858-1942) was an internationally renowned American anthropologist.

3   Note on L. Harap, *Social Roots of the Arts* (New York, 1949)

7   H.L. Mencken (1880-1956) was a leading figure in 20th century American journalism, especially during his period as editor of *American Mercury* from 1924 to 1933.

10   Note on Julien Benda, *The Great Betrayal*, trans. R. Aldington (London, 1928)

14   The Marquis de Vauvenargues was an eighteenth-century French moralist and essayist.

20   Note on Wyndham Lewis, *The Art of Being Ruled* (New York, 1926)

24   Note on H. Baynes and H. St L.B. Moss, eds., *Byzantium: An Introduction to East Roman Civilization* (Oxford, 1946)

30   Wright (1872-1944) was an American author, painter and clergyman.

37   Note on J.B. Bury, *History of the Later Roman Empire*, vol. II (London, 1923)

41   Koster was a Dutch printer, contemporary to Gutenburg.

42   Note on Samuel Butler, *Further Extracts from the Note Books of Samuel Butler*, ed. A.T. Bartholomew (London, 1934). Gill was a twentieth century sculptor and a designer of type faces.

43   Note on *Autobiography of a Journalist*, ed. Michael Joseph (London, 1929)

25

1950

1   Eleusis - about 14 miles from Athens - worship of Demeter - teaching
     transmitted orally and kept a secret by initiates. How far Hebrew and
     Christianity with emphasis on writing destroyed religions of oral tradi-
     tion - Druids and pagan religions - and how far did oral tradition in
     ceremonial and ritual of early religions persist in liturgies of Christian-
     ity?

2   Worship of Isis outlawed 391 [A.D.] came to an end at Philae under
     Justinian 527-65. Pyramid texts compiled in latter part of Old Kingdom
     2400-2240 [B.C.] and inscribed on stone walls of five pyramids at Sag-
     garch. With Middle Kingdom large portions of pyramid texts copied on
     sarcophagi of kings and nobles - changed and added to - Coffin texts.
     In 18th dynasty beginning 1580 B.C. religious literature including Pyra-
     mid and Coffin texts brought together, re-edited, painted on coffins and
     written on papyrus becoming the Book of the Dead. Last recension of
     Book of the Dead in 26th dynasty 663-525 [B.C.] - used to end of
     Egyptian civilization. Development of writing under Hebrews permits
     escape from link between man and nature in absolute morality and
     under Greeks an escape in absolute intellectuality. Myth and sculpture
     overcome by moral courage of Hebrews and intellectual courage of
     Greeks. Importance of art in Egypt and Babylonia - sculpture especially
     Egypt and architecture linked to character of government - place of
     king - ceremonial, oral ritual - spoken word - with Hebrews escape from
     link between art and government or problem of king in integrating hu-
     manity and nature by emphasis on writing rather than art and conse-
     quent belittling of man and nature. Language in Egypt linked to con-
     crete with architecture and art - limited effectiveness in dealing with
     abstract. Once language linked to speech and writing as with Hebrews
     and Greeks concern with architecture and art less important. Linking of
     ear and eye in alphabet meant revolution from writing of limited effic-
     iency with need to depend on ceremonial - oral tradition and architec-
     ture and sculpture - need for kingship as a link declines with rise of co-
     hesion between speech and writing. Emphasis on concrete reflected in

myth even after language perfected as an instrument – link of myth and sculpture in Greece. Limited evidence of deification of kings in Mesopotamia reflects power of priesthood. Interest in religion in controlling the senses – sight use of temples and sculpture, hearing use of songs, liturgy, smell use of incense, taste use of wafers, speech confessional. Power of religious or of other institutions varies with technological developments affecting communication by one or other approaches of senses.

3   Weakening of nationalism evident in spread of ideologies suited to spoken word and to new systems of government than those characterizing nationalism or adaptability to printed word. Importance of nationalism in cheapening raw materials for communication, i.e. Canada as source of supply of newsprint implies operation of competitive forces in bringing prices down – on the other hand provincial crown lands may enable provinces to raise prices of raw material and become a check to communication. Opposition to vertical integration extended from paper mills to papers but not to downward integration of newspapers and newsprint mills – *Chicago Tribune*. Possibility of nationalism as basis of diversity and escape from danger of totalitarian world – checks control of single group or a double group.

4   Dangers of Christianity with emphasis on individualism and constant threat of individualism in search of individuals for power – demand for change and instability. Strong impress of Rome on church. State a device by which military groups acquire control of resources – culture possible where no strong centralized political power based on force – France, Italy.

5   Athanasius, bishop of Alexandria, reflected tenacity of Egyptian tradition in opposition to Constantine and Constantinople.

6   Gothic cathedral 'The Bible of the Poor' (Emile Male).

7   Importance of monopoly of communication developed along bias of a medium and implications to civilization – emergence of new medium to offset bias, i.e. appeal to eye rather than ear, to space rather than time.

8   Importance of dominance of religion by state evident in persistence of Byzantine empire, also of England under Henry VIII – religion under control of state implies conservation of energy. Problem of change in religion – Constantine to escape from Roman gods assisting Maxentius – relied on Christianity. Facilitated despoiling of pagan temples and use of gold to support currency – paralleling Henry VIII and monasteries.

9   Effect of writing and printing on other arts - tendency to destroy them - to preserve them but not to encourage active interest. Energies drained off in writing about art and architecture. Sculpture, painting, architecture flourished when existing as distinct interests absorbing energies of those concerned and not checked by writing and printing. Architecture in spite of Hugo tends to break through, i.e. skyscrapers - Hugo over-emphasizes print. Shaw tends to be influenced by print as compared with Shakespeare, i.e. in writing novels. Division between arts influenced by eye and by ear - latter oral tradition, music, poetry, drama. Eye - architecture, sculpture, mathematics, painting, writing, printing, prose. Plato - danger of oral tradition - expulsion of poets - dangers of music in military interests, i.e. bagpipes.

10   Tendency of news in paper to be built up to support the headline. How far monopoly tendencies in paper industry? International Paper Company 1898 - followed by monopoly tendencies in newspaper industry - building up chains to strengthen position against paper trust.

11   'I have been convinced that a democracy is incapable of ruling others' - Cleon in Thucydides in protesting against reluctance of Athenians to take harsh measures against captives.

12   Shakespeare's plays sold by companies because of difficulties of theatres and general poverty.

13   Relative power of Caesaropapism in Byzantine empire implied check to growth of monasticism evident in iconoclastic controversy in east and intensification of monasticism in west - also feudalism in west and not in east. East not exposed to long swell of history - feudalism and renaissance. Iconoclasts - supported by Judaism - attack on myth, sculpture, architecture, based on book - scriptures - monotheism - Mohammedanism - Koran. Image worship in west with Trinitarianism, development of cathedrals, reluctance to depend on book until Protestantism. Importance of tradition in church - oral tradition. Babylonian civilization dominated by brick in architecture and writing - sculpture limited in seals. Power of gods such as to compel recognition by conquerors and kings, i.e. Assyria proceeding to Babylon.

14   Religion the dope of the past and the press the opium of the present (Kingsley Martin).

15   Progress - that kind of improvement that can be measured in statistics (Mallock). Man began to wish to live beyond his income (Butler). Moral difficulty for barristers seldom arises in criminal cases but rather in civil

cases - if barrister convinced of guilt of client in latter case unable to drop him. In criminal case duty to defend prisoner against prosecutor (p. 12). House of Commons with labour party has different languages working men and gentry - mutual annoyance and difficulty of debate with mixture of styles (216).

16   Contrast between ear and eye in effective communication - children born deaf have much more difficult time than those born blind. Writing tends to divide between those who write and read and those who read - passive and active - more effective division than between speaker and listener but speaker may assume active role.

17   Time - emphasis on saving and thrift an indication of attempt to strengthen position of appreciation of time (Bentham) in contrast with collectivism and wiping out of individual interest.

18   Significance of writing in crystallizing meaning, i.e. contracts and statutes covering meaning and limiting it - raises questions as to non-contractual elements not covered by writing or printing in a contract or statute. Problem of courts in defining fringe or margin of meaning of contract or statute.

19   Veblen - pecuniary or industrial interpreted as influence of writing or printing, i.e. Gras interest in administration. Economic systems reflection of consistency writing and monetary systems.

20   Marriage alliances important in banking history as basis of growth and continuity - also in land under conditions of feudalism - significance of marriage in business as a device for continuity.

21   Importance of printer and publisher to have a range of interests or a list - Fust and Schoeffer - especially the latter emphasized religious and law books, botany. Printing profoundly influenced by locality in early stages - problem of transportation of folios. Schoeffer and others, i.e. Mainz, emphasizing theology. Leipzig later in century active in science - emphasis on territorial specialization with quartos and octavos greater interest in wide market. Significance of capital - operating plant to capacity - adaptability of Bible and large books or advantage of press most evident with large books. Interest in large books accompanied by interest in broadsides as between large projects. Printing reflected powerful impact of economic motive - printer estimating size of market and exploiting it - strengthened groups best adapted to its demands.

22   Significance of writing and printing to economics - spread of writing in Greece in 5th century brought shift from politics and community to economic individual. Economics based on communication.

23   Dangerous fiction of political entities as a result of interest in statistics,
      i.e. comparison between nations - collections of statistics with regard to
      national boundaries.

24   Epigram a half-truth expressed in such a way as to be annoying to those
      who believe the other half.

25   'Freedom of the press from government interference under the first
      amendment does not sanction repression of that freedom by private
      interests. ... Surely a command that the government itself shall not im-
      pede the free flow of ideas does not afford non-governmental combina-
      tions a refuge if they impose restraints upon that constitutionally guar-
      anteed freedom.'

26   'For the ear trieth words as the mouth tasteth meat' (Job 34:3).

27   'And every man has so inviolable a liberty to make words stand for
      what ideas he pleases that no one hath the power to make others have
      the same ideas in their minds that he has, when they use the same words
      he does' (Locke).

28   Importance in common law of stability 'stare decisio'. Also of elaborate
      debate in parliament and in procedure to enable steps to be taken well
      in advance and to make it possible to discount economic implications of
      legislation.

29   'In primitive thought the name and object named are associated in such
      wise that the one is regarded as part of the other. The imperfect separa-
      tion of words from things characterized Greek speculation in general'
      (Herbert Spencer).

30   Implications to rise of individualism of writing - sets individual apart in
      ability to write and to read writing, i.e. in Greece.

31   Common law 'that ancient collection of unwritten maxims and customs'
      (Blackstone).

32   'Language is not a device whereby knowledge already existing is com-
      municated, but an activity, prior to knowledge itself, without which
      knowledge could never come into existence' (p. 41).

33   Glanville Williams argues legal memory determined rule of seven years
      absence as presumption of death became ridiculous with writing - also
      rules as to precise times and amounts.

34 How far swing from priesthood to kingship in Babylonia part of weakness of priest and succumbing to various invasions of force under king leading to development of new religions – meant emphasis on priests among Jews resenting aggression? Restoration of emperor concept under Alexander and Rome – declining and leading to supremacy of church – again restoration of political power in Middle Ages and defeat of church or priests.

35 Significance of control over time exercised by religion in holidays – during Middle Ages interest of church in periods of truce – struggle with state insisting on more working days, i.e. iconoclastic controversy opposition to monasticism – right of individual to decide on disposal of time. Interest of churches in Sundays.

36 Tenacity of culture – Sumeria to Mongol invasions. Egyptian concept of kingship imposed on Hellenistic princes, Roman emperors whereas in Sumeria kingship restricted by religion – city state – limited power of kingship reflected in position of religion of Hebrews – constant struggle between concepts of Babylonia and Egypt. Duality in divinities reinforced by conflict of cultures – old deities driven underground and regarded as forces of evil – new deities given position – Apollo and earth goddess, i.e. male vs. female. Babylonian culture apparently provided place for deities of conquered because latter powerful but Persia apparently attempted to drive deities underground. Greek conquerors made peace with conquered and did not drive them underground but gave them feudal structure – retainers and followers. Christianity drove pagan deities underground.

37 Lord Beaverbrook (Nov. 12, 1950) claimed he had no use for [Edward VIII] Duke of Windsor but anxious to embarass Baldwin. Could have displaced Baldwin if King had stood firm. 'The cock wouldn't fight.' A curious attitude toward the Crown – willing to use it to suit journalistic purposes.

38 Dr Spooner claims Osler did great damage to medicine in Canada – text paid little attention to treatment – medical doctors pessimistic whereas surgeons more apt to be optimistic. Recent development in anti-biotics gave medicine a fresh start – escaped influence of textbook.

NOTES

6 Note on Emile Male, *Religious Art in France: XIIIth Century* (London, 1913), retitled in 1958 *The Gothic Image*

14   Martin was a prolific author, best known as the editor of the *New Statesman and Nation* from 1930 to 1960.

15   Note on Dean Inge, *Diary of a Dean* (London, 1950). W.H. Mallock (1849-1923) was a British novelist and political writer. Butler is possibly Henry Montagu Butler (1833-1910), master of Trinity College, Cambridge, from 1886 until his death.

19   N.S.B. Gras was a Canadian-born economist, contemporary to Innis, who taught at Harvard and wrote on the subject of business history. Innis is possibly referring to Gras's article, 'Types of Capitalism,' N.S.B. Gras, ed., *Facts and Factors in Economic History* (Cambridge, Mass., 1932).

21   Johann Fust (1400-66) together with Peter Schoeffer (see 28 / 70) founded the first commercially successful printing firm.

25   Note on U.S. *v.* Associated Press, Mr Justice Black 325 U.S. 20

32   Note on R.G. Collingwood, *The New Leviathan* (London, 1942)

33   G.L. Williams (b. 1911) is a leading British authority on English law.

38   E.T.C. Spooner (b. 1904) was a British professor of medicine. Sir William Osler (1849-1919) was a Canadian medical professor whose text *The Principles and Practice of Medicine* (1892) was highly influential over a long period.

26

Probably 1950. During much of 1950 Innis was preoccupied with his duties on the Royal Commission on Transportation. During the latter part of the year he became gravely ill but largely recovered by its end.

1   Exploitation of freedom in U.S. - religious freedom exploited, i.e. Brooks Adams, *Emancipation of Massachusetts* [Boston, 1887] freedom of expression of press and speech - guarantee of Bill of Rights. Search for truth and not the truth (Lecky).

2   Danger of influence of book on Germans and Japanese - translations and influence of Mahan.

3   Polanyi argues that man separated from stability of land and becoming concerned with industry and trade - necessity of substituting social legislation as basis of stability for land.

4   Modern history about four centuries old.

5   Toughness of Jewish religion result of persecution - impact on law - [American Supreme Court Justices] Cardozzo, Brandeis, Frankfurter - struggle of Jewish lawyers against Catholic judges in Ontario - aggressive political support of Jewish community in election of members - enthusiasm of religion.

6   Importance of teaching to politics - enthusiasm of students as politicians - held responsible for Noseworthy's election against Meighen - also Aberhart. Paid political workers of doubtful value compared to enthusiasm of religion. Liberals capitalize types of enthusiasm - Jewish appointment to Quebec bench by Abbot's influence.

7   State linked to political law - becomes in part a creature of writing (see MacIver.

8   Senator Fraser organized constituencies or sought out individuals for nomination when executives of ridings unable to find suitable candidates.

Necessity of finding candidates belonging to large numbers of organizations and consequently popular and with a prospect of support from organizations. Importance of getting good well-known popular men – explains number of sportsmen as members. Liberals recognize new hierarchies, i.e. sport to offset that of families, etc. of Conservatives. Son of general manager of railway from Picton to iron mines controlled by S.J. Ritchie interests – Cleveland – Edison, Ingersoll and others friends of Ritchie visiting railway. Picturesque figure settling difficulties of party – preventing independent candidates running and split nominations and securing nomination of suitable members. 'As useful as last year's birds nest.' From a rooster to a feather duster.

9 Oral tradition evident in attitude of church toward faith – Gnosticism fell into discard as combination of Greek and Hebrew thought and development of abstractions with symbols and emphasis on Word. Church seized on literature and added concrete personal elements to strengthen oral tradition – growth of hierarchy and possibilities of corruption – leading to return to writings or abstract in reformation. Gnosticism – constant extension of oral tradition – recent dogma on Virgin Mary. Break between written and oral – overemphasis on written leads to overemphasis on oral – lack of balance between two – problem of church and state with writing. Rise of business organization in relation to writing.

10 Problem of division in professions – general practice in medicine in contrast with specialization. Specialist develops techniques in contrast with general practitioners at expense of patient. Lack of co-operation between two groups. General practitioner a broker of specialists – decides for patient as to specialist best suited to needs. How far specialists develop new lines and build up monopolies – controlling entry of other specialists by examination? Apt to become racket at expense of public. Difficulties of development of medicine with dependence on oral diagnosis. Problem of reporting accurately by patient symptoms of disease or of stating what he thinks the doctor wants to know or what he may wish to conceal. With development of tests – temperature, pulse and the like, medicine in a position to make rapid strides.

11 Intense respect for human life attributed to Christianity probably brought from India where carried to greater lengths – consequent dislike of war in India compared with Christian countries.

12 Sexagesimal system – problem of arranging shifts of working days – 8 hours or 6 hours emphasis on shortening number of days rather than hours – forty hour week.

13 Painting Impressionism 1870 to about 1900 - Fauves (wild beasts) 1904-8. Cubists 1907-13. Dadaists (Bavaria) 1916. Surrealism 1922. Suggested that impact of idea of evolution led to rapid succession of schools and to disappearance of schools at present time. Painters with idea of evolution hastened to create new schools.

14 Impact of instrument on writing - wax tablet - Greek alphabet, pen on medieval writing - uncial, etc. Metallurgist made important contributions to printing alloys for metal - mint - engraving and gunstocks - engraving significance of metallurgy to print - impact of metal on knowledge - metallic age, machine industry. Introduction of printing spurred writers to fresh activity also painters - with defeat of writers printing sagged back - lack of initiative crucial developments at point of struggle between two media. High price of paper possibly favoured Gothic as type felt to take less space than roman - more words to page and fewer pages to book.

15 Cultural activity characteristic of courts, i.e. in period of tyrants in Athens - probably similar development politically in Florence, also in Paris, Vienna, and Moscow.

16 Significance of rise in photography to development of impressionistic painting in France - latter avoided detail as brought out by photograph and emphasized impression. Colour used in painting and eye compelled to do work of fusion whereas previously emphasis on mixing of colours by artist. Development of ideas in relation to impressionism - high point reached by Cezanne.

17 Cremation perhaps greater significance for family as ashes could be conserved in small space. Inhumation on the other hand significant to community - city state and necropolis. Importance of death to political institutions - use of sacred ground to strengthen power of church.

18 Emphasis on symbols of British sovereignty - use of Crown on highways - an indication of the penetration of American life - the greater the emphasis on form the greater the indication that the substance is inadequate - danger of intense interest in symbols - obscuring of basic factors.

19 Problem of minorities in following defeat in rebellion or civil war. Cohesion of force in war enables groups to continue and eventually to dominate in Civil War in England and defeat of puritans but persistence in Whig, Liberal, Labour tradition. In U.S. defeat of Democratic party or of south meant persistence and eventual success of Democratic party - able to dominate north - bipartisan foreign policy, etc. - Roosevelt and Truman. Danger to foreign policy - reliance on force and use of force to

prevail in domestic as well as foreign policy. In Canada suppression of
W.L. Mackenzie - reorganization of Liberal party under grandson
[Mackenzie King] to position of dominance. South Africa - defeat of
Boers but attempt at compromise under Smuts - eventual success of
Boers under Malan.

20   Tragedy of Germany - religious revolution but not a political revolu-
      tion; tragedy of U.S. - political revolution but not a religious revolution.
      Importance in England of revolution religious and political but problem
      of Tudors in delay of political revolution. In France revolution religious
      and political and hence more deeply rooted and continuation of uncer-
      tain combinations of elements, i.e. continuation of revolution in relig-
      ious and political terms. Russia - revolution similar to that of France -
      continuation of political revolution and weakening of religious institu-
      tions. Culture possibly a development at point of balance between
      religious and political intensities - France, Russia, England.

21   Cemeteries - interest in heroes, great men. Westminster Abbey reflects
      tenacity of nationalism - large municipal cemeteries break down control
      of church.

22   How far booksellers interested in magazines as means of advertising
      books, i.e. *Gentleman's Magazine* 1731 started partly to compete with
      Wilfords' Catalogue and *London Magazine* started 1732 by bookseller
      to carry Wilfords' notices of books - i.e. rise of magazine from book-
      seller's catalogue? Significance of advertising to improvements in com-
      munication - large-scale technological changes undertaken at a loss be-
      cause of advertising value of the change in itself and cumulative increase
      in business with advertising for the sake of association with change.
      Persistence of influence of early means of communication, i.e. use of
      capitals based on inscriptions in stone of Romans.

23   Importance of oral tradition in 19th century evident in accounts of
      clubs, meetings, gossip - reminiscent of Greevey, Hardmann, Milnes -
      familiarity with similar groups on the continent - Paris, Berlin. Signifi-
      cance in refusal of Tories to consider dealing with the press, i.e. difficul-
      ties of Henley as an editor and a Tory. Advantage to U.S. of having able
      visitors analyse and comment on society - De Tocqueville, Bryce, etc.
      De Tocqueville's artistic interest in political development in contrast
      with Anglo-Saxon or North American interest in economic development.

24   Oral tradition permits painters on vases to attempt to show several
      scenes at once but written tradition compels a concern with time and
      painters use scenes with fixed space and time. Dominance of scribe over
      painter corresponds in development with drama in fifth century using

scenes of fixed space and time. Drama, also dialogue, an attempt to find compromise between oral tradition and written tradition. Oral tradition depends on memory and use of repetition to give sense of time and continuity. Written tradition accentuates continuity and time. Later with papyrus roll at Alexandria - illustrations worked out in cycles to show time, i.e. balance of space and time. Illustrations in text assure continuity and strengthen text in papyrus roll. With parchment and use of columns with edge for codex, margins left for illustrations and commentaries. Development of miniatures and demand for space leads to separation of illustrations from text, i.e. collected at ends of manuscript or brought together. Large codex manuscripts Bible, Septuagint and Homer and demand for illustrations probably mean relying on papyrus rolls - illustrating conservative influence of Bible in perpetuating artistic design from papyrus to parchment. Ornamentalizing of book by Irish wiped out 3 dimension landscape illustration and adapting of ornament to two dimension writing. Antipathy of writing to perspective or space. Conflict between literature and other arts, i.e. weakening of sculpture or arts concerned with space. Oriental empires emphasizing capitals, architecture, space in contrast with Sumerians emphasizing time in writing. Impact of printing on other arts, i.e. those concerned with space.

25   Slowness in development of measurements for time. Writing limited [up] to Cicero's period because of power of oral tradition.

26   Company of stationers 1557 enabled Mary to exploit self-interest of printers in a monopoly - to respect her views and suppress competition of other opinions - early monopolies a device for authorities to exploit commercial activities of members. Within stationer companies - monopolies of certain book granted to individuals - especially serious works. Consequently new literature - lyrics and drama under Elizabeth - printed by small printers unable to obtain monopolies - pressure of small printers on new types of literature in opposition to monopoly of Crown - power of press to break through its own monopoly (?). Oral tradition of court weakened after Civil War and coming of Hanoverians - consequently literature got out of line, i.e. into hands of booksellers leading to deterioration of language under Johnson in 18th century.

27   Skill assumes that within a generation new innovations come in, i.e. scribes vs. printing machine attendants. Religious works advantageous - short, constant demand, quick turnover - significance to printing. Demand for highly elaborate descriptions parallel the demand for pictures and photographs. As reproduction by illustrations developed with cheap press new types of activities - emphasis on state weddings and funerals also rise of exhibitions which can be photographed or reproduced. Illustrations create the type of phenomenon which can best be illustrated. Enormous influence of illustration devices in creation of shows and exhibitions - indirect significance of photography.

28 Protests of French Canadians about inability to secure positions in upper brackets of civil service - telephone a symbol of status and very few telephones in name of French Canadians in civil service. This leads people in Quebec to become more nationalistic and to withdraw from interest in wider sphere.

29 Danger of lawyers placing reliance on meanings of words and abhorrence of possibility of going beyond obvious meanings - necessity of a fixed meaning over a long period.

30 Pride an essentially Christian vice with emphasis on individual and hence necessity of St Augustine emphasizing its significance in weakening religion and in weakening the state.

31 *Jim Farley's Story* (1948) gives illuminating account of decline of old machine tactics. Organization across country - routine appointment as Postmaster General - decline in influence with Roosevelt as latter became more powerful with radio - fought old guard over Supreme Court - attempted purge of democrats. Farley's stand for presidential nomination in opposition to third term extremely significant. Replaced by Hopkins who had 'never even attended a county meeting and wouldn't know how to get into one. Now here he is taking over a national convention. It's disgraceful' (Ickes on 1940 convention) (p. 297). Wallace as New Dealer as vice-president replacing Garner opposed to third term significant of break with old newspaper politics.

32 Emphasis on Bible reading in Early Christian church among Greeks explains concern of orthodox church in translations and development of nationalist literature - power of religion in east in relation to language. Contrast with west placing Creed above Scriptures and emphasizing apostolic order of bishops and apostolic rule of faith. Innocent III with power of church prohibiting reading in vernacular - Waldenses and Albigenses. Emphasis on Bible reading also supported monasticism 300 and 400. Protestants returning to Bible reading - Luther a monk. Parallels between England and Byzantine empire. Church of England, women rulers, influence of Greece on reformation.

33 Farrell argues movies and radio concerned with selling commodities - similar threat appearing with reprints - linking up with movies - large-scale reprint houses during war boom - control over magazines. Claims book the freest medium of writing but neglects commercial background of book.

34 Delphic Oracle an intelligence bureau giving information about colonies - oral tradition built up by Alcmaeonidae after expulsion by tyrants from Athens - secured support of Spartans particularly sympathetic to Delphi. Tyrants in Athens built up Sybilline books and cultural level to offset Delphi - probably influence felt with growth of writing in Athens.

35   Devices by which organizations becoming concerned with time mono-
      poly - celebrations of anniversaries, writing of histories, emphasis on
      architecture. Public relations and employee relations designed to
      strengthen continuity - possibility of certain types of organizations able
      to build up time monopoly at expense of those unable to emphasize
      time.

36   Virginia in 1717 protested against postal charges imposed by parliament -
      taxation without representation - first evidence of break linked to postal
      administration (p. 245).

37   Use of death to perpetuate family, i.e. tombstones, eulogies, cemeteries.
      Monarchies emphasize capitals or changing names of capitals - Lenin-
      grad, etc. Federal governments establishing capitals as means of empha-
      sizing continuity.

38   U.S. attacks on communism a device to make imperialism a matter of
      puritanical conscience. Penalty of American revolution in emphasizing
      animosity to maintain unity - dependence on animosity continued in
      Civil War. Difficulty of shifting from animosity toward England exploit-
      ed by Irish to friendship and need of emphasizing animosity toward
      Russia. Revolutions France, U.S., Russia destroy stabilizing elements.

39   Impact of movie industry on books - latter 'famoused up' and supported
      by movies to provide advance advertising by publishers. Tendency rein-
      forced by large scale book production and interest in marketing through
      large wholesalers and publishing houses - book of the month clubs, best
      sellers. Influence of periodicals on books especially during war - paper
      bound reprints sold on news stands or with periodicals ransacking of
      published books for entertainment industry. Development in trade
      books gives university press an opportunity to produce serious books
      for libraries. Trend of large-scale production and distribution evident in
      concentration of book sales in northeast - accentuating differences in
      cultural levels of different centres or regions in U.S.

40   Common law - constant adaptation of words to meet changing facts
      but with significant lag and moulding of facts to suit words. Roman
      laws - written less adaptable and moulding facts to writing.

41   Modern scholarship to some extent showing interrelation between
      highly specialized fields - necessary to break down specialization -
      room for synthesis between fields.

42   Calligraphers concerned with Roman script - printers followed in pro-
      ducing classics for humanists but market exhausted in 1472 in Italy and

printers turning to Gothic or books printed in Gothic, i.e. theology, medicine, law - finally turning to Roman after 1525 or in 16th century - reflected change in type of book - enormous implications of displacing generation of writers - skill tending to die out with people - depreciation through obsolescence in skill requires a generation in contrast with capital equipment. Impact of renaissance in classical books - rapid spread over Europe single culture and Latin read and written. Printing destroyed unified culture. Illustrated book abhorred by Renaissance and used for works in vernacular but humanists admitted ornamentation, i.e. Roman architectural devices - columns, arches, medal, also from Byzantium. Problem of illustration with printing - dependence on wood cuts. Complete revolution in culture with encroachment of printing - commercial in character moving from one type to another, exhausting most profitable markets and turning to others. Art of medieval manuscript in unity torn apart by printing. Query as to extent of commercialism - rise of publisher and trade mark rather than change in character of thought suggested by Goldschmidt - following Max Weber pattern - need for recognition of technical background or middle ground between Weber and Marx. Weber neglects technical aspects.

43   Contempt of court lawyers for other lawyers. Enormous significance of writing to development of law or rather significance of words and development of language - words must be subjected to interpretation in administration of justice and expected to mean the same thing to those concerned.

44   Excellence of Canadian commercial intelligence service result of late development of diplomatic service - early establishment meant escape from demands of latter.

45   Interest of French Canadians in culture, language, and tradition evident in nationalism a reflection of the continual interest in time, i.e. influence of religion and church.

46   Maine's 'status to contract' a description of a change from an emphasis on time to an emphasis on space.

47   Problem of South American countries related to dominance of church and control over time. In the west generally division between church and state a reflection of the break from a monopoly control over time to one over space.

48   Contrast with U.S. - abolition of appeals to Privy Council in Canada [1949] leads to greater emphasis in Canada on written constitution particularly with importance of civil rights in provinces.

49   Advantage of U.S. in international negotiations – emphasis of sport and game – in industry, commerce, etc. constant reference to team work and to infinite possibility for substitutability – ability to wear down opposition by team work. Practice in local industry of emphasizing game approach carried to international conferences. A separate team from U.S. to meet each nation and possibility of resources wearing down other participants. Small nations unable to provide numbers and ability to meet resources of U.S. in numerous committees. Futility of conferences in dominance of American delegates with large number of committees and sub-committees and overwhelming numbers of Americans with emphasis on finding formulae receiving general approval and avoiding minority reports. Attitude of common law lawyers – wearing down opponents by extending length of hearings and compelling weaker ones to withdraw. Also in case of hearings on religious questions tempers the fanaticism of religions – similar to army.

50   Decline in power of church with regard to time but retaining control over period after death – refusal of burial in sacred ground.

51   Problem of law – equipment, books in central areas with best lawyers paid by largest corporations and impetus to centralization – necessary to offset centralizing tendency of monopoly of knowledge in hands of experts, arguments of economists and appeal constantly to necessity of considering handicaps of outlying regions. Tendency in economics for best economists to come from richest countries – necessity of sociology to offset limitations of concentration on economics or of constant emphasis on national policy. Danger of logic in law and advantage of common law in recognizing necessity of constant adjustment – oral traditions. Changes in economics, i.e. Keynesianism, to offset danger of monopoly of knowledge in economics shown in depression. Problem of linking economics to law or checking danger of combination of law and economics – law in danger from dogmatism of economics. Possibility of political process offsetting dogmatism of law and economics – function of parliament. Statutes in themselves apt to become rigid.

52   'News is what a chap who doesn't care much about anything wants to read' (p. 69).

53   Monopoly of time under church in Middle Ages followed by monopoly of space under political organization. Interest in Virgin Mary in Middle Ages result of attempt of Franciscans to bridge gap with vernacular particularly in relation to women. Force against religion producing law, i.e. space against time.

Chinese language restricted possibility of continued control by invaders – emphasized literature rather than science. Chinese writing with brush meant slow artistic work compared with rapid block printing of Buddhist. Paper – emphasis on space – political organization in China. Mohammedans – iconoclastic controversy in east and crowning of Charlemagne in west compelled fusion of church and state but at expense of church in east and to advantage of church in west. Parallel Byzantine Empire and England – women on the throne. Iconoclastic controversy and destruction of monasteries. Sumerian city states followed by empire and polytheism.

NOTES

3   Note on K. Polanyi, *The Great Transformation* (New York and Toronto, 1944)

6   J.W. Noseworthy of the CCF defeated Arthur Meighen in the South York by-election in 1942. D.C. Abbot was a senior Liberal cabinet minister in the 1940s.

7   Note on R.M. MacIver, *The Modern State* (London, 1928)

8   Ritchie was an American businessman with interests in Canadian mines and railways who worked for commercial union with Canada during the presidency of Grover Cleveland. C.E. Ingersoll (1860-1932) was an American railway president.

9   Note on C.G.A. von Harnack, *Bible Reading in the Early Church*, trans. J.R. Wilkinson (New York, 1917). See also 26 / 32.

22   Note on C.L. Carlson, *The First Magazine: A History of The Gentleman's Magazine* (Providence, R.I., 1938)

23   Sir William Hardman (1828-90) was editor of the *Morning Post* and founder of the Primrose League. R.M. Milnes (Baron Houghton) (1809-85) had been a member of the 'Apostles' and was well connected with both literary and political men both in England and on the continent. W.E. Henley (1849-1903) edited several journals including the *National Observer* and the *New Review*.

24   Note on Kurt Weitzmann, *Illustrations in Roll and Codex: A Study of the Origin and Method of Text Illustration* (Princeton, 1947)

31   Note on J.A. Farley, *Jim Farley's Story: The Roosevelt Years* (New York, 1948)

32   Note on Harnack, *Bible Reading.* See 26 / 9.

33   Note on J.T. Farrell, *The Fate on Writing in America* (New York, 1946)

34   Note on P.F.S. Paulsen, *Delphi*, trans. G.C. Richards (London, 1921)

36   Note on A.F. Harlow, *Old Postbags* (New York,1928)

39   Note on W. Miller, *The Book Industry* (New York, 1949)

42   Note on E.P. Goldschmidt, *The Printed Book of the Renaissance* (Cambridge, 1950)

46   Reference to H.S. Maine, *Ancient Law* (London, 1906)

52   Taken from Evelyn Waugh's *Scoop: A Novel about Journalists* (London, 1948)

27

1951. Accompanied by his son Hugh, Innis went on a holiday to Europe in 1951 which took him to Ireland, Scotland, England, and France.

1 Chartres - beautiful stained glass - 12th and 13th centuries, very intricate stone carving. Gothic structure - unfortunate intrusion in one place of elaborate altar and numerous candles - also intrusion of flags reflecting encroachment of state. An unhappy cross of wood near the entrance of cathedral. Even the pipe organ seemed out of place and altogether too loud. The church particularly effective in supporting monopolies of dynasties, of power as linked to family as basis of aristocracy and monarchy but in conflict with army as source of power and demands on efficiency of administration.

2 Importance of French language to politics - contributes to numerous parties as they reflect need for precise expression. Fixed terms of election compel constant shifting of parties based on elected and explain to some extent constant renewal of parties. Rise of republics an attempt to destroy dynastic influence but throw necessity for organizing time on bureaucracy. Overcome patronage of family and marriage alliances but emphasize other types of organization in army with limited bureaucracy as in U.S.

3 Great advantage of giving flat increase for service - simplifies problems for consumer and stimulates waiters to sell and to make good impression for business.

4 Enormous contribution of monarchy and of Napoleon I and III to buildings and layout of Paris - support of Napoleon III to Haussmann and large-scale planning. Power of French culture to achieve great projects - Eiffel Tower - and yet remain intensely individualistic.

5 Nationalization of railways in England possibly not followed by full advantage of eliminating wastes of monopoly, i.e. high rates and good service via Folkestone or Dover and Calais and Boulogne exploit advantages of quick service - longer routes, i.e. Dieppe, etc., at lower rates

and greater length of time - a most effective device for exploiting luxury traffic between London and Paris.

6   College de France 1536 by Francis I to offset narrow theological interests of Sorbonne. How far legal separation of church and state an extension of state monopoly at expense of church, i.e. education and how far does it permit increased friction between time and space?

7   Diderot Encyclopedia - exhibition (July 2, 1951) Bibliothèque Nationale - illustrating difficulties of publication and tremendous controversy aroused with books and publications for and against, particularly by Jesuits - latter expelled after 1763. A great row against monopoly of knowledge of church especially Jesuits and for the organization of secular knowledge preceding revolution and undermining position of state and church - precursors of encyclopedia especially in technical field - in industry and arts. Sound of horse neighing at Madeleine typical of French contrasts. Extent to which encyclopedia may tear knowledge apart and pigeon-hole it in alphabetical boxes - necessity of constantly attempting a synthesis to offset influence of mechanization - possibly basis for emphasis on civilization as a whole.

8   Schumpeter claimed Mitchell wrote a book without formulating a question - Schumpeter's argument that perfect competition made for complete instability and that stability could be considered only in terms of monopoly.

9   Common law protection of monopolies compelled concentration on competition as a means of evading burden. Roman law emphasis on administration and planning with efficiency in transportation offsets costs of monopolies. Socialism inevitable with increasing costs of inefficiency of transportation as in London in contrast with Paris.

10 Conference between academic people - in Anglo-American historical [tradition] imply use of written papers of not high quality to maintain oral tradition. Similar conferences of academic administrators, but those less justified as papers not particularly significant. Problem of arranging conferences between scholars but again these not successful.

11 Disastrous effects of politics on character - Tawney a conscientious scholar compelled to defend policy of Socialist party as to rearmament - a necessity for vigorous opposition to communism - would object to appointment of communists on staffs of universities.

12 Chapelon - socialists the trustees of capitalism. Socialism and capitalism brought together by force or private enterprise in U.S. or army in U.S. -

rearmament essential to full employment in both socialist and capitalist countries. Perhaps socialists more dangerous from standpoint of armament and war than capitalism.

13 Writing official history bound to be one of omissions regarding details affecting lives of officers concerned - official history written too quickly and inevitably involves lying.

14 Flood lighting most effective on Gothic architecture.

15 Enormous importance of communications to state evident in provision for relays, roads, post office - subsidy to newspaper, i.e. significance in American revolution.

16 Lack of elevators - restrictions in height facilitated or compelled a spreading out of cities - horizontal transport instead of vertical transport explains vast area of London - also Paris - city developed before skyscrapers, early rail development accentuates spreading out of cities - monopoly of railway evident in prohibition of building's height above certain level - in London for example.

17 Importance of decline of worship of forest to growth of settlement and agriculture.

18 Problem of advertising in France possibly limited to policy of concessions - a certain metro station may be given to an advertiser and the same advertising appears on all the walls of the station - also on metro cars - the same product will be advertised in one car. How far does this make for inefficiency in advertising?

19 Simeon (French economist) largely responsible for disappearance of Cournot tradition in France according to Perroux.

20 Hard cover of books in English speaking world reflects influence of libraries whereas paper cover of French suggests practice of book reading and limited library development for readers with more limited newspaper expansion and cheaper paper for book purposes. Influence of libraries in English-speaking world checked development of pocket book and Penguins. Problem of French provincial weeklies necessity of respecting political and religious views and taking part as political and religious papers restrict circulation possibilities and in turn advertising. Emphasis on serials especially for winter season when subscriptions largest, emphasis on local news. Problem of emphasizing goodwill of newspaper staff possibly checks growth of unions in newspapers - similar to department stores.

21 Did very high profits of J.M. Dent and Son in 1926 lead to their subsidizing *Canadian Forum*?

22 Problem of labour in printing industry – reluctant to favour nationalization as it would involve bureaucratic dictatorship but favouring control
over press and preventing use of press to injure trade unions – background of Royal Commission report on press – state of division in labour
movement as to nationalization. 'Love your neighbour, yet pull not
down the hedge' (George Herbert).

23 Not until 1939 were births, deaths, and marriages replaced by principal
news in *Daily Telegraph* front page.

24 Printing followed calligraphy until latter part of 15th century in Italy
and after 17th century printing regarded as department of engraving except in Germany. Morison's 'Art of Printing' – slavish following of
manuscript in 15th century, i.e. monopoly of form. Special presses with
problems of royalties tend to emphasize classics in literature especially
for collectors. Significance of establishment of newspapers in spread of
price system and introducing stability to market, i.e. *Gloucester Journal*
(1722) prices from London. Taxes imposed on established paper may
be carried by advertisements or by a monopoly control over circulation
without difficulty particularly as threat of competition checked but effects of newspapers on price system checked. With removal of stamps a
large number of competitors may suddenly emerge and period of active
competition eventually followed by weeding out of papers and new
monopoly. How far does relative stability of information in price system cut down number of papers? Role of papers in establishment of
price system or of price systems in establishing newspapers.

25 Conventions of House of Commons – catching eye of speaker from
floor but not between benches – hence tendency to oration and probably use of Latin quotations. Pocket borough system possibly cause of
situation in which in England members can represent different constituencies whereas in France and U.S. members tend to represent region
with which they are familiar. Shift from king to prime minister meant
strength of party to select leader or strength of party to determine
representation.

26 Enormous increase in numbers of books by journalists in late twenties
and thirties – probably effect of war and continual impact of newspapers – see museum catalogues.

27 Impact of newspapers also in Encyclopedia Britannica and book club.
New journalism drove *Times* into book field and brought clash with

organized booksellers under net book agreement - *Times'* emphasis on printing Encyclopedia - defeat and falling into hands of Northcliffe, i.e. imperfect competition. Peerages, etc. of popular press result of need of advertising the press or part of phenomenon of journalism.

28 George III not Wellington said 'I know not what effect these troops may have upon the enemy ... '

29 Significance of political organization to economic organization, i.e. setting up of various trade bodies with representatives from trade and various committees. On continent administrative bodies copied more obviously by business.

30 Publisher interprets price or decides on price at which books will sell which determines character of requests to printer, i.e. publisher part of price system. Significance of paper cover and uncut pages in Europe - makes possible system of sending out books for sale or return to bookseller - English books affected by library.

31 Lecture on frontiers of Roman empire - Rhine because of extent of river which was deep, swift flowing and relatively free of ice in winter - a relatively inexpensive frontier. Troops about 300,000 in 28? legions.

32 Dutch dislike jury system as less fair than continental system with learned judge; also critical of English boast of love of animals and yet very fond of fox-hunting and shooting.

33 Academic life of London suffering from pressure of city - business, politics - divided with politics - conservative free enterprise, and pro-American socialist - latter violently anti-communist. Inability of academic individuals without roots in England to obtain objective approach. Ability to understand corruption of German academic life after seeing England. Abhorrence of communists a most unhealthy sign - fresh effective remarks of Chapelon as communist, France an American state, socialists trustees of capitalism. Indirect influence of Americans on other countries - Tawney appointed at suggestion of Winant to bring British embassy into closer relations with American public.

34 Dangerous effect of festival [Festival of Britain] on British - reinforcing their ego.

35 St Bartholomew the great near Smithfields market - oldest church - Norman architecture - rounded arches - Gothic later. In France lighter ironwork an indication of 17th century - ironwork heavier in 18th century and more elaborate. In 16th century red brick used on large scale as at St Germain in palace of Francis I and around Place des Vosges, formerly Place Royale.

36   Dependence on monarchy as in England meant vacillation in power to the advantage of parliament, i.e. Henry VIII with great power, Edward VI with limited power - dynastic limitations in time overcome by steady increase in power of parliament as a continuous body.

37   Was Lawson's attack on finance a prelude to prosecution under Hughes of insurance companies?

38   Use of sexagisimal system accompanied by development of exchange tables for consultation.

39   Large colleges at Cambridge - interest of royalty - Henry VII in Kings and Henry VIII in Trinity intended to be one of the largest and absorbed property formerly held by monastery - triumph of courts over monasteries meant increasing concern with writing influenced by oral tradition or subject to change in contrast with religious writing emphasizing continuity, i.e. scriptures. Kings using universities to offset church and monastery. Universities an indication of a concern with the oral tradition in teaching - strength of oral tradition at Oxford and Cambridge compared with London. London - able to appoint scholars who are not gentlemen.

40   Ely Cathedral - combination of Norman and Gothic but without skill of French at Chartres in stone sculpture - hence resort to painting on ceiling and to elaborate wood carving.

41   *Times Literary Supplement* gains reputation from late reviewing of learned journals - use of younger men with less interest in reputation but also an ambush to protect thinly disguised assassins.

42   Enormous significance of overhead costs in printing with an established plant easy to expand output at proportionately less cost, i.e. amount of type necessary less than increase in presses. With development of enormous prestige and power in press, i.e. Northcliffe, a tendency for other Napoleons to emerge and exploit their names, i.e. Horatio Bottomley. Danger of emphasis on great names and threat of influence lead to emergence of concept of trust, i.e. in *Times*. Probably explains decline in influence of Lords. War brought enhanced importance of newspapers.

43   Significance of printing laws in various colonies, i.e. encroachment of printing on oral tradition of common law of Great Britain, meant development of separate tradition but also establishment of printing plant with excess capacity and development of press and postmaster.

44   'Merry Wives of Windsor' – tremendous gusto of the age of Shakespeare
        – probably result of the temper of the time – after Spanish armada, com-
        parable to period after defeat of Persians in Greece – temper of age
        essential to production of drama.

45   Irish rebellion a reflection of influence of metropolitan growth of Dub-
        lin, and six counties – a reflection of the metropolitan power of Belfast.
        Population in Ireland almost stationary over long period – first slight
        increase in present year after long period of decline – urban develop-
        ment at expense of rural areas. Strong pagan tradition – belief in ban-
        shees also in ghosts – continuance of wake although effort of church to
        stamp it out because of drink. Proud of Joyce but reluctant to praise
        him. Influence of elevator – houses of Dublin and European cities limi-
        ted to 5 and 6 storeys in contrast with American apartments and hotels
        following use of elevator. Attempt to revive Erse – compulsory teaching
        – apt to produce illiterates in both languages.

46   Complaint that Roosevelt more effective with army than navy and left
        army experts greater freedom of decision. For Churchill's attitude to-
        ward experts see Sherwood (page 601).

47   [James] Joyce possibly developed break through English language by
        familiarity with Celtic or Erse or realization of significance of another
        language – also importance of clash between English and Roman Catho-
        lic and Celtics – nursery of literature. Canadian papers not bad enough
        though well on the way – too much catering to high-brow and assump-
        tion of intelligence. Dublin advantages in separation, i.e. prestige, income
        from embassies, escape from German bombing, and possibly heavy de-
        fence expenditures.

48   Sexagisimal system protects English and Irish from cash registers and
        slot machines but reliance on individual probably makes work slower –
        possibly less accurate.

49   Adam Smith first to purify concept of profit.

50   Renaissance – in part a result of fall of Constantinople – a reassertion of
        belief in empire in the west – ambition to recapture prestige.

51   Great division between Babylonia with emphasis on knowledge and
        Egypt with emphasis on religion, i.e. reference to immortality. History
        of west a conflict between two – political and religious.

52   Revolt against principle of what traffic will bear evident in nationaliza-
        tion and socialization and demand that equality be generally recognized
        contributes to problem of capital equipment – first-class passenger cars
        on British railways completely inadequate.

53 Glasgow largely dependent on thick brown sandstone - building of city without moving enormous quantities of heavy stone blocks, fairly easily cut - presumably soft - into long thing uniform slabs - quick to turn grey and leave drab appearance to city.

54 Importance of religion in shifting of emphasis on time by Puritans church in reformation - sudden transfer of interest from control over time by church to control over time by individual - made possible saving and escape from demands of Rome - basis of capitalism.

55 Importance of cathedral to music - gives effect not possible outside of buildings.

56 Intense pride of Scotland in Edinburgh - war memorial. Emphasis on literature - monument to Scott - also Dugald Stewart but Hume and Adam Smith neglected. Like Ireland Scotland largely escaped Roman empire but control from England by land more effective than by sea. Objection to nationalization and centralization in London evident of growth of Scottish nationalism. Enormous improvement in food within last two or three years probably more than offsets effects of higher prices. Tax structure emphasis on utility - heavy purchase tax on all luxuries and no purchase tax on utility goods, i.e. suits of clothing and so on. Importance of marriage as a device for solving problems of England and Scotland in royalty. Princess Margaret daughter of Henry VII wife of James [IV] of Scotland - grandmother of James VI and I of England.

57 English use of discarded luxuries - dining room of Olympia transferred to White Swan Hotel, Alnwick, when broken up. Viscount Ridley, land owner, moved one of Wembley buildings to Durham county as recreation for workers.

58 Railway bridges built across rivers on way to Edinburgh 1849-50.

59 Alnwick - seat of castle of Percys - largely intact - though numerous castles destroyed by Cromwell and others. Reformation accompanied by destruction of ecclesiastical buildings.

60 Holy Isle 1634 - apparently mission started by St Aidan from Iona - civilization returning from Ireland. Roman influence extended to England chiefly through ports - near mouths of rivers - York on Ouse. Roman wall ending at Newcastle - Chester - London - accessibility of England from continent via rivers left England exposed to invasions and with power to dominate.

61 Decline in control of Britain in India and far east means damming back of flow of administrative ability and possibly accentuates bureaucracy

in England - accompanied by centralization and by counter movement of regionalism. How far was this true of Roman Empire - retreat from outposts accompanied by increasing bureaucratic tendencies? Extent to which concentrated power of British propaganda effective, i.e. spread to U.S. and commonwealth, and how far enormous propaganda of vast areas such as U.S. can be resisted by Great Britain? Enormous importance of aristocratic hierarchy to industrial revolution - taking over of population trained to respect authority. France apparently had no such outlet as industrial revolution and political revolution a result.

62   Simplicity and efficiency of British railway systems - extent of rock ballast - bolts in ties to which cradles of rails attached - rails in cradles held by small blocks of wood or iron coil - these easily removed in case of replacing of rails. Small cars - spoked wheels - light equipment. Brakes applied automatically through bumpers - no complication of air brakes - latter used on passenger trains. Advantages of nationalization in railways - eliminating competition between separate companies at expense of convenience of passengers. Through-line York to Oxford compared with numerous changes Nottingham to Oxford in 1948.

63   'No one ever went broke underestimating the taste of the American public' (Mencken).

64   Colleges in Oxford admitted to university when they become completely self-governing and all other influences than that of teachers dropped, i.e. church, business, etc. - remain halls until meet requirements of university to become colleges. Effective drive for continuing oral tradition and continuity - oral tradition also evident in oral examinations. Danger of inbreeding of fellows or of conservative tendencies of education met in part by competition between colleges.

65   Tremendous emphasis on columns to celebrate Nelson and Wellington possibly a result of position of great figures and limited importance of press - difficult to think of interest in heroes extending to point of great columns of stone at present day - also Blenheim (Marlborough).

66   Long slow painful adjustment of political geography to demand of languages - emphasis on coherence of language and political boundaries developed in relation to it.

67   Unique position of executive in U.S. and tendency of power to collect in his hands explains to some extent the number of assassinations.

68   Enormous significance of David picture of Napoleon crowning himself - with Pope Pius VII in the Chair - undid the work of Constantine and

Charlemagne – belief of force – opened way to break between church and state – emphasized force and right of republic to create situation in which individual could reach highest position.

69 Interest in Keynes in biographical sketch of great [lovers?] Harrod contested seat as a conservative – wrote Keynes' life possibly with a view to restoring his liberal position and to prevent socialists claiming all his contributions.

70 J.A. Roebuck argued that high stamp tax implied a monopoly and limited purchasers to ruling few and consequently arguments appealing to the ruling few. Necessity of reducing stamp taxes to destroy monopoly.

71 Problem of accumulation of media – part of monopoly difficulty, i.e. stone – striking architectural buildings. Archives – sense of continuity – when did problem of conservation of media develop? Emphasis on micro-film – use of new methods of preservation – tendency to stress accumulation rather than synthesis. Struggle against burdensome accumulation of materials. Revolt against preservation – Shaw and others on cremation.

72 Once a policeman, never a gentleman – saying in England – habit of looking into other people's affairs difficult to overcome.

73 Stonehenge – probably built for religious purposes and use of stone reflects interest in time. How far did Romans suppress Druids (also Jews?) as means of killing oral tradition – see Salisbury handbook.

74 Socialism weakened by monopolistic encroachment of private enterprise, i.e. railways built up under private enterprise building up monopoly of territory – possibly accentuated by position of unions – difficulty of achieving economies essential to reamalgamation and danger of perpetuating limitations of private enterprise in interests of labour – steel possibly a duplicate of railways.

75 Enormous pressure of huge industrial and trading population on production of world especially through exchange control and trade agreements – regions producing consumption goods compelled to accept demands of large purchasers and regions other than dollar countries encouraged to produce increasing quantities of goods as substitutes for goods from dollar countries. Policy probably accentuates policy of U.S. in armaments as a device for maintaining employment in U.S. – labour drained into army or into industrial plants – also true of Canada – leads to emphasis on propaganda regarding isolationism.

76 Harvington Hall - manor house with moat and numerous hiding places so that priest could hide with all ceremonial paraphernalia during period of persecution of Catholics. Rigorous repression of Catholicism probably important in maintaining sense of ultimate unity but also providing base for non-conformists and tolerance of Anglicanism.

77 Enormous respect for authority in England - persistence of Victorian patriarch family - influence of aristocracy as a result of invasions in development of discipline - a basis of factory system. How far racial problem behind Labour government? Churchill's fine words probably source of annoyance to people who did the work and won the war.

78 Cemeteries gradually rise above surrounding territory with generations of interments.

79 Position of Labour in England partly determined by respect for authority incidental to several invasions - this provided background for industrial revolution - respect for hierarchical management. Geography also a very important factor in background of industrial revolution - great diversity of regions - topography, geography, climate compels specialization, i.e. breeds of animals, and makes large-scale control and uniformity impossible.

80 Brick houses an indication of cheaper supplies of coal or of industrial revolution - Georgian period. Stone, i.e. in Cotswold, stone shingles rural and pre-industrial.

81 Rick stones - mushroom shape to put under ricks and keep rats out.

82 Cultivation lines on the hills of the Isle of Man and elsewhere as a measure of the influence of development in Canada, Australia, and other regions, i.e. wool production in Australia means competition and moving out of people or abandoning upper fields of mountains and hills.

83 Relative lack of interest of democracy in arts - consequent reluctance to spend money on sculpture, painting and so on on public buildings - demos niggardly in its interest in the arts.

84 Narrow English roads suited to small English car - in possibility of passing each other. Types of cars suited to capital outlay in roads.

85 Manx motor races - amateur in September - professional in May - largely sponsored by Norton, manufacturers of motor cycles - pick individuals to run races and pick motor cycles - usually winning and enormous advertising value.

86   Latin alphabet spreading in Roman period to margins in form of og-
      hams of Druids and runes of Scandinavians or Norse - Bishop of Sodor
      and Man apparently established from Norway.

87   Heavy cost of immigation to Canada, i.e. in terms of illiteracy of imi-
      grants incidental to limitations of education - advantage of Scottish im-
      migration incidental to more adequate education facilities. Imperial
      problems incidental to mental attitude of illiterate immigrants.

88   We attempt to drown our real fears of the United States by shouting
      about imaginary fears of Russia. The United States steadily destroying
      the resisting powers of nationalism in Europe. Destroying freedom by
      shouting about its merits.

89   Heavy cost of cloth-bound library book - monopoly choking spread of
      information and consequently exploited by paper covered books.

90   Ecclesiastical profession emphasized oral tradition and legal profession
      writing, i.e. contrast Cody and Smith.

91   Effects of Colt revolvers on dictatorships, i.e. history of assassinations -
      influence on governments in U.S., Italy, also South American republics -
      also on industry, i.e. Frick - rise of protected government heads - secret
      service - Roosevelt, etc.

92   Shakespeare wrote in and for a group of players - later playwrights
      writing for reading or whoever wishes to play. How far writers handi-
      capped by writing, i.e. taking elaborate notes and using them as a stock-
      pile - Arnold Bennet, Sinclair Lewis - in contrast with writers con-
      cerned with direct and immediate impact of mind?

93   Technological jerkiness of mass production with disastrous effects on
      culture - monopolistic technological gaps - book and newspaper left
      way open to Penguins and pocket books - mass production - newspaper
      writers turning to pocket book writing or older books hammered into
      adaptable length and form for mass production purposes. Emphasis on
      subjects neglected by newspapers and library books - also in movies -
      concern with sudden impacts.

94   According to Johnson, Goldsmith never said a wise thing and never
      wrote a foolish thing, i.e. break between oral and written tradition -
      exacting demands of latter. How far did Boswell supplement Johnson's
      memory at period when latter affected by age? How old was Johnson
      at the time?

95 How far Jewish sentiment responsible for Nuremburg trials and their outcome?

96 Important for economists to travel extensively to acquire impressions not registered in books and to interview extensively. Economists like Prometheus bound between short- and long-term trends.

97 Significance of low fixed rents in Paris - Giraud pays $80 a year for apartment - possibly leads to high price of food - little building and little changing of residences - possibly explains subsidy to transportation and low price of Metro - need to travel long distances cheaply - possibly also low wages - stenographer 18,000 francs, average workman 27,000 francs monthly. Low fixed rents may explain strength of communism. Elected deputies in communist party pay salaries to party and receive average workingman's wages to check political careerists.

98 Tendency socialized railways France and England to exploit private enterprise in luxury travel - Thos. Cook reluctant to give access to tourists to 3rd class travellers [third class railway carriages], i.e. no reference to location tickets for seats - presumably these bought from railway agents but Cook's might notify people of them - excellent third-class cars enabling middle class to travel by them. Metro exploiting foreign traveller paying 22 francs for single ticket whereas French traveller familiar with system pays 150 francs for 10 rides. Food apparently cheaper in England possibly because rents lower in contrast with Paris - French meals roughly 500 francs or slightly less. English meals say 6/6 or $1.00 whereas French nearly $1.50. Consequently English able to build houses and limited housing development in Paris - population more stationary in size and emphasis on efficient system of transportation in and outside of Paris. French tourist industry explained by inflation, i.e. Paris taxi drivers insistent on tariffs and not on tips - English taxi drivers still robbers - French insistence on equality - percentage charge for service - English servility.

99 Have movies developed largely in relation to demand of women, i.e. as papers have turned to emphasize women's interest were newspapers primarily of interest to men and has consequent monopoly facilitated development of cinema for women? In article on Canada, U.S. - see St John Ervine - arguing the movies' attempt to be international made them stupid.

100 'Much of what is called progress has lain in the discovery of substitutes.'

101 Significance of interest in preservation of papers, i.e. destroying of paper records in public administration.

02 How far [Samuel] Johnson through work on dictionary of English words became obsessed with written tradition and influence of Latin and hence endangered English oral tradition? Absolute supremacy of parliament a reflection of power of oral tradition - steady encroachment of printing, i.e. Cromwellian regime - Milton's *Areopagitica* [1644] - American revolution, printing to control power of throne, i.e. act of settlement or to check encroachments on oral tradition.

03 Painting - shift from tempera to oil, Florence to Venice. Emphasis on colour in 19th century and escape from darker pictures in impressionism.

04 Savagery of cinema - necessity of features in which fighting occurs - knocking people down - settling of disputes by force rather than law - extra-legal characteristics.

05 Economics of institution of marriage - role in feudal rearrangements - accompanied by illegitimacy - bureaucracy and favouritism peculiar to courts - with puritanism more stable arrangement - see Westermarck, also article *Encyclopedia of Social Sciences*, 'Illegitimacy.' Property limiting size of families - France and elsewhere. Family versus joint stock company - floating family concerns. Beecham's pills apparently made joint stock company by catering to Sir Thomas Beecham's taste in port.

06 Technological jerkiness - mass production - adapting products of early technology to demand of later - giant books crowding type - small books - padding paper, etc.

07 Problem of language in modern Greece - literary classic language of aristocracy against demotic of people - newspapers in different writing - struggle between oral and written or printed tradition reflected in political parties. Voting dependent on membership in Greek orthodox church.

08 Economic or military consequences of the American constitution - gap between executive and legislative - emphasis on military presidents - Harrison - propaganda against communist impact - Great Britain Bevan's document. More austerity decline in purchase of Canadian goods.

09 Persistence in Egypt of monasticism, i.e. following Buddhism (?). Impact on western world, i.e. discipline of church, liturgy and ritual.

10 Significance of architecture to religion, i.e. emphasis on height - ziggurats in Sumeria, also pyramids in Egypt - height assumes necessity of

concentrating on one place – Parthenon – (temple?) emphasizes proportion – rectangular. Contrast with emphasis on vault in Rome – circle –
presumably in contrast with Greece – use of cement – collections of
people in circular amphitheatre – evident in stage in Greece. St Sophia
in Constantinople carried over Roman concept of administration to
church or use of vault and dome. Development in west – Gothic – rectangular – continued in parliament buildings in England – conflict with
dome in Italy – compromise in St Peter's – also St Paul's in London –
state emphasized dome in U.S. and in capital buildings of western provinces and elsewhere. Rectangular and emphasis on authority of a centre
or altar – dome an emphasis on assemblies – theatres, speeches, parliament.

111   Interest in poetry in Scotland and old world – monument to Burns and
to other poets reflects power of oral tradition – compared with lack of
interest in new world.

112   Long-run effects of first World War – break in structure – Russia; Germany – Hitler; U.S. – Roosevelt; G.B. – coalition – gold standard; Canada –
King, Hepburn, Aberhart, C.C.F. Age of violence.

113   Enormous significance of architecture to hierarchy – place of meeting
important in northern climates – hence restrictions of number in assembly meetings and emphasis on hierarchy or on means of selecting those
who could enter.

114   North of Ireland much more mountainous than south – relatively short
distance Belfast to Glasgow – less than an hour by plane – Belfast dominated by influence of Glasgow.

115   Radar greatly increases speed of boat with difficulties of fog – C.P.R.
steamships improve schedule – disappearance of ship's concert with
shorter passages. Hamburg line boats – traffic declined sharply with
persecution of Jews – offered to sell them to C.P.R. about 1937 to oper-
ate out of Quebec.

116   Full employment – enormous pressure on travelling facilities and on
capitalism in relation to luxury trades – old equipment inadequate and
necessity of government intervention and socialism – difficulty of getting hotel accommodations of modern type through cost of renovation.

117   Protestants with balance of power able to determine position of parties
under system of proportional representation – opposition to Costello by
Protestants who helped to elect him because of attempt to take Ireland
out of Commonwealth – Protestants refraining from voting helped De
Valera.

18   Support of universities to order of time, also aristocracy, hereditary in-
        stitutions emphasizing continuity, celebrations. Control over monopoly
        of knowledge exercised by range of universities throughout world –
        especially in building of libraries and more recently laboratories. Mono-
        polies of past built up to extend and control future – encroachments on
        future – revolutions a result of attempt to dominate future – freedom a
        result of attempt to keep channels open – disaster when means of keep-
        ing channels open becomes a monopoly.

19   Adam Smith – a product of political union – genius of British political
        rather than economical – bold imaginative strokes enabling Scottish to
        participate in British trade. Macfie holds that Adam Smith turned to
        develop economics because other branches of philosophy monopolized –
        law and philosophy.

20   Sex books – illustration of impact of mechanization on most intimate
        details – Havelock Ellis replaces phallic symbol but with less human
        results.

21   Predictions as to Landon election destroyed *Literary Digest* and estab-
        lished Gallup and Roper (p. 82). Roosevelt never mentioned opponents
        in political speeches as it gave them advertising and helped people to
        remember their names when voting. Alert to photography tried to have
        Hopkins near him when photographed (99). Shifting of enormous relief
        funds toward armament preparations in 1938 (101). War preparations in
        part a result of depression and need for employment. Even reputable
        journalists, i.e. Krock of *Times*, not above using imaginary conversations
        to damage politicians, i.e. Hopkins (102-3). Roosevelt preferred Roper
        to Gallup polls – limitation of polls evident in 'don't know' answers
        (105). Hopkins appointment Secretary of Commerce announced at
        Christmas time to avoid unfavourable comment (107) – Roosevelt's
        sense of timing. Quincy Howe – writing on British propaganda in World
        War I (130). Britain avoided appearance of propaganda of World War I
        in the U.S. in the Second World War (131). Enormous power of presi-
        dent, i.e. in intervening in war in spite of public opinion and congress –
        importance of military factor and of leadership by a single person – as
        in case of president – control over patronage and party. Wilkie a poor
        radio voice – 'the radio the supreme test for the presidential candidate'
        (184). The radio – Roosevelt's 'only means of full and free access to the
        people' (186). Newspaper publishers important in support of Wilkie
        (187). Wilkie's advisers largely amateurs. Early, a newspaperman,
        handled Roosevelt's relations with press with great skill for headlines.
        Bureau of Budget transferred from Treasury department to Roosevelt –
        gave him access to all activities of government. Every word in Roose-
        velt's speeches judged not by appearance in print but by effectiveness
        over radio. Problem of accurate timing in having exact number of words

and rate of delivery (217, 297). Claim that German and Japanese planned striking attacks at time of Roosevelt's speeches to offset effects. Churchill accustomed to speeches in parliament dictated speeches (261). Position of president in U.S. - compelled to use powers with wide discretion and to lead or force congress to accept them in contrast with Great Britain - coalition government with complete support of parliament and damping down of politics. Churchill turned out but Democratic party continued. Churchill and Roosevelt both in naval tradition. Contrast between American and British system of negotiation - latter relying on directives of cabinet. See also Keynes (361). Roosevelt very sensitive to religious views (384). Churchill dominated chief of staff more than Roosevelt (446). Hopkins extraordinary official position (457) similar to House with Wilson - points to power of president against State department. Far too great a gap between president and congress - Roosevelt widened gap between executive and legislative branches - hence the place of Hopkins (931-3) - particularly with development of use of radio. Tragedy of break between executive and legislative evident in death of Roosevelt and necessity of complete break in Cabinet with Truman's return - clash between lack of continuity and continuity of British and Russians. Hopkins never underrated radio audiences - friend of broadcasters (835).

122 Conditions of freedom - age, i.e. disappearance of older men with influence and authority and gradual realization of freedom.

123 How far bias of communication on monopoly centring about space and time contributes to progress or to advance as joining of monopolies may contribute to stability, i.e. Byzantine empire? Tenacity of empire in Persia possibly result of excellent pasturage for horses - alfalfa.

124 Movies - possibility of dividing time giving story from different angles or from viewpoint of different people - speeding up or slowing down. American movies emphasize violence - the hero slugging the villain and deteriorating whole atmosphere of stage - incidents which could not happen on stage and possibly with difficulty in English or continental movies - recognition of violence as a basis of justice. George Orwell's *Nineteen Eighty-Four* (London, 1949) - so horrible a reader can hardly finish it - reflects sensitivity of author to present conditions in English-speaking world. Concerned with problem by which democracy develops perpetuation or sense of time and solves problem of continuity or duration - continued anti-semitic - antagonism to Goldstein.

125 Significance of accumulation of historical knowledge by 19th century (p. 205-7). Hereditary autocracies short-lived compared to adoptive organization like Roman Church (211). Destruction of time. Poetry (English) - lack of rhymes in language determined history of English poetry.

126 Importance of theory in social sciences - time saving device giving social scientists time to engage in wider interests - Schumpeter in economic history.

127 Would it be possible in 1951 for Clarence Darrow to produce his 'Argument of Clarence Darrow in the case of the communist Labor party in the criminal court, Chicago' (Chicago, 1920)?

128 Teggart emphasizes importance of wars of defence to nationalism and bureaucracy - Egyptian wars against Hyksos - defence of Chinese - Schumpeter - imperialism based on offence - organization of militarism. Horse - basis of separate class - conservatism of nomads - professional soldiers and imperialism. How far does Marx consider time element? i.e. Schumpeter holds imperialism a product of past not present conditions of production.

129 Simmel - chapters on secrecy - writing destroys secret societies, i.e. oral tradition - protection by ritual and hierarchy. Problem of dictatorship that of destroying secret societies - developed techniques of discovery. Cabinet system in England based on secrecy - ease of securing of agreement and oral tradition. (This apparently also true in committees in House of Representatives.) Difficulties of U.N. or of arranging peace treaties so long as negotiations open to public press. Oral tradition of religion - struggle between Protestant and Roman Catholic - latter greater emphasis on oral tradition - problem of Protestants with emphasis on writing evident in constant divisions.

130 Monopolies fall of their own weight rather than being kept down by competition - entrepreneurial system a type of monopoly in itself. Emphasis on decadence rather than on activity of entrepreneurs - breakdown of administrative bureaucratic control - failure or inability to keep monopoly together the significant element rather than the activity of those concerned with competition - reverse theory of Schumpeter and of Cole - crucial point that in which profits and prospects of a new monopoly in evidence.

131 Problem of crossing class boundaries partly solved by illegitimacy - physical attraction - virility of progeny - William the conqueror, George Simpson and so on. Warfare as a device for singling out ablest individuals. 'The fair sex, who are the sovereigns of the empire of conversation' (Hume).

132 Significance of Jerome's translation of the Bible - provided basis for consistent copying and weakened position of classical tradition with its emphasis on stone and temples.

133   Free trade probably emerged in England as result of competition between ports and rotten borough system – ports competing for ablest representatives and those pressing for removal of restrictions to strengthen competitive advantages, i.e. John Gladstone with Canning and Huskisson.

134   Problem of breaking control of religion over space, i.e. sanctuaries, religious capitals, sanctified sites, i.e. St Paul as against St Peter, Methodist chapel, also St Andrew, Scotland. Salvation army – attempt of state to destroy control over space, i.e. separation of church and state. Importance of belief in immortality to army – stimulus to give up lives in battle. In Egypt belief preceded military expansion of empire, also among Druids and among Mohammedans. Attack of Lucretius – lack of imperial growth of Greece.

135   Triffin held difficulties of International Monetary Fund in part a result of American insistence on permanent membership of board in conflict with British demand that membership should be temporary and reflect changing views of country sending representatives – with permanent board in Washington only Americans changing representation.

136   Problem of representation in popular assembly at Rome after Italians enfranchised increased dominance of Romans and rise of demagogues supported by army. Possible influence of Greece, i.e. Plato's belief that philosopher king had wisdom to govern – weakening trend toward absolutism of Roman emperors.

137   'In politics nothing so uncertain as a sure thing' (Bob Ingersoll). 'Reading next to sleeping the best way to rest the mind' (Dooley). Enormous impact of Henry George on reform, i.e. Tom Johnson's fight in Cleveland for municipal ownership and free trade in Congress – strengthened by obsession of Republican (Mark Hanna) with national field – support of Democrats – Newton D. Baker, Frederick Howe. Scripps press strengthening municipal reform and opposing position of Associated Press in interest of monopoly and private enterprise. Enormous advantage to capitalist system and private enterprise. Cheap transportation in city – Cleveland advancing at expense of other Ohio towns – significant of Republic state.

138   Enormous importance of back list to publisher – sales without advertising – should provide backlog and bring profits to offset losses on books. Pressure of overhead costs of distribution leads to emphasis on agreements and associations of publishers – conservatism – keeping down numbers of books published, i.e. authors of books on publishing emphasizing difficulties of entering field, i.e. Michael Joseph.

139   Oral tradition among primitive peoples gives evangelical religions great advantage since they also have a large element of oral tradition. Oxford Movement a return of oral tradition of church - protest against influence of state - attempt to escape interference of state in England became a movement to separate church and state in papacy - latter lost temporal power and largely through Manning's influence adopted doctrine of papal infallibility.

140   High prices of books at first impression result of circulating libraries - involve limited individual sales - high prices accentuate libraries and limited sales produce remainders and cheap books at second hand. Penguins exploited high price of established titles and wide sale of remainders - able to publish their own books on basis of reputation - also assisted by limited housing space for private libraries and reduction in sale of clothbound bulky books. Influence of architecture on books - small houses limited room for private libraries and rise of Penguins. Impossible for radio to be critical in reviewing books.

141   Struggle between oral and written tradition accompanied by violence such as led to death of Tiberius Gracchus - as abuse reduced to writing it became effective - as a base for suits in the provision of evidence - empire meant emergence of measures to check attacks in writing and censorship. Oral tradition permitted abusive attacks, i.e. of Cicero.

142   British army as a base of reform - Blatchford got ideas of socialism from it. Cobbett got ideas of reform. Strength of radicalism in Saxon, i.e. Cobbett, Blatchford. Appeal to lower ranks free of classical intrusion - Labour party movement as supported by language - conflict of dialects in parliament press brought lower classes to surface in political change. Language cleared by Blatchford to reach underdeveloped minds - new approach to graduates of 1870 act - basis of socialism. Emphasis of Blatchford in *Clarion* on variety. John Burns on Blatchford - 'a yellow press scribe lying like a gas meter'. Blatchford - 'I can't speak but I can write' - reflects power of writing in lower classes. Rev. Philip Wicksteed converted Shaw to Jevonian criticism of Marx's theory of value.

143   Construction of monumental buildings in Rome to celebrate triumphs - Augustus after 29 B.C. building roads instead of buildings for the same purpose - a reflection of limited influence of writing, i.e. dominance of architecture - archives housed in it and golden age of Augustus meant dominance of writers by patronage. Accumulation of buildings meant turning to empire and bureaucracy.

NOTES

8	J.A. Schumpeter's (1883-1950) most famous book was *Capitalism, Socialism and Democracy* (1942). W.C. Mitchell (1874-1948) was an American economist who wrote widely, but is perhaps best known for his work on business cycles.
12	Marcel Chapelon (b. 1904) was a French communist editor and publisher.
19	Francois Perroux (b. 1903) taught political economy at the Collège de France.
24	Reference to Stanley Morison, *The Art of the Printer* (London, 1925)
33	R.H. Tawney (1880-1962), a distinguished British economic historian, was adviser to the British Embassy in Washington from 1941-42. J.G. Winant was American ambassador to the United Kingdom from 1941-46.
37	Lawson was possibly Ray Lawson, lieutenant-governor of Ontario from 1946 to 52. Hughes may have been P.J. Hughes, a Supreme Court Justice in New Brunswick.
42	Bottomley (1860-1933) was a controversial British journalist, financier, and member of parliament.
46	Note on R.E. Sherwood, *Roosevelt and Hopkins: An Intimate History* (New York, 1948). See also 27 / 121.
70	Roebuck (1801-1879) was a radical British member of parliament.
90	Sidney Smith succeeded Henry Cody as president of the University of Toronto.
91	H.C. Frick was engaged in a famous struggle with organized labour during the Holstead strike of 1893.
99	Note on Iris Barry, *Let's go to the Pictures* (London, 1926). For Ervine, see St John Ervine, *The Alleged Art of the Cinema* (Shrewsbury, 1934).
105	Note on E.A. Westermarck, *The History of Human Marriage* (New York, 1922), and Clark Vincent, 'Illegitimacy,' *International Encyclopedia of Social Sciences*, VII, 85-9
119	A.L. Macfie (b. 1898) taught political economy at the University of Glasgow from 1930-1958.
121	Note on R.F. Sherwood, *Roosevelt and Hopkins*. See also 26 / 46
125	Source not identified.
128	Possibly F.J. Teggart, *The Processes of History* (New Haven, 1918); also J.A. Schumpeter, *Imperialism and Social Class* (Oxford, 1951)
129	Not identified.
135	Robert Triffin (b. 1911) had been a senior employee of the International Monetary Fund.
137	Bob Ingersoll (1833-99) was active in Republican politics. H.S. Dooley (1871-1932) was a Democrat. Henry George (1839-1932) was a famous tax reformer. T.L. Johnson (1854-1911), mayor of Cleveland from 1901 to 1910, was an advocate of George's single tax. Mark Hanna (1837-1904) was a Republican senator from Ohio from 1897 to 1905. Newton D. Baker (1871-1937) was Secretary of War from 1917 to 1921. F.C. Howe (1867-1940) was active in municipal politics in Cleveland.
142	Robert Blatchford (1851-1943) was a British utopian socialist and journalist. Burns (1858-1943) was a labour leader and politician who rose to office in the Campbell-Bannerman administration. Wicksteed (1844-1927) lectured and wrote on a wide range of topics, including political economy.
143	Note on F.W. Shipley, *Agrippa's Building Activities in Rome* (St Louis, 1933)

28

1951

1   'Trade, sir, could not be managed by those who do manage it if it presented much difficulty' (Dr Johnson).

2   'The outstanding mark of an education is the ability of a person to hold his judgement in suspense in unsettled questions' (Newton D. Baker).

3   Music not the universal medium generally supposed - rather an index of a civilization - Spengler noted shift from unison to counterpoint as significant in west - importance of counterpoint to cathedrals. Shift from singing to use of instruments after 16th century - difficulty of understanding music as between periods with development of different instruments and between cultures - 22 notes of Indian music - 5 of chinese - incomprehensible to west.

4   Courlander - *Mightier than the Sword*, a powerful indictment of effects of journalism on journalist. Supreme individualism of journalism - Northcliffe found committees of political life repulsive and turned to journalism - sturggle between oral and written traditions - parliament or politics and new journalism. Significance of telephone to large newpaper - also large business organizations. 'A touch of brutality about journalism' (Leicester Harmsworth).

5   Oral tradition in Anglican liturgy apparently continued independently of continental liturgies - latter presumably made uniform by Charlemagne, i.e. Carolingian minuscule but Anglican regarded as purer and presumably not influenced by European - possibly by Eastern and German. Problem of Anglican church - imposing of printed prayer books on oral tradition of high Anglican clergy - with reform act an act in 1833 made Judicial Committee of Privy Council responsible for settling doctrinal disputes - probably contributed to Oxford tracts and to break of Newman and others. Gorham suit against Bishop Manning re: infant baptism in 1847 settled 1850 by Privy Council and Manning left church. Prayer book controversy settled by parliament - intended to adapt

prayer book to demands of oral tradition of high Anglicans. Maynooth College - defeat of Macaulay. Byzantine problem of relation of church to Rome - dissidents protesting against members of parliament including many other than members of Anglican church - necessity of preserving exclusiveness of oral tradition by Jews, Christians, Protestants, Anglicans - encroachment of writing - Sadducees, Christians. Importance of royal supremacy to empire. 'As it was in the beginning, is now and ever shall be, world without end' - reflects influence of time - conquest of church over death and eternity.

6   Difficulty of extending history or projecting bias of historian back to period in which a different type of bias inevitable. Creation of series of fictitious histories running in a flat line or plane uniform surface and difficulty of creating uneven surface adapted to periods of history with different types of bias.

7   Importance of oral tradition checked development of printing among Mohammedans. Did Chinese pictographs and complex writing seem to give scholars a basis of continuity and of constant selection of able individuals? Importance of priority of religion on political organization - religion earlier in Babylonia, dominated politics. Politics - earlier Roman empire dominated Byzantine empire though balance permitted dual relationship one influencing the other. British politics dominated Anglican church. Ireland most distant probably began with use of parchment and oral tradition. Writing was strongly entrenched and presumably favoured printing in Germany and England. Paper - restricted script. China - scholar administration - gap available for Buddhism - development of printing - alphabet - west - printing - wide dissemination - nationalism.

8   Translation implies adaptation of product of one culture to the peculiarities of another culture - papyrus to parchment, paper from China to Europe. Accentuates importance of cultural factors. How far writing makes possible retention of certain basic elements throughout history of civilization and thus introduces a relatively uniform element by which later civilizations become familiar with earlier civilizations and information in varied character passed from earliest to latest - in China with little change in script it can be passed on more or less intact? In regions where translation necessary modification develops and restricts borrowing over long period or adapts material borrowed making for greater efficiency.

9   'Popularity is the only insult that has not yet been offered to Mr. Whistler' (Oscar Wilde) (p. 99).

10 Mind affected by political hatred becomes conscious of its 'own passion, formulates, sees it, with an accuracy unknown to the same sort of mind fifty years ago' (p. 8). Political passions 'divinized realism' (27). Europe many less chances of civil wars and many more chances of national wars (28) – see Quetillet. 'Let us leave politics to the diplomats and the soldiers' (Goethe).

11 Emphasis on space – danger of geography or regionalism.

12 Most imminently civilizing effects of all works of art – self-examination to which every spectator is impelled by a representation of human beings which he feels to be true and solely occupied with truth – destroyed in novels and drama by emphasis on politics.

13 Chinese script restricted Buddhism in relation to writing and possibly compelled Buddhism to emphasize sculpture and charms – mass production – paper suited to mass production in China and in Europe (p. 53).

14 Initiative of printer – Charles Whittingham led to displacing of bulky volumes selling at big prices by handy duodecimos (p. 34). Possibility of approaching study of press from one price system, i.e. one cent on low price and relation to varying elements – circulation, size of paper, advertising, etc. Better paper with Fourdrinier, better press Stanhope, better ink and inking made possible work of Whittingham in using woodcuts and offsetting advantage of convenience of copper engraving. Woodcut – uneven pressure in contrast with copper – even pressure.

15 Incentive to arts connected with printing in extensive classical literature – i.e. Shakespeare – printers created classics.

16 'I spent Saturday taking a comma out of something I had written and I had to spend Sunday putting it in again' (Wilde).

17 Sorel infused class struggle of Marx with vitalistic élan of Bergson – proclaimed inevitability of revolution. Kohn – unrest of industrialism, science, democracy implied destruction of time (p. 50). Nationalism centred around barracks, socialism around factories (58) – each a symbol and model of teamwork and discipline (65).

18 One must not get so high up in the ivory tower as to be blinded by the glare from the ivory domes below.

19 Speed of print or of eye as compared with ear or oral tradition but elaborate training necessary to seize at a glance what has been written

as compared with listening. Persistence of lecture in handling more abstruse material and presumably being more effective and less final than in printed material – problem of technique of lecturing and adapting material to level of audiences.

20   Few 'rise above the vulgar level of the great' (Voltaire) – vulgar level of great enormously increased with printing and demand for biographies and autobiographies.

21   Importance of war in U.S. creating presidents – strengthening executive.

22   Ezra Pound constantly concerned with outgrowing of small groups and small periodicals or ahead of monopoly established by universal press. 'English is halfway between inflected languages and Chinese letters' (p. 303). Pound in face of cramping of literature went from U.S. to England and to France and Italy – England succumbed to control of W.H. Smith and Son. On the other hand a frontier product working back across civilization and releasing literature – Eliot, Joyce, Wyndham Lewis. Attack on monetary system because of control over publishing and swing to Social Credit. Revolt of the artist against the economic system – probably supported Keynes against bankers.

23   Strachey's interest in spacious character of Whig aristocracy in the 18th century and his contempt for the qualities of the Victorian period or following the reform act.

24   Problem of names in relation to time – i.e. papal names – also of kings. Louis in France, George, Edward, Henry, William in England.

25   G.V.F.'s [George Ferguson] story of telegrapher taking down story of Hatrack at time of censorship trial of *American Mercury* in Boston.

26   Cassell's suffering from competition of Harmsworths. Art of novel opposite that of short story – American more brilliant in letter (p. 38). John Cassell one of the first to sell tea in shilling packets – 1841 – printed tea labels to fight alcohol and became a publisher (50). Printed Bible and sold in penny parts – significance of Bible to printing and publishing. Savage reviewing continued in England from Addison and Pope to 1900. Arnold Bennett's reviewing put *Jew Süss* on the map in England and Europe. T.P. O'Connor could make books in M.A.P. (228). Sweden produces more books per head than any other country – Ireland a close runner-up (256).

27   Greatness comes to those who live long enough. Biographies largely a development of 19th century – following revival of interest in Greek – i.e. Plutarch. Autobiographies – St Augustine.

28   Influence of Philip Kerr on Lloyd George weakened reparations position
(p. 235). On position and problems of U.S. in Peace Treaty see Keynes
(238). Second World War 'unnecessary' (Churchill) (269). *Manchester
Guardian*, New York *World*, Baltimore *Sun* proposed Keynes represent
them in Disarmament Conference (307). Hubert Henderson - editor
Nation to 1929 (336).

29   Italian practice of castrating boys to make them good adult singers continued until Leo XIII in later part of 19th century - sacrifice individual
to ceremonial.

30   Acute demands for space in densely populated areas - need for land on
which to raise food - i.e. development of planning in England to avoid
building on fertile soil.

31   Extension of the power of the book over stone - i.e. conclusions drawn
from work of archeologists and contentions in higher criticism - but
probable that even flexibility of language not adequate to an understanding of civilization dependent on another medium, i.e. stone - or
has oral tradition remained sufficiently powerful to check impact of
writing? Story of Princeton graduate school with no one competent to
teach literary classics but with experts in epigraphy - extending work
beyond literary or oral tradition.

32   Enormous importance of long-range projects, i.e. in Canada - building
the C.P.R. - or in Paris, Haussmann - the need for a strong central power
to enable projects covering long periods to be carried out. Toronto sub-
way, planning Canberra, Ottawa, Washington capitals - importance of
municipality as base of credit or of large fortunes - Rockefeller Center
or strong central control - limitations of emphasis on private enterprise - danger of attraction of militarism. Pericles beautifying Athens
and emphasizing time previous to emphasis on militarism. Problem of
cities facing serious geographical difficulties - Amsterdam - Toronto
extension north. Significance of large-scale government control or central power in city planning.

33   Technology pressing on literature, i.e. architecture - Rondelet's book
[*Discours pour l'ouverture de cours de construction à l'école spéciale
d'architecture*] 1816 followed by encroachment of engineer on architect. Construction furnished new incentive to architecture for growth
(p. 148). Department store - effects of advertising - mass production -
French use of perforated buildings and light court in Bibliothèque Nationale - light for reading - developed in department store (176) - also
British Museum. Development of glass before electric light. Break between engineer and architect - Polytechnique and Beaux Arts in early
19th century - first healing of breach in Chicago office buildings in 80's -

significance of demands of administration in architecture - light and space - iron skeleton and great glass surfaces.

34 Importance of vices of individual being checked by other vices and need for law and government - check each other, i.e. economics. Mandeville, Smith, 18th century deism or importance of virtues of individuals - i.e. doing good and becoming basis of Christianity.

35 [U.S. Supreme Court Justice O.W.] Holmes's concept of deciding what people can do without getting into clutches of law.

36 Importance of U.S. restrictions on immigration - backing up of labour in countries of Europe - i.e. Italy - consequent unemployment and communism in Southern Italy. Importance of labour unions in U.S. checking immigration creating problems in European countries. Consequently labour turns to armament economy or to industry designed to check spread of communism. After defeat of other theories, i.e. fascism, which emerged to attempt the solution of unemployment created by U.S. immigration restrictions.

37 Names - chiefly of monarchs preserved - also in Roman church - names of popes following state tradition - names suggest breaking up of commercial organization and emphasis on individual - Christianity emphasis on name. How far novels written to be read aloud - did this stop in latter half of 19th century - i.e. Meredith, James, etc.? Dickens gave readings - period of lamp and family centre. Did handicraft period in printing coincide with reading aloud period and machine industry bring writing for reading?

38 Problem of biological factor in relation to administration - University of Toronto - control of Brebner in relation to small college followed by Fennell. Smith in relation to university following Cody. Gilley following Dunlop - change corresponding with age of retirement.

39 Oral tradition persisting in Roman Catholic church and to less extent in Protestant services, or in religious aspects of civilization - also in law but with tendency of writing and printing to weaken it. Transmission by teaching - spoken word - lecturing in university. Spread of written or printed tradition. Incredible reports in *New Yorker* of meetings in Truman's office and interview.

40 'A sheep in sheep's clothing' - Max Beerbohm on Sturge Moore.

41 Language as a factor in 18th century, i.e. Latin influence - [Samuel] Johnson checking possibility of revolution perhaps more than claim that

Wesley diverted energy from political channel. Enlargement of power of
state with financial policy – no longer capable of resisting power through
control over property – capacity of state to make available taxes by
which it supports itself – is this the essence of bureaucracy? Protection
of fundamental law of McIlwain disappears with extended powers of
state – control of state by military authorities in industrialism – particularly propaganda. Problem of approach to history as basis of history.
Belief in rationalism makes for rationalism. Belief in miracles affected
whole approach – escape by development of new medium, i.e. paper to
position of science – printing and paper new type of dissemination.

42   Sir Edward Morris member representing a constituency in St John's,
      Newfoundland, over long period – apparently became member of House
      of Lords – claimed to have held constituency by assiduous attendance
      at all funerals.

43   How far spread of Dionysus an attempt with wine to escape inhibitions
      of civilization – i.e. emergence of drama – catharsis escape from civiliza-
      tion? 'Death where is thy sting?' – typifying period in which death and
      monuments to dead no longer used to indicate importance of time.
      Divinity with death strengthening dynasties. Christianity also religion
      of Egyptians destroying monopoly of pyramids and of death. Periodic
      overcoming of death as reflected by religion or by temporal devices –
      significance of belief in immortality.

44   Significance of geometry to interest in space. Nationalism emphasizing
      space – i.e. capitals, architecture, sculpture. Imperial expansion emphasis
      on space with capital and communication. Problem of astronomy in
      relation to geometry – interest of state and in relation to time or calen-
      dar interest of religion. In Egypt national capital probably had astro-
      nomical and calendrical offices.

45   [Karl] Mannheim – *Ideology and Utopia* [London, 1936] – sociology of
      knowledge.

46   W.C. Mitchell types of economic theory.

47   Character of state as an economic factor – i.e. Russia swinging between
      Byzantine concept and western concept – with speeding up of Russian
      development to catch up with west implied necessity to concentrate on
      Byzantine approach. Importance of war to industrialism – jerky develop-
      ment of Russian industrial growth. Return to collectivism paralleling
      earlier serfdom in relation to state.

48   Walras (father and son) – contribution of family, i.e. Clark, Keynes –
      two generations in Walras and Clark.

49   Bérard law of isthmuses – easier to follow land than sea – importance of
      isthmus of Corinth to Athens – reversal of later tendency where sea
      easier than land.

50   Decline of influence of priesthood and religion in Athens – particularly
      evident with Pericles but followed by individuals with less pre-eminence
      competing among themselves, flattering public and neglecting interest
      of Athens – Cleon, Alcibiades – weakening of character of individuals –
      rise of trade and commerce centring around Piraeus.

51   J.W. Root built Montauk block using steel rather than stone foundation
      to save space – steel used in walls in Rookery – skyscraper era began
      (pp. 109-10). Louis Sullivan leader of secessionist movement in archi-
      tecture of Chicago's World's Fair [1893] (133). French cathedrals –
      highest reach of feudal ideal (151).

52   Dominance of architecture over sculpture – Egyptians emphasized relief
      for interior and Greeks statuary for exterior – need for foreshortening
      to suit demands of architecture favoured fast development of group
      statuary – broke law of frontality which had dominated sculpture. Fore-
      shortening meant development of movement or introducing function
      and time element to space element. Temples in themselves a concern
      with space to offset time influence of religion (F.H. Robinson).

53   Problem of United Nations in finding arbitrators of disputes since all
      become part of struggle and resolution impossible other than by force.

54   Military organization – phalanx of Spartans extended as basis of politi-
      cal organization – i.e. significance of space – epoch in Europe. Use of
      pay in Roman army followed by displacement of phalanx by manipular
      legion especially in Punic wars – also implied tax system or use of mon-
      ey or treasury. Apprensiments shifted land to notary in 312 B.C. (?)
      Religion used to influence politics – augurs to decide whether meetings
      to be held. Weakening of time and religion and oral tradition and rise of
      empire. With oral tradition political power assigned to king and council.
      Organization of assembly developed from army. Importance of industry
      to army recognized in political assembly based on organization of force
      in Rome. Individual voting probably suggested by orderly military array
      of comitia centuriata (p. 211). Act of pontifical college 472 regulating
      intercalary month inserted on bronze calendar (238). Significance of
      struggle over debt as a political factor – i.e. a result of the spread of the
      price system (313). After 219 B.C. restrictions on capital outlay for
      senators drove money into land – probably accentuated slavery system
      (336). Control over calendar 191 by pontiffs used to favour party (358).
      Control over land became problem of Gracchi reforms. See Mommsen
      C.I.C. 12, 203.

55 Creation of images or mirages in literature as guides as in discussion of Babylonia.

56 Concept of being in contrast with writing and emphasis on time or concept of becoming – geometry and arithmetic?

57 'Ambition is the cheapest of all human qualities' (p. 63). 'My Mercury book review department is terrible this month, fit for Scribner's, but I've been having so much trouble with one thing and another down here that it's a wonder I didn't shoot myself long ago or start writing for the *New Republic*' (H.L. Mencken). 'Readers of *Century* liked Beerbohm's stuff – always fetches school teachers ... our customers ... too sinful to be intrigued by literary sinfulness. The mere name of Beerbohm will not land them. They are hep to all the old magazine dodges and we can never fool them with gaudy names as Hearst does' (G.J. Nathan) (100).

58 Problem of printing in 18th century – influence of publisher – dividing manuscript among several printers and hence unable to secure uniform interest in fine printing because of need of haste.

59 Increase in number of subjects leading to matriculation recognizes stepping down of material in subjects – a fact recognized by textbook writers. Importance of avoiding pages of print to junior students – must be broken down into paragraphs, sentences and indents to avoid frightening them, i.e. also newspapers.

60 Possible importance of blindness in development of minstrel – unable to do usual work consequently concentrating on memory and recital – stories – how far do epics reflect lack of interest in colour and emphasis on music and sound?

61 Disappearance of developments designed to strengthen position of time. Even death no longer effective – i.e. Westminster Abbey or shrines of national interest – cemeteries.

62 Economic significance of extension of space inclusion of new diversities – uniformity of speech possible – also trade – mixture of races – hence political expansion probably followed by economic advantages – British Empire.

63 Significance of names in history of religion – importance of continuity and probably anonymity in history of Babylonia – beginning of names in Egypt but with reference to a place.

64   Pound anxious to have communists in Russia to take up [Major] Doug-
      las, i.e. as a phase of communism suited to countries already in higher
      state of technical development than their own. Douglas in technological
      phase, Communism in agricultural condition (p. 276). Pound attacking
      church of Rome - *Social Credit* March 20, 1936.

65   How far the oral tradition evident among Hebrews and Mohammedans
      responsible for opposition to images and iconoclastic controversy? - i.e.
      power of oral tradition evident in religion and especially in India. Prob-
      able interest in sculpture, limited interest in painting - latter became
      significant with discovery of perspective.

66   Significance of space to history, i.e. emergence of a great number of
      regional histories with little broad integration with that of other
      regions - influence of geography on history.

67   Selling of 'words' or mottoes to be framed. Northcliffe 'killed the pen-
      ny dreadful by the simple process of producing a ha'penny dreadfuller'
      (A.A. Milne). These cheaper papers developed rapidly after 1890. Lloyd
      George giving Northcliffe scoop on development of Roads Bill in 1909 -
      beginnings of attempt to dominate press (p. 88). *Ideal Home Exhibition*
      1908 emphasized *Daily Mail* as home paper - attracted advertisers of
      products for home - concentration on women as purchasers (99). Power
      secret - to time hardest blows when authority in confusion. Press direc-
      ted to strong opposition and to creation of discord in government when
      it can show effects of power most effectively - how far does radio check
      this? 'Kitchener's incompetence ... killed Asquith' (Bonar Law) (113).
      Children's features to strengthen circulation in short and long run - i.e.
      after children grew up. Serial stories attractive to women (116). Births,
      marriages, deaths - advertisements on front pages of *Times* most impor-
      tant news (125). Northcliffe complained of dominance of business other
      than newspaper but neglected his own interest in newspaper as most
      dominant of all. Northcliffe checked political bribery in raising wages of
      journalists. Emphasis on children's features as well as women. Resort to
      best sellers to learn preferences of readers for features - influence of
      book on newspapers Oxford Gazette 1655 - first to break from book
      format with double columns and a rule (33). *Daily Telegraph* - educa-
      tional paper (36). Press a vested interest in strong opposition in Parlia-
      ment as basis of freedom (34). Northcliffe on use of names - Lloyd
      George not L. George - Winston Churchill not W (58). 'A very intimate
      practical knowledge of a subject hampers a journalist'. His job 'to use
      the expert ... with a one tract mind' (59). 'Never be long winded with
      outdoor publicity, especially when it's mobile' (69). Serial story one of
      most successful in holding readers.

68   The curse of federalism - inability to solve problem of regionalism leads
       to concentration on war. Greece a possible exception with money spent
       on cultural development of Athens rather than power. War to some ex-
       tent becomes an instrument to secure centralization of federalism.

69   Savage attitude of Germany towards negroes in abhorrence of colour -
       comparable to that of Southern U.S.

70   Peter Schoeffer a calligrapher in Paris.

71   Telegraphs and telephones weakened position of correspondence -
       letters in particular.

72   Theatre world in awe of the press (p. 52). *Vogue* led field of high fash-
       ion with Hearst's *Harper's Bazaar* second. For interviewing on the air
       actors the dullest people (231). A man didn't know as much as God but
       he knew as much as God knew at his age (244).

73   Discipline, cogency of reasoning, thinking probably inseparable from
       writing. Science, i.e. extension of writing in symbols, tends to destroy
       speculative thought by widening expression.

74   Conservative character of printing - improvement in 19th century print-
       ing result of interest of scholars and publishers and not printers. In 18th
       century printing developed under publisher's printers - in early 19th
       century printers separated from publishers.

75   Tendency for occupations to develop hierarchy in relation to 'dirty
       work' and for upper brackets to lift themselves into administration -
       reflects power of writing in paper industry to lift individuals in upper
       brackets out of dirty work of different stages and to form bureaucracy -
       i.e. Veblen's pecuniary and industrial. In universities importance of
       evading scholarship and becoming an administrator.

76   Possibility of collecting information on religious revivals.

77   Humour - closeness to spoken word - the medium by which interest is
       best developed in U.S., i.e. bridged gap between oral and written tradi-
       tion and west and east.

78   Overwhelming importance of printing in cultural life of first immigrants
       and of North America - especially the United States. Check of printers
       on size of editions - removed with increased mechanization and conse-
       quent flooding of market. Extent to which printing overwhelmed public

evident in feelings of limitation – i.e. retreat to unconscious – Bryson intuitive, Freud subconscious. In novels emphasis on new territory beyond the prudery line – D.H. Lawrence, emphasis on unconscious in Joyce.

79   Possibility of printing with relentless pressure leading to revolution – building of libraries of works of past and adjustment to new demands. But probably in French revolution – salons' oral tradition facilitated effectiveness in small groups more than encyclopedia. Power of oral tradition evident in Revolution – orientation of Mirabeau, Danton and others.

80   Check of court tradition in Charles II – emergence of blend in Addison and Steele.

81   History with seams of space and time – not seamless. Egypt – space and time – oral tradition – ultimate success of time on religion – problem of empire. Separation of space and time in west – balance in east. Monopoly of space in west with paper – mechanization – mechanization of space. Paper penetrated west by Mohammedism and by trade and undermined parchment and Christianity.

82   Widely disseminated system of communication – writing and printing makes it possible for individual to develop belief in individual and hence to give energetic drive to society in contrast with limited system, i.e. pyramids which limits possibility of belief in individual and emphasizes belief in society.

83   Remains of a culture apt to be the writing of the conquered with a consequent bias.

84   Does parchment imply a land civilization and papyrus one based on sea? Emphasis on permanence of material linked to problem of time, i.e. stone. Separation of problems of space and time and escape from absolutism – i.e. Egyptian monuments, Versailles, etc. Egypt space – Old Kingdom – pyramids followed by time – priesthood – Middle Kingdom.

85   Struggle over holidays – fast days – saint days – extent to which church able to control time and how far monopoly of time in feast days led to economic inefficiency and in turn monopoly of time of state – shorter hours, shorter weeks? Problem of time in whole problem of interest theory – development of probability – insurance, etc. – conflict of pecuniary interest in time and industrial interest in place.

86 Tremendous handicap of print and writing. Turn to science an escape from sacred scriptures. Veblen argues science emerges when dualism of knowledge in animism and matter of fact generalization converge. Veblen's early essay on *Critique of Judgement* argues that *Critique of Pure Reason* had notion of strict determinism according to natural law and *Critique of Practical Reason* had notion of 'freedom in the person', mediation between the two indispensable to free activity. Veblen argued inductive reasoning necessary to mediate between theoretical knowledge and moral action, but Kant did not link *Critique of Judgement* with inductive reasoning.

87 'The inmates of a house infested with fleas are not to be envied.'

88 Emphasis on water in Egypt and Mesopotamia as substratum may explain Thales' belief in water.

89 Importance of music to Jews in psalms – taken over by Christians – oral tradition.

90 Monotheism and terrific glare necessitates intervention of intermediaries – Christianity, Mohammedism, Protestantism – need for umbrella – return to less intervention in Puritanism, Protestantism, Mohammedism – relation to iconoclastic controversy.

91 See Montaigne (chapter on Conversation) [*Essays*, Bk. III, ch. VIII] apparently point reached at while it was necessary to take interest in conversation – see also Bacon – oral tradition in Montaigne conversing with reader. Importance of salons, i.e. women at courts in developing oral tradition. Descartes destroying monopoly of scholastics or reflecting power of printed word over written word, also La Bruyère, *Les Caractères* [Paris, 1688] chapter on society and conversation.

92 Solution of problem of trinity unable to save Egypt and east from Mohammedism.

93 Technology of communication making for constant disturbance and shift in balance between faith and reason.

94 Tragedy of collapse of Germany that of loss of civilization based on books – attack on west from North America via newspaper. Salvation through abandoning concept of state, i.e. in France and Italy – possibly means of offsetting influence of church but also because custodians of earlier civilizations – importance of saving Paris.

95   Difficulty of borrowing between cultures with vested interest in printing.

96   Chinese ideograph developed through fairs into half-phonetic half-
       ideograph with rhyming – apparently basis of literature 1000-700 B.C.
       Drift of phonetics from words or lack of adaptability of words in con-
       trast with alphabet meant continuation of short terse written language
       and great variety of spoken languages. Literature becomes written
       rather than oral. But continuity of written languages resists influence of
       time whereas with alphabet adapted to sound script drifts with sound
       and it becomes necessary to study other languages as well as one's own
       at earlier date. Poetry apt to flourish at periods before writing crystal-
       lizes or influences language. Basic English apt to destroy poetry – alpha-
       bet tends to destroy continuity – imposes penalties of translation. Im-
       plication of flexible language to social and political institutions – empha-
       sis on change.

97   Significance of death, i.e. tombstones, monuments, inscriptions throw
       light on life of period or on attitude toward death – enormous bias of
       archaeology as influenced by study of cemeteries – beginning with
       pyramids – escape from death by extending influence in papyrus – belief
       in immortality – use of monuments to show power and continuation of
       dynasties – political continuity strengthened by devices to emphasize
       control over time vested interest in immortality channel of control over
       entrance – significance to politics. Creation of saints – struggle for con-
       trol over time between church and state.

98   Jack Cade 'the first thing we do, let's hang the lawyers' (p. 126). A lie
       'an abomination in the sight of the Lord but a very present help in
       every time of trouble' (127). Prominence of country lawyers in public
       affairs – boys choosing profession above average intellectual endowment.
       Law requires assiduous study – trains men in debating, keeps them con-
       stantly in public eye (135). Conventions should be in halls with seating
       capacity limited to 3000, 1000 delegates, 1000 reporters, 1000 alter-
       nates and for visitors, or be abolished and presidential and vice-presiden-
       tial nominations made by primary elections – no possibility of delibera-
       tions with 15-20,000 (140). U.S. par excellence the land of orators
       (189). Age of oratory gone (347). Joint discussion for foes and friends
       but stump speeches with audience of political friends gave little oppor-
       tunity for proselytizing (356). Two-thirds rule of Democratic conven-
       tion device by which pro-slavery men secured friendly presidential can-
       didates for a quarter of a century. Since they controlled over a third the
       two-thirds rule used (405) – nominated Van Buren, Cass, Pierce, Buch-
       anan – rule defeated Clark in 1912 – Bryan refused to support Clark as
       long as New York vote was for him (413). Rise of convention raised
       problem of rules and slavery domination. Clark defeated as machine

man from west but from book obvious that Wilson a better choice. Monopoly of Republican power culminated in Cannonism and break of Republicans prior to 1912. Principle of cheap money broke Democratic party under Cleveland in 1893. Divided west from south and gave Bryan opportunity and precluded tariff as chief southern item from occupying crucial place after Cleveland elected – Cleveland's eastern financial interests destroyed Democratic party.

99 Balloon frame – cheap nails 1828-1850 thin studs, unskilled labour instead of exacting mortar and tenon. Danger of literary architectural education evident in destruction of principles of Chicago school (p. 314). Painter showed way to architecture in Europe – cubist, space, time development after 1910. Rational geometrical versus irrational and organic methods of mastering environment. Country outside the city – Versailles, Industrialism – squares in London, Haussmann's rue corridor in Paris after 1850. Cubist painting and destruction of perspective – enlarging of space – emergence of slab surface – bridges, Rockefeller Center. Separation of residential, traffic, pedestrians, i.e. breakdown of perspective – ferroconcrete and glass. Height and greenery. Does this involve wiping out of time, i.e. fixed character in relation to perspective – emphasis on speed?

.00 Children of the blind bard – reciters – emphasis on blindness and on ear-hearing. Also Latin reading of mass by priests (p.447). Episcopalian chain of tradition in apostolic succession – writing introduced to protect and establish property rights. Writing itself permitted copyright.

.01 English of north look to south, i.e. to French – Germans isolated with difficulties of language. Neglect of significance of communication to changes in thought.

.02 Man did not even possess the idea of freedom in communities of antiquity.

.03 Descartes reflected influence of printing press as did Bacon in breaking up time.

.04 Physician cannot dissect a patient in order to make a diagnosis. [Kant] *Critique of Judgement* (1790) (p. 170) a decisive break in asserting autonomy and methodological independence of biology without giving up connection with mathematical physics – prior to Kant physics based on biology according to Aristotle but Descartes demanded a universal mathematics to include all problems and phenomenon of biology. *Critique of Judgement* to prove no antinomy whatsoever between two forms of order (1) to refer phenomenon to universal dynamic principle of causality and (2) to regard phenomenon from point of view of purpose and to organize and arrange them accordingly. Kant rejected solutions of both Aristotle and Spinoza - i.e. biology and mathematics. Principle of formal purposiveness and Kant's conclusions as to adaptation of nature to our judgement - in formal purposiveness the logician of Linnaeus' descriptive science. Conquest of historical world one of great achievements of enlightenment (217).

105   The fundamental corruption of the commercial spirit - increasing influence of commercialism in C.N.R. being made over in image of C.P.R. English aristocracy reinforcement against commercialism and consequently possibility of socialism in England in contrast with U.S. Press given freedom in U.S. accentuates commercialism - importance of law in offsetting commercial influence. Effect of commercial spirit on attitude of lawyers and other professions.

106   History of theatre an attempt to give effective expression to oral tradition - restrictions of print in criticisms writing for public, struggle with church, of theatre - Voltaire, Shaw.

107   Printing an enormous impetus to reading and accentuating division between reading and writing consequently raising problems of heresy. The Middle Ages becoming brighter as the modern age becomes darker. In 17th century books widely advertised in almanacks.

108   Northcliffe insistence on employing young people - businesses grow old rapidly (p. 138). Great emphasis of Northcliffe on keeping in touch with common man - newspapers exploited contact with vernacular but at appreciable cost - use of spies and informers (148). Northcliffe 'lack of character' (199). Wrench young, enthusiastic, success with postcards - absorption of business and of Wrench by Amalgamated Press - absorbed in *Daily Mail* - Imperial Press Conference 1909 (225). Northcliffe becoming obsessed with power 1909 - allowing his name to appear in his papers (225). Wrench converted at funeral ceremony of Edward VII to empire (235). Problem of newspapers producing unstable character - built up to great levels and starting movements. Wrench - oversees *Daily Mail* - English Speaking Union. [Sir Norman] Angell *Great Illusion*, W.T. Stead.

109   Isadora Duncan began in Chicago early 90's - magic touch gave vigorous push to weary and stuffy formalized art - brought dancing back to the stage - significance of Chicago skyscrapers (p. 195). W.B. Griffin - Chicago architect won prize for Canberra plan (210). Few poets accomplished musicians. Music possibly less close and intimate than architecture, sculpture, painting - but poets must have knowledge of metre.

Architecture and poetry basic – other arts more or less lack essential stimulus – music and drama from poetry (209). Radical artists – revolt against 19th century realism – disgust with camera, outrage over superficial smoothness covering up the weakness of structure (215). Obsession of visual – reading – neglect of oral or poetry (242). Imagists contemporaries of post-impressionists and futurists but nothing in common with them (297). Sense of freedom from time limits and space limited – sense of sudden growth – experienced in greatest works of art – sudden liberation (298). Is great art the indication of a proper balance between space and time – bias of communication reduced? Imagists destroyed Victorian weakness and excess, repetitions, clichés, archaic formalities of diction and techniques (302). Importance of capital in giving authority in arts – Paris, London (328). 'Times when religion seems to me the greatest curse in human history, the first cause of wars, of persecutions, tortures, of ethical confusions and errors, the enemy of reason, of tolerance, of courtesy' (451).

10   Effectiveness of actors in formal plays, i.e. Shakespeare.

11   Significance of holiday celebrations as an indication of the role of the state and the church. Increasing importance of first of the year as a holiday for example in France. Celebration of Christmas an indication of power of church. Possibility of study on holidays as an introduction of a shift of control between church and state.

12   Lytton Strachey on Macaulay's style – 'with its metallic exactness and its fatal efficiency, was certainly one of the most remarkable products of the industrial revolution'.

13   Walt Disney the only artist existing in a world of his own creation without tradition or snobbism. Printing and publication of musical scores leads visual conception to become confused with oral execution (215). Music – definite vibrations in time. Neglect of form a neglect of time – Sibelius important as from margin of Finland. Gap between Beethoven and Sibelius – spread of romanticism and impact of African and Mongolian music in Spain and Russia weakened classical tradition.

14   Galbraith – literacy of English Kings in medieval period – seal preceding writing, i.e. a symbol accompanying oral tradition – change in government reflected by change in literacy of kings – use of seal related to literacy. Importance of period in which people become accustomed to ideas reflected in writing before learning to read and write – problem of shift from oral to written tradition of enormous difficulty.

28

115 Limited effectiveness of Spanish church in new world possibly a result of rigid organization in Spain and of strength of cultural organization of Indians, i.e. reversal of Mexico to communism and weak character of church. Limitations of marriage as a device for increasing territory as contrasted with Mohammedans and polygamy - consequent recognition of divorce and expedients of Henry VIII.

NOTES

4   Note on Alphonse Courlander, *Mightier than the Sword* (London, 1912)
5   G.C. Gorham (1787-1857) won his case in the Judicial Committee of the Privy Council for institution with the Church of England after it was refused him because of his Calvinist views on baptismal regeneration. Maynooth College refers to the large Roman Catholic seminary. T.B. Macaulay (1800-59) was a leading British historian. The Sadducees were a Jewish sect at the time of Christ which insisted on the obligation of the traditional oral law.
9   Note on J.A.M. Whistler, *The Gentle Art of Making Enemies* (New York, 1934)
10 Not identified
13 Not identified
14 Note on Arthur Warren, *The Charles Whittinghams, Printers* (New York, 1896)
17 Note on Hans Kohn, *The Twentieth Century: A Mid-way Account of the Western World* (New York, 1949)
22 Note on Ezra Pound, *The Letters of Ezra Pound, 1907-1941*, ed. D.D. Paige (New York, 1950).
25 George Victor Ferguson, Innis's close friend and confidant, was editor of the *Winnipeg Free Press* and later of the Montreal *Star*. Innis drew heavily on Ferguson for insights and gossip about both journalism and politics. Ferguson published a biography of J.W. Dafoe in 1948.
26 Note on Sir Walter Newman Flower, *Just As It Happened* (London, 1950). John Cassell (1817-65) entered publishing to supply instructional material to the working classes. Arnold Bennett's attack on *Jew Süss* made the work famous. T.P. O'Connor (1848-1929) was a British journalist and politician.
28 Note on R.F. Harrod, *The Life of John Maynard Keynes* (London, 1951). Kerr was Lloyd George's private secretary.
32 The Baron de Haussmann (1809-1891) was responsible for modernizing Paris during the Second Empire.
33 Note on Siegfried Giedon, *Space, Time and Architecture: The Growth of a New Tradition* (Cambridge, Mass., 1941)
38 A.B. Fennell was registrar of the University of Toronto in the thirties and forties. Sidney Smith was Henry Cody's successor as president. James Gilley and William Dunlop both held senior positions in the University of Toronto's extension department.
41 C.H. McIlwain of Harvard was author of *Constitutionalism: Ancient and Modern* (Ithaca, N.Y., 1940).
46 See 29 / 11.
49 Possibly note on Victor Bérard, *British Imperialism and Commercial Supremacy* (New York, 1906)

51	Note on Harriet Monroe, *A Poet's Life* (New York, 1938). Root (1850-91) was an American architect of the Chicago school and a pioneer of skyscraper architecture. See also 28 / 109.
52	Not identified.
54	Note on G.W. Botsford, *The Roman Assemblies from their Origins to the end of the Republic* (New York, 1909). C.I.C. is possibly a reference to Mommsen's edition of the *Corpus Iuris Civilis*.
57	Note on *The Intimate Notebooks of George Jean Nathan* (New York, 1931). Nathan was an American writer, an associate and collaborator with H.L. Mencken.
64	Note on *The Letters of Ezra Pound*. See 28 / 22.
67	Note on Tom Clarke, *Northcliffe in History* (London, 1950). See also 29 / 1.
70	Schoeffer (1425-1502) was an early German printer.
72	Note on Ilka Chase, *Past Imperfect* (London, 1943)
75	Possibly note on Henry Hughes.
78	Possibly a reference to Lyman Bryson (1888-1958) who wrote on science, philosophy, and religion
86	Note on Thorstein Veblen, 'Kant's Critique of Judgement,' *Essays in Our Changing Order*, ed. L. Ardzrooni; first published in the *Journal of Speculative Philosophy*, vol. XVIII (July, 1884)
98	Note on Champ Clark, *My Quarter Century of American Politics*, vol. II (New York, 1920)
99	Note on Giedon, *Space, Time and Architecture*. See 28 / 33.
100	Identified by Innis as a work by (Solomon?) Gandz
104	See 28 / 86
108	Note on Sir J.E.L. Wrench, *Uphill: The First Stage in a Strenuous Life* (London, 1934)
109	Note on Monroe, *A Poet's Life*. See 28 / 51.
113	Note on Constance Lambert, *Music Ho! A Study of Music in Decline* (London, 1937)
114	Note on V.H. Galbraith, *The Literacy of the Medieval English Kings* (London, 1936). See also 29 / 42.

29

1951 / 52. In 1951 Innis was elected President of the American Economic Association. He had completed correcting the proofs of *Changing Concepts of Times* and was still working on his Presidential Address when he died in November 1952.

1 'Advertisements are news' (Northcliffe). 'The discovery of advertising was bound ultimately to revolutionize the Press by changing the balance of power from the directly political to the directly commercial.' 'Women are the holders of the domestic purse strings ... men buy what women tell them to' (Northcliffe) (p. 149). Northcliffe destroyed hegemony of editorial department with pretensions of interest in public welfare. Did this become basis of welfare state? - public could no longer feel newspaper interested in them and turned to political party - short-run view of newspapers, i.e. emphasis on consumption goods - hence war becomes essential to give full employment to producers industries - possibly greater tendency under nationalization than otherwise. Co-operation of all departments of newspaper in production and control. 'If it's flattery to show the man-in-the-street his own importance, then we are flatterers' (Northcliffe). 'We don't direct the ordinary man's opinion, we reflect it' (Northcliffe) (153). Use of spies inside and outside to keep him informed of details - how far essential to large organization? Weather 'Britisher's greatest talking point' (181). 'Every extension of franchise renders more powerful the newspaper and less powerful the politician' (Northcliffe) (187).

2 'The ass is a noble animal but when infuriated they will not do so.'

3 Massacre of communists by Thiers in Paris and destruction of possibility of reform as an explanation of discipline of Communist party.

4 'If I told all I know not a man who read it would henceforward leave for war' (Clemenceau). 'I doubt if any object is worth the horrors of war. It may be that your only object should be - using an English phrase which may displease you - 'Peace at any price.'

5   Problem of dramatic criticism - press 'don't be afraid of slating 'em'
     meant that criticism of play or actors brought talk and circulation but
     unfair treatment of drama (p. 253); or on the other hand if actors com-
     plained newspapers followed policy of Delane. 'The real fact is that
     these matters are of too small importance to become subjects of discus-
     sion' (254). [W.S.] Gilbert a despot - left no scope for acting. 'People
     are becoming less and less disposed to patronize entertainments de-
     manding thoughtful attention from the spectator' (267). Attack of
     Thompson, 'Dangle', on entrenched monopoly of London's West End
     managers - may have helped in development of provincial theatres.
     Chief hope of British drama in repertory companies and growth of ama-
     teur societies (270-1). Revolution in theatre essential to socialism and
     labour's success, i.e. oral tradition. Actor managers keep centre of stage
     to themselves - from Kean to Tree (277).

6   Oldest London bookshop - exploited position of British museum as
     buyers of old rare books - continuity maintained by apprenticeship less
     than by family suggesting importance of skill and of training. How far
     was oral tradition significant in apprenticeship or as a basis of apprentice-
     ship and guild system especially in printing and bookselling industries? -
     destroyed by writing and printing of instructions.

7   Shakespearian audience - enormous importance of an ear-trained audi-
     ence in contrast with modern eye-trained audience - difficulties of
     theatre with printing - emphasis on memory and on time.

8   Continuity of English prose in works of piety from pre-conquest to
     post-conquest period - developed by R.W. Chambers.

9   Goidelic or Q Celts as Helvetii migrated westward from Switzerland and
     invaded Ireland - making language Q and dividing whole Celtic language
     into unintelligible languages P and Q - Celts and weakening Celtic lang-
     uage in face of English. Divisions of oral tradition follow emphasis on
     force, i.e. changes of language - survival in oral tradition a reflection of
     success of force and ability to dominate conquered language unless
     protected by religion.

10   Newspaper offices 'fact faking factories'. Significance of sport - Hulton
     started with single sheet of racing news to meet demands of sporting
     north (p. 41). 'Men who live and die without a name are the chief
     heroes in the sacred list of fame' (Swift). Sport as basis of socialism -
     Blatchford and Thompson on sports papers - style close to public -
     informality of *Clarion's* style - sporting journalism broke through early
     journalism and emphasizing socialism evaded abstractions of Marx -

socialism a product of English vernacular and of journalism and education act. Class war more definite and acute between propriety and im-
propriety than between property and poverty - Northcliffe exploited
writing of Blatchford and Thompson. Objection of labour to Thompson
consorting with Northcliffe and latter using him. Success of state ownership in Germany of mines a precedent for England. Blatchford 'More
like an old Tory squire than a modern journalist' (Northcliffe).

11 Lecture notes on types of economic theory as delivered by Professor
Wesley C. Mitchell argues that important economic theorists those very
deeply concerned in problems of period - but this probably a reflection
of Mitchell's bias of present period - economics 'a series of dealings with
current problems of outstanding importance' (p. 5).

12 Juxtaposition of oral and written law and importance of oral tradition
in Rome with dislike of statutes demanded great emphasis on interpretation (p. 82). Dislike of legislation, i.e. written law, meant development
of judge-made law. Detailed minutiae of early writing a reflection of the
precision of verbal formula and the oral tradition - a device for protecting rights under oral tradition - followed by dangers of rigidity in written law hampering justice. Oral tradition linked in courts with *dies fasti*
[days when business can be transacted], i.e. *legis actiones* [oral and cus-
tomary proceedings] accompanied by declines in number of days in
which courts could be held - probably hastened *formulae* [a document
which replaced *legis actiones*] not limited except in cases where it took
over *legis actiones* to *dies fasti* - writing probably developed under pressure of court work and oral tradition.

13 Gladstone's campaign against 'them Bulgarian atrosites.' 'Equality of
educational opportunity is more essential to social justice than equality
of fortune - and more easy of attainment' (p. 39).

14 Problem of 18th century - an attempt of printers to escape slavery to
booksellers - hastened development of newspapers - periodical printing
first step in emancipation - Strahan 1771, Richardson. Could this be
developed in emphasis on pecuniary versus industrial? In 18th century
unrestricted competition - small number of large presses and pressmen
with small presses exploited by book-sellers - situation favoured compilations and division between large presses and booksellers. Do compositors favour small type and small books and printing masters larger
type and larger books? Does size of books indicate relative position of
compositor to printer? (p. 23) Prestige to *True Briton* and *Craftsman*
with aristocracy's concern with political journalism. Wharton, Boling-
broke. Large and expensive books published in period of 1725. Domestic production of paper and type followed by standardization of book-

making. Printing became trade rather than profession – but where printers enslaved to booksellers before 1750 they had recognized presses after 1750. How far large government contracts gave printers backlog and relative independence, i.e. Richardson? (254) 'The Tyranny of Booksellers' (265).

15   Primogeniture for king established in England only in 13th century but general rule in Normandy (p. 97). England acquired by conquest and kingship elective (98). Normans adopted ruler-worship in England as it had travelled from Byzantium to west (4). Heraldry to distinguish men with faces covered in armour developed in 12th century (24). Writing in England in 12th century with small population accompanied by minutiae of detail especially in direction covering cultivation of land (42). England – sheep-raising country provided exports for wool and parchment for growth of administration. Cistercians contributed to expansion of sheep farming (84). Crusades brought windmill and black rat to Europe (95). Feud and private castle made for anarchy in 12th century (150). Struggle in England between church and king. Clergy brought by Normans – arrogant treatment of native clergy and native customs – a factor in later opposition to Rome. New monastic orders part of European organizations increased power of papacy (184) – papacy favoured York as independent see and King insisted on supremacy of Canterbury – papacy (divide and rule). Cistercians (1098) spread rapidly with puritanical emphasis in England especially after St Bernard joined them (187). Anarchy of Stephen's reign – soldiers plundered land and endowed monasteries – rapid growth of latter. Becket a product of the struggle between law and clergy – 3rd clause Constitution of Clarendon giving right to try criminous clergy opposed by Becket and papacy chiefly because a custom put in writing – law and writing vs. church and customs (206-7). Shock of Becket's murder (214). Did lax discipline and loose morals of English clergy explain absence of heresy and orthodoxy? (230).

16   'The Pulpit was the cradle of English prose' (p. 253).

17   Magna Carta developed in part as a result of demand by barons that they should not be expected to fight abroad, i.e. an emphasis on space or land.

18   Problem of conflict between periods emphasizing offensive or defensive in military strategy and periods emphasizing time and space – periods emphasizing time will be favourable to defensive and space offensive.

19   Galbraith argues that writing developed with government and reflected type of government.

20   'One may derive art from life but not from art' (Jean Cocteau).

21   Narrative and music, i.e. time and oral tradition. Picture with narrative element unpleasing because trying to present time by cutting a section through it in space. Industrial revolution - large buildings - effects of architecture on music. Art must be parochial in the beginning to become cosmopolitan in the end (George Moore). Nationalism rather than romanticism destroyed classical tradition.

22   Imperialism of Great Britain based on aristocratic background - administrative efficiency of appointment of foreign service in contrast with U.S. - artistic interest in bringing regions to self-government - U.S. opposition to aristocratic - second-rate appointments to foreign service.

23   Heaton argues that austere character of cathedral and inability to get warm emotional feeling from pipe organs an important factor in explaining place of chapel with music and especially singing. Cathedrals adapted to choral singing but ceremony discouraged communal singing.

24   C. Reinold Noyes formerly St Paul graduate of Yale under Sumner took on family business - sold out at time of slump 1929 for cash retired - at Johns Hopkins with Dunlop to locate physical basis of ego or vanity - the third of Sumner's drives, i.e. hunger and sex. Dissatisfied with textbook economics from business - wrote *Economic Man* [1948] - attempt to provide physiological basis - chairman of National Bureau of Economic Research - an illustration of manner in which core of hard subject attacked - from Yale rather than Harvard - sociology rather than economics - business rather than abstract approach.

25   Catholic church regards greatest enemy not communism but degospelized humanism of the United States. Emphasis on church or on gospel - emphasis on latter brings revolution and on church stability, i.e. oral versus written tradition.

26   Danger of imposing economic system emerging from industrial society to societies essentially agricultural - giving PhDs to Chinese and other students, i.e. language. Western system basis of PhD unsatisfactory to all concerned. Approach to limitations of economics - fur trade - fashions, fishing, industry - religion.

27   A town is never the same after it has been subjected to an anthropological survey. Social behaviour a term used to separate history from psychology, social psychology - impact of this on foundations. Need for some action on part of universities to protect themselves from foundations' prostitution. Need for rules of game by which social sciences or universities attach new sources or potential sources of funds.

28   Economics essentially à democratic subject and difficulty of getting co-
operation with hierarchical subjects – bias of subject of economics
against leadership – study of economics of foundation grants to various
social science subjects – oligopolistic competition – problem of working
out projects of a size which will appeal to foundations – problem of
foundations in resources available for allocation – small grants are too
expensive. Technological basis of research grants, i.e. significance of
steel – Carnegie – of oil – Rockefeller and of automobiles – Ford – unsatisfactory character of technological impact on learning, i.e. social
sciences – also reflection of government – agricultural pressure, labour,
etc.

29   Representatives of undeveloped, 'have not' countries take an objective
view of problem – colleagues becoming corrupted and neglecting economic analysis – problem of priesthood – reason the slave of the passions
or of the wishes of foundations and government grants – latter more
serious. Government grants – importance of science – skill and importance of architecture and laboratories – weakness of social sciences and
humanities. Problem of manipulation of stupidity to impress sources of
funds. Problem of suppression of leaders as device for increasing widespread interest – danger of charisma on the one hand and of priesthood
on the other.

30   Significance of Orphicism – influence on Pythagoreans and Plato and in
turn on eastern religions, i.e. Mithraism, Isis, Christianity, Judaism compelling them to conform to Greek ideas. Reality of Plato had inferior
imitation in nouns and verbs – reason for Plato's rejection of poets –
Plato appealing from oral tradition – developing philosophy in terms of
ideas, i.e. result of prose and writing (p. 88 – Goodenough seems to give
wrong interpretation). Oral and religion versus law and written tradition.
Allegory to link written and oral tradition, i.e. Jewish and Greek. Elasticity of thought incidental to mingling of oral and written tradition of
Jews, i.e. Philo. Translation of Pentateuch to Greek probably changed
conceptions of God (237). Philo attempting to free law of Jews from
religion or to emphasize oral as contrasted with written tradition. Allegory a device to bring together various religions. Put off corruptible to
put on incorruptible one of earliest Orphic motifs carried on in Hellenistic Judaism through Philo. Oral tradition – liturgy absorbs other oral
traditions based on writing. Written law to check tendency toward pan-
theism and polytheism – given by God. Mysteries saved oral tradition in
face of written. Greeks opposed mutilation and hence circumcision
thus emphasizing ritual.

31   Did development of military wind bands weaken grand orchestra and
lead to development of annual exhibitions, sea side resorts, public parks?

32   Did crowning of Matilda 1068 with Laudes by which English King had absolutely equal rights and status with Emperor and King of France follow development in Byzantine empire (p. 31)? Inability of Norman kings to play off York against Canterbury - their position was strengthened (41). Normans changed coronation ceremony to reflect element of hierarchy in society in contrast with Teutons. Ceremonial in the oral tradition in a land of feudalism - recognition of members of court at coronation gave validity to rights - particularly important to a land conquered by king - in France Capetian kings after 1200 no longer filled court offices and avoided pressure from feudatories in court (66-7). Significance of canonization of King Edward in 1161 and of Louis IX at end of 13th century as contrasted with failure of Emperor to secure canonization for Charlemagne. Dynasties of England, i.e. Henry I, and France, given special position (123) - ability of kings to work miracles - King's evil in England and France put church at disadvantage (133). Migrations favoured monarchical principle and consanguinity as basis of selection (142). Principle of division of inheritance disappeared as idea of state came to be considered as separate from private law (144). Dynasty versus election, i.e. time versus space - king and parliament - time and space - weakening of church as time element. Emphasis of France on male descendants and exclusion of daughters - meant foreigner could not become king. Teutonic ideas regarded law as a whole without distinction between private and public law, i.e. oral tradition (161). Beginnings of charters in 1101 (Henry I) to supplement coronation oath, i.e. intrusion of written tradition. At coronation of Edward II parliament distinguished between Crown and person of King.

33   'Makes a practice of observing the most recent customs' (Kai Lung).

34   English literature raided for movie plots.

35   'Am at Wolverhampton where ought I to be?' [G.K.] Chesterton's telegram to his wife.

36   'The House of Commons hates a lawyer' (Charles Masterman).

37   Emotions of a mule accepted as an entry to the Derby: 'loving it all, and only wishing I felt more at home in it'.

38   Story of Brodrick, Warden of Merton. Gladstone - 'Brodrick, won't you speak to me?' Brodrick - 'Gladstone, when you can tell me that you have repented in all sincerity of your flagitious conduct in the matter of Ireland, our relations may be what they formerly were.' F.H. Bradley regarding the Warden's injured hand: 'I expect he's been trying to hold his tongue'. Brodrick suggested that a student choose 'that career in which imposture was likely to be most serviceable'.

39   No proof of Bacon having taken bribes. 'We know only that he said he
     did.'

40   'A war cannot be carried out without atrocity stories for the home mar-
     ket' (p. 164). T. Roosevelt systematically rid name of all association
     with aristocratic refinement - F.D.R. profited by this (198). Handling of
     Irish question broke Liberal party, i.e. raised to height interest in sensa-
     tionalism - F.E. Smith and Lord Hugh Cecil howling down Asquith in
     House of Lords debate. Liberals created distrust by 'long display of
     fumbling insincerity' (205). Intense religious hatred in Ireland - 'prac-
     tice of religion ... the consecration of hatred' (206) penetrated English
     life. In election of 1910 'Black Bread' linked to protection - campaign
     held Germans up to contempt as consumers of Black Bread due to pro-
     tection - accompanied by Blatchford's letters had serious effects on
     German opinion (209-11). Hatred the strongest motive in political life
     (Ellen Wilkinson). Book trade claims public not interested in stories
     about newspaper life - possibly belief that journalists too specialized
     (218). 'What Anglo-Saxons call a Foreword, but gentlemen a Preface'
     (Hilaire Belloc) (219). Did *News* suffer from Cadbury ownership and
     insistence of Quakers on principle? Hardness of nonconformists not
     adapted to new journalism - Lehmann and Herbert Paul left *News*
     (224-6). Journalism stepping stone in civil service. Herbert Paul and
     Vaughan Nash - latter with Campbell-Bannerman (226-7). In England
     Revolution without the 'R.' Bentley clinging to office with teeth and
     toenails. Printers trade union enormously powerful in London (240).
     Kaiser showed too much favour to Jews, i.e. Ballin, and with disappear-
     ance of Court - anti-Semitism developed against international conspir-
     acy (300-1). Tendency against long leaders in papers (317).

41   Spirit of lawlessness in rebellion at Ballarat 1854 followed by general
     defiance of law (p. 13-15). In 1909 Sir Joseph Ward Prime Minister of
     New Zealand told by Roosevelt regarding settlement of Irish question:
     'It is most essential to furtherence of friendship between America and
     Britain' (226). 'There is more joy in Fleet Street over one lover who
     cuts his sweetheart's throat than over nine hundred and ninety just men
     who live happily ever after ' (A.P. Herbert) (315). Winston Churchill to
     fascist: 'If I had been an Italian I am sure I should have been with you
     from the beginning to the end of your victorious struggle against the
     bestial appetite and passions of Leninism' (352). Function of press to
     provide journalists obsessed with news and possibilities of exotic, i.e.
     C.V.R. Thompson for *Daily Express* in U.S. - foreign correspondents
     generally. Lack of interests in common among papers in British Com-
     monwealth hence Imperial Conference in 1909 in London emphasized
     theme of fear of Germany.

42   The state 'an artificial contrivance' - 'growth' proceeds by a series of
deliberate innovations (Galbraith). Hume and other writers made 'past
exist for the sake of the present' (p. 6). 'Early society is ordered and
governed by oral tradition' (26). Cross used by witness a recognition of
serious character of document. Ceremonial and spectacular cruelty a part
of oral tradition - ceremonial declined with printing. As documents became more plentiful meaning changed - enhanced value at early stage
(26-7). Spread of writing and decline of ceremonial, i.e. pyramids, hieroglyphics - Egypt. Precision of oral tradition in persisting ceremonies of
church. Significance of length of life to oral tradition - if average length
short written tradition built up slowly - with greater length of life books
by individuals increased. Penetration of writing from top down through
society. Enormous transformation of administration 1140-1210 only
comparable to 1800-50 in first marked extension of writing and in second of paper and printing (71). Significance of parchment to development of government in England, i.e. rolls permanent and subject to constant search - permanence strengthened rights of those involved (83).
Emphasis on accessibility for administration - especially after 1372
(85). Care of records marked belief of Middle Ages in past and neglect
with Tudors reflected sharp break with preceding age (88). Domesday
book an epoch in use of written word in government (90). 'An attempt
to replace mere memory and the spoken word by a *jusscriptum*'. How
far writing a part of conquest and reflection of limitations of oral tradition? - neglect of oral tradition in government (103). Domesday book
legalized greatest spoliation in English history - provided title deeds of
new nobility, i.e. linking of writing to force (107). Magna Carta like
Domesday book 'a landmark in the transition from an oral to a written
society' (123). Enormous prestige of government records in early 13th
century.

43   English prose, like Greek and Latin prose, established before Conquest
of William I and Teutonic invaders - prose a test of written tradition
(lviii). Illumination - informal richness, naive vigour of figure representative in 10th and 11th centuries (lxxi). Alliterative poetry became oral
tradition for 9 centuries and revived in 14th century - English prose
slower to come back after conquest. Significance of women to vernacular, i.e. nuns in conquest demanding intelligible reading (xliii). Conquest
meant English in France and French in England - both disappeared in
15th century. Importance of prose with support of king, i.e. Alfred.
Prose of religion adapted to 15th and 16th century - basis of authorized
version on the one hand and of Shakespeare on the other - but power
of vernacular evident throughout. Appeal of Shakespeare primarily to
working men, i.e. 1*d* admission - consequent emphasis on vernacular
and ability to quote and memorize - influencing emphasis on verse -
power of oral tradition persisting as in case of alliterative verse driven
underground for 6 centuries. Enormous significance of oral tradition in

English life. Importance of Crown in Shakespeare's plays plus economic
independence provided by working classes - Harbage - balance between
action and reflection a balance between written and oral.

44   Polytheism of Rome and Greece permitted emergence of Emperor as a
God - addition to pantheon - monotheism weakened position of emper-
or - Julius Caesar recognized as god by Senate - largely of his nomination and after his death Octavian secured recognition of Caesar's position as Divus Julius and in turn of his own position as adopted son -
immortality became a support to the dynasty (p. 99). Rise of Emperor
strengthened position of women - Fulvia wife of Anthony, Livia Agrip-
pina - rise of women in empire and court (116) - Octavian claimed
Apollo as special patron - a precedent for Constantine (118) - Apollo
associated with Greek god - Octavian linking himself with Greek deities -
how far a result of Greek influence? Struggle between Octavian and
Anthony a continuation of struggle between Apollo and Dionysus leading to supremacy of Apollo (138). How far the history of Rome the absorption of Greek and eastern culture? Culminating in Constantinople -
Augustus control over Apollo's temple and Sybilline books meant support of Greek rites - especially as Augustus had Sybilline books purged
(77). November 11 selected to mark end of war. How far did Greeks
attempt to meet dynastic problem by anthropomorphism linking gods
to kings - consolidation of empire in space (Augustus) accompanied
consolidation in time (232). How far did religion tend to centre around
a place in Rome and compel a break with Constantinople and acceptance of a new religion - Christianity (242)?

45   Lincoln and Douglas debates captured attention of nation for Lincoln -
period of oral tradition - press still largely an instrument - Lincoln constantly alert to possibility of using press - an artist in diseminating publicity (p. 37) - master in art of planting information (75). Impact of
American journalism on England began with civil war and decline of
Times, i.e. items unfavourable to North planted in *Times* to be printed
in U.S. papers against Lincoln and paper becoming an arm of the South
(98-9). Possible influence of newspaper on military strategy - Greeley's
'Forward to Richmond' - probably first challenge of force to press in
attitude of generals toward editors (103) - complaint that Southern
generals learned of army movement from newspapers (136). Forney
supporting Lincoln - one of first editors to realize value of printed
propaganda as a weapon (111). 'Continue this administration in power
and we can all go to war, Canada, or to hell before 1868' - M.M. Pomer-
oy in *La Crosse Democrat* (229). 'The ceremony was rendered ludicrous
by some of the sallies of that poor President Lincoln' - London *Times*
report on Gettysburg address. Lack of political sense - Greeley thought
Seward would be nominated and that Lincoln could not be nominated
for second time.

46   Did anointing begin as part of Merovingian coronation ceremony and
      used by Carolingians and followed by church? Charles the Great with
      support of Rome attempted to suppress it but it persisted and event-
      ually spread to Rome where it gained acceptance and spread elsewhere.
      This suggests that anointing of king spread to church rather than in op-
      posite direction as suggested in Schramm on coronations - but this de-
      pendent on Merovingian origin (Ellard).

47   How far did coinage compel emphasis on authority of state and contrib-
      ute to emergence of emperor? Romans in contrast with Greeks viewed
      past in golden majestic light magnifying great men into lofty figures.
      Caesar in last year of life first to have portraiture on coinage while liv-
      ing, i.e. change from Republican Imperial coinage (p. 8). War lords using
      'imperatorial coinages' for self-advertisement and to pay armies - appear-
      ances of private army - concept taken from East and used by Caesar at
      principal mint at Rome - drive of coinage toward centralization - also
      of trade. Coinage, poet, historian, inscription emphasized time element
      of dynasty (27). Augustus's realization of danger of state depending on
      one person - interest in problems of dynasty - position of Senate - how
      far was this accentuated by uncertainty of life? Was cremation impor-
      tant to idea of divinity - eagles flying from burning fire, i.e. Augustus?
      Sejanus paved way to making *aes* into a suggestive imperial gazette (103).
      Neglect of monetary policy, i.e. issue of coins at beginning of each new
      reign - importance for propaganda possibly overcame adjustment of
      supply to demand. Coinage performed an informative function (137).
      Fire at Rome under Nero 64 A.D. led to inflation - reduction of weight
      of gold *aurus* and silver *denarius* (164). Coinage the device for reaching
      more distant areas (181).

48   Relative powerless character of force as compared with press in Amer-
      ican civil war but recognition of dangers of press by generals evident.

49   Introduction of ransom in feudal system - beginnings of impact of price
      system on war. Persia - great wealth - monopoly destroyed by new mili-
      tary tactics of Alexander. Conservative character of militarism - hence
      part of monopoly of knowledge - especially in defensive period - rapid
      change to period of offensive. 'Ever and ever again true belief regarded
      the machine as a devil' (Spengler). 'In the operations of war use of
      fraud ... praiseworthy and glorious' (Machiavelli). Gunpower - centraliz-
      ation of power, monarchies, state above church - standing armies. 'Gun ...
      the starting point of a new type of power machine ... a one cylinder
      internal combustion engine' (Mumford). Price system effective in gen-
      tlemanly wars - defeated by Keynesian emphasis on full employment
      with totalitarian war including ideology and savagery. Dominance of
      artillery after 1750 - greater costs, industrial growth - factory organiza-
      tion (p. 102). Armies and factories became masters - mass struggle
      Darwin, Marx, Clausewitz.

1	Note on Tom Clark, *Northcliffe in History*. See 28 / 67.
3	Louis Adolphe Thiers (1797-1877) was chief executive of the provisional government at Bordeaux which made peace with Prussia and crushed the Paris commune in 1871.
5	Note on A.M. Thompson, *Here I Lie* (London, 1937). See also 29 / 10, 13. J.T. Delane (1817-79) edited the London *Times* from 1841 until 1877. 'Dangle' was Thompson's *nom de plume*. Charles John Kean (1811-68) and Sir Herbert Beerbohm Tree (1852-1917) were important figures in the British Theatre.
7	Note on H.S. Bennett, 'Shakespeare's Audience', *The Proceedings of the British Academy*, XXX (1944) 78-86
8	Note on R.W. Chambers, 'The Continuity of English Prose from Alfred to More and his School,' in *Harpsfield's Life of More*, ed. F.V. Hitchcock (London, 1932). See also 29 / 43.
9	Note on T.F. O'Rahilly, 'The Goidels and their Predecessors', *The Proceedings of the British Academy*, XXI (1935), 323-72
10	Note on Thompson, *Here I Lie*. See also 29 / 5, 13. Sir Edward Hulton (1869-1925) was a successful newspaper proprietor, at one point owning as many as fourteen periodicals. R.P.G. Blatchford (1851-1943) founded the *Clarion* with Thompson in 1891 after being dismissed by the *Sunday Chronicle* for his socialist opinions.
11	Note on W.C. Mitchell, *Lecture Notes on Types of Economic Theory*, (New York, 1949), vol. I.
12	Note on A.H.J. Greenidge, *Legal Procedures of Cicero's Time* (Oxford, 1901).
13	Note on Thompson, *Here I Lie*. See also 29 / 5, 10.
14	Note on W.M. Sale, Jr., *Samuel Richardson: Master Printer* (Ithaca, N.Y., 1950). William Strahan and Samuel Richardson were London printers; Richardson was also an important novelist. The *True Briton* and the *Craftsman* were eighteenth century political newspapers. The Duke of Wharton and Viscount Bolingbroke were influential political figures, usually in opposition to the government.
15	Note on A.L. Poole, *From Domesday Book to Magna Carta, 1087-1216* (Oxford, 1951)
16	Identified by Innis as by A.G. Litle
19	See 29 / 42.
20	Cocteau (1869-1963) was a French poet, novelist, and playwright.
21	Moore was a British painter and art teacher.
23	Not identified
27	Note on Norbert Weiner, *Cybernetics* (New York, 1948)
30	Source by Goodenough not identified.
31	Note on H.G. Farmer, *Military Music* (New York, 1950)
32	Note on P.E. Schramm, *A History of English Coronations* trans. L.G.W. Legg (Oxford, 1937)
36	Masterman (1874-1927) was a British author, journalist, and Liberal politician.
39	Bacon was removed from office in 1621 on a charge that he accepted bribes.
40	Note on F.C. Bently, *Those Days* (London, 1940)
41	Note on Sir J.W. Kirwan, *My Life's Adventure* (London, 1936)
42	Note on Galbraith, *The Literacy of the Medieval English Kings*. See 28 / 114.
43	Note on R.W. Chambers, 'The Continuity of English Prose from Alfred to More and his School', see 29 / 8. Alfred Harbage was author of *Shakespeare and the Rival Traditions* (New York, 1942).
44	Identified by Innis as a work by H.O. Taylor
45	Note on R.S. Harper, *Lincoln and the Press* (New York, 1951)

46   Note on G. Ellard, *Ordination Annointings in the Western Church before 1000 A.D.* (Cambridge, Mass., 1933). For Schramm, see 29 / 32.

47   Note on C.H.V. Sutherland, *Coinage in Roman Imperial Policy, 31 B.C. - A.D. 68* (London, 1951)

48   Note on J.G. Randall, 'The Newspaper Problem in its Bearing upon Military Secrecy during the Civil War,' *American Historical Review,* XXIII (1918) 303-23.

49   Note on J.F.C. Fuller, *Armament and History* (London, 1946)

A

Collection of notes on universities, about 1948. Innis probably brought this material together with a view to writing a paper.

Large colleges at Cambridge – interest of royalty – Henry VII in King's and Henry VIII in Trinity intended to be one of the largest and absorbed property formerly held by monastery – triumph of courts over monasteries meant increasing concern with writing influenced by oral tradition or subject to change in contrast with religious writing emphasizing continuity, i.e. scriptures. Kings using universities to offset church and monastery. Universities an indication of a concern with the oral tradition in teaching – strength of oral tradition at Oxford and Cambridge compared with London. London – able to appoint scholars who are not gentlemen.

Support of university to order of time also aristocracy, hereditary institutions emphasizing continuity, celebrations. Control over monopoly of knowledge exercised by range of universities throughout world – especially in building of libraries and more recently laboratories.

Position of university as a destroyer of new ideas or as creator and destroyer of ideas – new ideas being taught lose freshness and vitality. University of Paris had restrictive effect on ideas – England escaped restrictive effect through separation of universities from capital and division between universities.

Interest in modern history at Cambridge overshadows other subjects as does interest in law in Paris. Tendency for best man to be attracted to Paris and for provincial universities to be weakened and in turn for students to go from provinces to Paris.

Problem of scholarship – French insist on high standards of knowledge of language in severe examinations. Difficulty of creating understanding through scholarships – English students in Paris almost all in modern languages. French-Canadian students bothered with widely different accents – avoid too much contact with French in Paris.

Oral tradition – Gay, Bullock – individual doing very little writing but exercising a profound influence over students – stimulating them in teaching.

Heard French-Canadians – Madame Garneau attacking clerical control of education in Montreal. Reporting Gilson as saying university would never flourish under clerical control.

Scottish universities more influenced by Bologna than English - University of Glasgow constitution follows that of Bologna - basis of student election of rector who becomes chairman of court in Glasgow though seldom taking chair. Explains election of rector at Queen's in Scottish-Italian tradition. University of Glasgow founded by pope.

Universities in British Empire apt to overemphasize power and political influence and to overlook outstanding significance of France or to make it difficult to appreciate position of France - important to develop philosophy of western culture.

Oral tradition in France - universities - richness of language and precision. Escape from drains of dual language - Latin and vernacular - and emphasis on vernacular made for rich development of literature.

Impact of increasing knowledge and number of facts shown in growth of libraries and increasing registration in universities - largely concerned with retailing facts. Government support to large-scale marketing of facts.

Universities in relation to tradition. Oxford, Cambridge, Harvard. Scotland dominated by Roman law emphasized philosophy in universities. Scottish universities early to use vernacular - Hutcheson - Scottish tradition not acceptable to common law. Significance of Adam Smith. England - back of revolt of English against James and Charles I or Stuarts. Regional approach to intellectual thought - important with decline of Latin and universal position of University of Paris.

Tyranny of erudition - characteristic of American scholars - necessity of creating impression by knowledge - neglect of human relations with students in order to impress knowledge.

Education apt to become a building up of mazes - teaching students to go through the maze and using the maze to test capacity. Examinations studied as system of mazes and various approaches covered by best teachers - emphasized memory. Neglect of training of intellectual capacity - ability to meet and solve problems.

Printing industry steadily burying work of past except for reprints of work regarded as more valuable - problem of libraries and index makers to keep ahead of flood. Universities and libraries a fight against pressure of steady output of paper and print. Textbooks, etc., tend to mean neglect of basic minds - models of arrangement and manipulation rather than emphasis on original thought.

Danger of any one point of view in university such as Toronto - precisely because it is a leading university it cannot afford to follow fads.

Carver - could trust opinion of common man if he were not uninformed. English tradition - we must educate our masters or French belief in democracy and realization that we do not have final answers. Importance to scholarship and universities. Overemphasis on politics

and economics. Importance of drawing in England and Europe - Denmark and Sweden. Adult education developed during depression period.

University - centre where one has the right and duty not to make up one's mind.

Increase in numbers of books and growth of book civilization makes for more extensive hierarchy - those who know more books than others and development of universities to foster book knowledge and create hierarchies - difficult for adult education to make impression on it and difficult to develop new points of view - cramps freshness and vitality.

Textbooks - constant revision reflects news character of university education and pressure of printing press - necessity of rapid turnover with large overhead costs.

Science makes for rapid continuous obsolescence of its literature - each new advance implies disappearance of old literature - humanities on the other hand involve retention of the past - scriptural writings and difficulty of overcoming bondage of written word. Increased burden of religious institutions' rigidity even strengthened by influence of science, i.e. increase in printing - U.S. - newspaper journalism means rapid dropping of tradition - humanities brought more clearly into line with science. Science compelled to pull enormous burden of humanities' rigidities.

Necessity of university making available standards of western civilization.

How far break from oral tradition to written shown in freshness of Greek civilization paralleled by growth of oral tradition in development of universities and emergence of Aquinas and Abelard? Tendency to crystallize in written tradition. Augustine at beginning of parchment tradition. Renaissance of paper and printing. Each new development of communication giving freedom to develop new point of view.

Implication of closing of gap between written word and vernacular with newspaper to university - tendency to reduce significance of learned language - Latin, Greek - and reduce possibility of class based on language - emphasis on science - difficulty of understanding literature of past - obsolescence of great books except for prestige purposes. Increases difficulty of securing universal approach in face of nationalism, communication, etc. Machine industry emphasizes regional civilization and difficulties of broad understanding. Emphasis on vernacular of printing press accentuates problem of university in maintaining bridge between world view and a shifting base of vernacular. Universities overwhelmed by vernacular and common interest with little prospect of maintaining interest in problems of civilization.

Significance of Gothic architecture to universities - developed in cathedrals and facilitated development of education in contrast with monasteries.

Universities developed with basis of science and compelled to emphasize elaboration of learning, i.e. PhD theses take place of Roman Catholic ritual in Roman Catholic Church - worship of learning rather than church.

Decline in influence of church and in numbers of highly trained clergy leaves problem of humanities to university and necessitates importance of scholarship. Problem of irony and other forms of literature with mechanization of communication - impossible to be ironical with enormous numbers - assumes sophistication.

Monasticism spreading from Egypt in protest against absolutism made encroachments on family or *pater potestas* of Europe though this had been weakened by Roman law. Restriction of learning to monasteries favoured outburst of oral tradition in universities and finally breaking through in Reformation. Monopoly of monasticism and church gave tremendous significance to coming of Greek and classics in Renaissance - attempts to dam back Greek influence in St Thomas Aquinas, etc. failed with migration of manuscripts and printing or emphasis on Hebrew and scriptures and puritanism as against church and cathedrals.

Importance of oral tradition among Greeks meant easy absorption with scarcity of parchment in scholasticism in Middle Ages - emphasis on oral tradition in universities.

Usher deplored decline of essay writing by students and consequent illiteracy - problem of over-worked students in compulsory subjects and over-worked staff. Administration fails to give proper attention to appointments with large teaching staff and staff overloaded with mediocrity.

Significance of lower interest rate to increasing numbers of students and emphasis on teaching and fees to offset lower income from endowments.

Rise of dialectic oral tradition appearing in universities - emphasis on logic and disputation.

Great accumulation of manuscripts - durable produced in monasteries during Middle Ages - available for printing and making for reading public before printing - development of schools and universities providing reading public.

Importance of cathedrals or expression in architecture in checking spread of Bible and of university - in England cathedrals did not grow into universities - Roman law not taught - common law in London.

Similarly in universities or hierarchies exceedingly difficult to use price system effectively as a moderating device - promotions apt to become personal matters - difficulty and danger of relying on publication tests.

Growth of towns favoured cathedrals and weakened rural monasteries. Cathedrals became more important as schools and drew on wealth of towns for large Gothic buildings - these became centres of universities and new types of libraries.

Problem of democratic tradition - infinite squabbling and flattening out of individual differences - exhaustion particularly in academic centres incidental to working out problems. Problem of knowledge and inability to reach a common point of view due to insistence on content and what to teach - implications to university policy.

Significance to England that universities not located in London where law predominated - consequently latter responsive to trade and not in cathedrals - consequently grew up as possible centres of movements in Oxford.

Franciscans - established in period when towns important in cathedrals in Europe and monasteries important in rural areas in England - reflection of lag in economic development. Arts tradition and division or specialization strong in England - law and medicine. Universities in Scotland associated with towns and trade - Adam Smith in Glasgow - use of English in lectures - Scotland absorbed Roman law, Calvinism. Glasgow University based on Bologna - student university.

Problem of universities in overcoming effect of mechanization. Communism - conflict of science and humanities - mysticism.

Universities escaping from book tradition by emphasizing enormous buildings. Tendency of denominations to centre around universities - religious organizations always attempting to seize strategic points of education - Dominicans - St Thomas always poisoning education at the source.

Over-emphasis on commerce and finance reflected in skyscrapers and architecture and encroachment on universities publishing and printing histories of banks and other institutions - importance of indirect advertising - brewers published Leacock's history of Canada - distortion of learning. Emphasis of commerce and finance on architecture, literature and universities carried to excess but paralleling excess of concern of church with cathedrals and rise of scholasticism. Universities systematically register effects of ground swells or affected by major waves in disturbances of civilization. Excess of religion paralleled by excess of commerce and finance.

Religion checks spread of ideas by communication through hierarchy of learning, etc.; universities, etc., restraint on competitive element.

Religion facilitates cutting across national boundaries - law apt to be bound to state and to differentiate and reflect interest of force in political boundaries. Worship of cultural past - learning may provide basis of common appeal - possible check to religion, i.e. philosophical approach - also to law or may be used to reinforce them. City state in Italy a strength of municipal development provided ground for absorption of printing whereas place of university, copying, etc., in Paris checked its expansion - accentuated religious differences between France and adjoining countries - press in U.S. as against press in England - developments on margin. Plan to emphasize U.S. as marginal development -

machine industry approached from outside - monopoly of knowledge compels development of external character.

University presidents giving each other degrees - a university not an institution designed to that end, or to give members of boards of governors degrees.

Constant reference to crises in writings of social sciences a result of necessity of appealing to fear and influence of news appeal. Place of learned class - universities to prevent domination of various groups - church, army, state - learned class - appreciation of necessity of limited power of groups.

Improved methods of communications facilitate repetition and build up ideologies which become extremely difficult to break down - position of defence in knowledge strengthened at expense of attack - with resistant ideologies necessity of resort to force - irreconcilable minorities reinforced by new propaganda technique make possibilities of philosophical attack difficult - inability to secure common ground. Necessity of universities to withstand pressure from irreconcilable minorities. Small islands in rising sea of barbarism. Inquisition of religion followed by inquisition of nationalism.

Power of university - restriction of court in 18th century accentuated emphasis of printing on encyclopedia.

Rise of universities meant struggle between them reflected in influence of geography and vernacular.

Hierarchy of oral tradition developed with limited written tradition - elaborate ceremonial an indication of limited written tradition. Church ceremonial and university ceremonial to reflect influence of oral tradition. Gradual decline of influence of church in university compels latter to emphasize its own ceremonial as a device to preserve oral tradition. Weakness evident in influence of church, army, business - difficult for university to find a footing.

Significance of oral tradition shown in place of Maritimes in Canada - intensive training facilitates adaptability of college presidents from Maritimes to larger universities of which scholars have been more concerned with oral tradition.

Recent emergence of word adolescent - result of industrial revolution emphasis on secondary schools. Proliferation of educational administration, i.e. division of presidents and deans, organization of universities (i.e. graduate schools) - devastating influence of administrative hierarchies. Impact on universities of medical schools with social health schemes - enormous expense of medical institutions. Menace of educational organizations - attitude toward academic freedom - crystallization of opinion against freedom. Professional education dominating discussion - details of income tax, government contracts - neglect of problem of university tradition. Abhorrence of a vacuum and necessity of reports annual and otherwise to keep printers busy - individuals fearful of being alone.

Threat of elementary and secondary schools to colleges and universities - demand for graduates of colleges to teach practical subjects or general education - emphasis on life.

B

Notes on Law, winter 1951-52, or spring 1952. This material does not come from the *Idea File*.

Endless time of lawyers cross-questioning on economic questions - paramount need of training in economics in the legal profession - part of the whole problem of government reconciliation between law and the social sciences. Significance of the legal profession exposing and entrenching fallacies - advantage of oral tradition in that constant change possible in the courts, criticism of witnesses and exposure of weakness of arguments presented in briefs more effective than economics since the latter pursue arguments to much greater lengths - lawyers in civil and criminal jurisdiction with traditions of procedure emphasizing oral tradition in sharp contrast with those of social scientists emphasizing written tradition. Importance of oral tradition tends to check extravagant statements by lawyers and others. Close adherence of lawyers to facts rather than principles. Public opinion reacts immediately on status of lawyers. The bias of courts and legislation reflected in history - facts distorted in relation to biases of common law courts. Importance of not over-working material in law, develop to the point of discovering law - a principle of British practice emphasizing brevity and avoids verbiage. Lawyers intensely interested in criminal trials - comparable to that of newspaper readers. Tradition of awe built up by courts in arrangement of rooms to emphasize power and authority. Never talk down to the bench - a useful maxim. Extent to which common law coming under influence of textbooks, commentaries and the like - becoming black letter law. Enormous production of printed material. Criminal legislation chiefly in codes. Lawyers concentrate on particular problem and then forget them. Lack of training of memory. Limitation of general principles and neglect of general theory. Legal profession in common law obsessed with immediate details. Necessity of economists studying immediate problems, if it is to be linked to law - the handicap to economics in the development of theory. Civil code emphasizes memory. Examination (America) emphasizes memorization of the code in contrast with emphasis on cases in common law - neglect of the time factor or considerations of continuity in time, training in law makes for a brittle, brilliant type of work. Function of legal approaches to delay proceedings - delayed application of rate case probably by eleven months - dilatory proceedings soften severities. Insistence on the dignity of the court, a room set off with a bar, rigid prohibition against smoking, opposition to reading of manuscripts by counsel. Varied interests in precedents, the story of citations by a lawyer to A.L. Sifton - the latter writing vigorously but discovered later he was only writing a series of his own signatures.

Lesson of economic theory in supplementing law without taking into account the beginning of historical development. Economic history supplements law by emphasizing time in contrast with emphasis of law on space. Common law tradition guarantees legislation by individuals with a common denominator of opinion - emphasis on facts. Consequent inability and ineffectiveness of intellectuals in parliament - compels intellectuals to isolation and renunciation of interests in practical politics - contrast with court tradition attracting abler individuals and offsetting influence of parliament or entering parliament and exercising influence of legislation. Lawyers shift from politics to bench (Ilsley) or from bench to politics (Carroll, over 70 years of age). Concern with immediate practical matters makes common law tradition favorable to scientific tradition (Bacon) reinforced by newspapers' interest in questions of the moment, difficult in securing recognition of time problem, or developing an interest in theoretical problems. The Roman law tradition, intellectual ability attracted to law, prestige of academic field in law - interest in theoretical speculation and in philosophical theory, designed to provide concern with time. The story of a lieutenant-governor (Saskatchewan??) refusing to permit transfer of funds by government from the bank of which he was a director. Max Weber and Toynbee neglect the influence of legal systems, comparison between legislation proceeding with emphasis on circumstantial evidence in common law countries in contrast with inquisition practiced in France and code countries. Parliament practice in Canada subsidized by the legal, business, and accounting profession.

Angus L. MacDonald complained of King's anti-British tendency - opposed Churchill's proposal to have Canadians trained on British cruisers - objected to use of Canadian division in Pacific beyond specifically stated longitude and latitude. MacDonald and Power, a committee appointed by cabinet at Ralston's suggestion as to the means of securing additional men. Power, as a result of attack of appendicitis, left MacDonald alone, the latter phoned various commandants but found a hard core of men resistant to pressure for services abroad. Commandants argued against Prime Minister making a personal visit and appeal. At meeting of the cabinet, Ralston offered to make an an appeal to the men but King suggested he would not have his heart in it and proposed that letter of resignation of Ralston's at the time of the plebiscite should be accepted and MacNaughton should be appointed in his place. Ralston advised MacDonald not to resign. All illustrations of King's insistence on freedom from British dictation in order to secure French support. In the army, MacNaughton opposed to interference of England in sending troops to Italy and breaking up Canadian army. Hence he agreed with King against Ralston who had presumably fallen under British influence as had been the case with Massey.

C.N.R. and C.P.R. hire lawyers to present case and to overcome the difficulties of their own counsel. They escape full responsibility of statement of their counsel and greater manoeuvrability given to the lawyers. Slow process of working through economic problems in contrast with demand for swift effective argument of the common law courts. Maritimes play up briefs and reports at great lengths - cheaper material than that provided by press associations and consequently the weaker areas have the more effective democratic discussion.

The importance of law to rise of individualism - emphasis on character and study of character from objective point of view, leading to a concern with the influence of the state on character and of character on the state. Lawyers prepare case, emphasize the character of witnesses and work out tactics with regard to the character of other witnesses, the shrewd sizing up of the individual.

Legal training in rapid mastering of facts important to parliamentary institutions with constant turning to new legislation. Protection of courts and interest of counsel in clients ensures that questions of fact of an embarrassing character can be brought out except in the case of clients unable to pay fees to good counsel.

The practice of China in giving the family an extremely important place making personal law and government extremely difficult.

Common law with background of tradition before reading and writing - insistence on oral evidence rather than written evidence compels contact with all classes of society including the illiterate - use of the jury system to this end. Possibly common law more effective than the church in maintaining contact with the illiterate, absence of liturgy and the scriptures though use of religion in extracting evidence, testimony sworn on the Bible and the penalty of perjury. Clash between lawyers in courts emphasizes competition of ability but influence weakened by restrictive considerations in appointments to the bench. Tendency for lawyers to prefer practice to bench in Canada. Separation of barrister and solicitor in England tempers effect of finance on legal profession. In Canada two combined in solicitor and consequently finance and business an important effect on law. English common law greatest emphasis on facts of legal systems - cross-examination - oral tradition designed to get at facts of case - illustrations of royal commission - amazing self-confidence of common law - chairman and two counsel with no knowledge of railway rates - members of commission with little knowledge, legal profession profound belief - it can master any evidence and insists on reducing all questions to adaptability of court. Legal profession dominates medium - doctors' cases and other professions - probleming of absorbing economics.

Economics probably in common law tradition under Adam Smith and steady emphasis on contract probably supported private enterprise economy. In present century common law carried as far as possible in private enterprise and leading to final breakthrough to legislation and administrative control with depression and Keynesian approach. Lawyers continuing to occupy an important place in legislation but laymen introduced on larger scale. St Laurent culmination of legal influence - former minister of justice and fully aware of possibilities of patronage - Mitchell - Ilsley's partner made judge in Demarais' constituency instead of Demarais and Demarais given position as junior counsel for commission, appointed to bench.

Common law countries based on oral tradition - able to carry out socialistic legislation - Roman law countries with written constitution reflect power of Roman law in concept of property. United States and Canada less suited to socialistic legislation - Roman law countries emphasizing property subject to revolutions.

English courts insist on accepting living person as authority but not a text by him unless he has died - power of oral tradition - insists person alive may have changed his mind from writing. In America difficulty of transporting English authority leads to gradual acceptance of text and whittling down of English rule. Joan of Arc reflected oral tradition of France and helped to defeat English and Plantagenets - expression of rationalism rather than dynasticism.

Legal self-confidence - difficult to get changes in the educational system of lawyers - importance of power over life and death - possible vested interest in capital punishment.

Overwhelming influence of lawyers and rate schedules in B.T.C. [Board of Transport Commissioners] cases and in railway position. Fundamental problem of legal versus economic approach - common law emphasis on facts unsuited to complexity of rate problem.

Comparison between litigious procedure with emphasis on circumstantial evidence in common law countries with inquisitional procedure in France and code countries. Max Weber and Toynbee neglect the importance of legal systems, i.e. common law and Roman law. Portrait painting in Canada subsidized by legal, business, and academic professions.

Effect of regionalism and religion in Supreme Court - one judge for Quebec and one for Montreal districts reflecting the importance of the code - one Irish Catholic for Ontario - one Protestant - one Maritimer. The reluctance of the bar to accept appointments because of the dislike of living in Ottawa. St Laurent refused to be appointed - others resigned after a short period. A weak Supreme Court handicaps the government with abolition of appeals to Privy Council.

Index

An asterisk indicates that there is a note associated with this reference.

Osborne, E.L. 11/25*
Osler, Sir William 25/38*

Pantaleoni, Maffea 11/48*
Papyrus 5/192; 6/4, 64; 7/29, 43; 11/22, 33; 28/97
Pareto, Vilfredo 8/10*; 15/16, 19*; 18/21 Paul, Herbert 29/40
Perroux, F. 27/19*
Philosophy *See* Philosophy in the topical index
Plato 2/24; 6/32, 51; 11/1, 2, 35; 15/7, 15; 22/9; 23/3; 24/6, 10, 20; 25/9; 27/136; 29/30
Poetry 2/24; 5/30, 179, 180, 7/32; 10/5; 27/111, 125
Polanyi, Karl 26/3*
Political Science 1/7; 4/9; 5/150, 216
Politicians 5/22, 38, 103; 13/8; 16/38, 50
Politics 2/21; 4/23; 5/36, 51, 147, 192; 7/36, 39; 15/3, 6; 16/62; 17/19; 18/4; 19/26; 22/2; 24/16, 26; 26/6; 27/11, 25, 33; 28/4, 7, 12, 54, 97
Popovich 5/222
Pound, Ezra 24/32; 28/22*, 64
Pound, Roscoe 5/13*
Price Systems *See* Price Systems in the topical index
Printing *See* Printing in the topical index
Puritanism 7/26; 11/2, 35

Quebec 1/16; 2/3; 4/13; 5/149, 152; 26/28

Radio-Television *See* Radio-Television in the topical index
Raymond, H.J. 2/4*, 13
Reid, Whitelaw 5/165
Reformation 5/203; 6/12; 7/8, 48; 9/19; 14/13; 18/54; 19/9; 26/32
Renaissance *See* Renaissance in the topical index
Religion 2/1; 2/40; 5/57, 110, 118, 157, 176, 192; 6/38; 12/29; 14/6, 10; 15/40, 65; 17/10; 18/7, 35; 22/2; 23/41; 24/40; 25/8, 14, 35; 26/5; 27/54, 134; 28/50, 54, 109; Appendix A *See also* Church in the topical index

- Buddhism 2/1; 5/28, 178, 181, 190; 7/31; 15/32; 16/29, 34; 17/10; 19/7; 28/13
- Confucian 2/1
- Jewish 1/9
- Protestant 3/14; 4/18, 25; 5/58, 99, 192, 200; 6/23, 25; 7/50; 8/9; 12/13. 29; 15/10, 14, 15; 19/9; 22 22/3; 23/33; 24/24, 32; 28/5
- Roman Catholic 2/1, 11; 4/2, 6, 33; 5/18, 52, 58, 192, 196, 204; 6/49, 54; 11/17; 15/13; 23/28; 24/32; 27/76; 28/39 *See also* Mohammedanism in the topical index
Revolution 2/30, 34; 5/121, 137, 142, 150; 7/8, 27; 9/14; 11/39; 13/3; 15/6; 19/4, 6; 28/41; 29/25
- American 1/13; 2/4; 3/14; 7/7, 8; 21/7; 26/38; 27/15, 102
- French 5/126, 139; 7/8; 17/17; 19/4; 28/79
- Industrial 5/88, 135, 137; 19/16, 35; 27/61, 79, 80; 29/21
- Russian 5/128, 139
Richardson, Samuel 29/14*
Riley, J.W. 11/40*
Ritchie, S.J. 26/8*
Rivarol, Comte de 23/23*
Robertson, H.M. 22/3
Roebuck, J.A. 27/70*
Robinson, F.H. 28/52
Roosevelt, F.D. 5/38, 64; 26/31; 27/46, 112, 121
Root, J.W. 28/51*
Russia *See* Russia in the topical index

Saint-Simon, Comte de 1/2*
Schumpeter, J.A. 5/16*; 19/22; 27/8
Schoeffer, Peter 28/70*
Science 5/215
Sex 5/201, 214; 7/29; 9/24; 11/3, 47; 12/27; 16/66; 17/28; 27/120
Shakespeare 5/21, 121, 130; 6/8; 8/16; 10/6; 22/6; 23/55; 25/12; 27/44
Shotwell, J.T. 5/41*; 15/31
Sifton, Sir Clifford 5/100
Silberling, N.J. 6/52*
Simmel, George 27/129*
Sismondi, J.C. 1/2*

Topical Index

'Extent to which encyclopedia may tear knowledge apart and pigeon-hole it in alphabetical boxes – necessity of constantly attempting a synthesis to offset influence of mechanization – possibly basis for emphasis on civilization as a whole.' (27/7)

I MEANS OF COMMUNICATION

Oral Tradition 1/15; 2/1, 24, 30, 32, 41; 3/5, 15; 4/2, 28; 5/3, 35, 37, 54, 77, 84, 99, 106, 162, 167, 168; 6/15, 20, 36, 45; 7/2, 20, 46, 51, 59; 8/4, 5, 19; 9/8, 23; 10/3, 5, 6; 12/10, 21; 15/35, 52, 72; 16/1, 11, 21, 24, 27, 33, 38; 17/1, 31; 18/32; 19/1, 3, 6, 23, 25; 22/9; 23/46, 53, 55; 24/5, 25, 31, 34, 35, 38; 25/32; 26/9, 23, 24, 25; 27/139; 28/5, 7, 39, 65; 29/12; Appendix A

Writing 1/8; 2/12, 30, 32, 41; 3/15; 4/2, 6; 5/3, 48, 57, 84, 99, 107, 113, 119, 125, 156, 172, 173, 179; 6/15, 20, 36, 43, 54; 7/2, 16, 31; 8/16, 23; 9/8; 10/5; 11/15, 41; 12/8; 15/9, 50, 63, 72; 16/29, 60; 17/30; 18/39, 52, 53; 19/14; 20/1; 24/5, 9, 18, 32, 36, 38, 44, 45; 25/9, 18, 22, 30; 26/26; 28/8, 82, 86, 96; 29/42

Printing 1/11, 12, 18; 2/4, 14, 22, 42, 43; 3/8, 14, 17; 4/3, 31; 5/3, 12, 21, 23, 55, 56, 59, 75, 77, 84, 85, 98, 111, 112, 116, 128, 130, 137, 139, 190, 194, 206, 210; 6/2, 53, 56, 60; 7/5, 8, 46; 8/3, 7, 8, 9, 12, 13, 14, 27; 9/9, 15, 24; 10/9; 11/18, 19, 32, 39; 14/13, 14; 15/23; 16/13, 56; 18/6, 34, 47; 19/32; 20/9; 23/50; 24/5, 45; 25/9, 21, 22; 26/14, 22, 24; 27/24, 43; 28/19, 26, 58, 79, 82, 86, 107; 29/14

Newspapers 1/12; 2/4, 23, 28; 4/11, 12; 5/9, 10, 24, 31, 36, 38, 55, 70, 71, 72, 90, 108, 120, 121, 125, 131, 134, 141, 145, 166, 175, 208; 6/11, 13, 14, 57; 8/15; 9/5, 10; 12/16; 15/4, 21; 16/5, 33; 17/30; 18/43, 47, 56; 19/37, 38; 20/8; 22/5, 7; 24/29; 27/27; 28/67, 108; 29/1, 10

Radio-Television 4/23; 5/10, 23, 36, 38, 64, 65, 71, 72, 139, 164, 205, 216; 6/22, 37, 58; 7/52; 8/15; 11/8, 38; 15/47; 18/11, 38, 41, 55; 24/33; 26/33, 39; 27/104, 124

Music 4/25; 5/225; 15/10, 39; 24/3; 25/9; 27/55; 28/3, 60, 89, 113; 29/21, 23, 31

Art 11/35; 12/18; 15/5, 25, 54; 16/2, 45; 17/23; 18/30; 23/44, 49; 24/4, 28, 32, 41, 42; 25/9; 26/13, 16; 27/83, 103; 28/12, 15, 52; 29/21

II POLITICAL ORGANIZATION AS THE FOUNDATION OF CULTURE

Church 1/4, 9, 13, 15; 2/1, 8, 11; 4/17, 24; 5/3, 5, 8, 11, 28, 32, 35, 38, 52, 55, 58, 61, 99, 121, 122, 163, 169, 178, 185, 192, 196, 199, 200, 201, 204, 205, 210, 211, 225; 6/16, 23, 28, 41, 49, 54, 59; 7/3, 17, 34, 35, 45, 57, 59; 8/7, 9;

III PRESERVATION OF CULTURE

IV CRISIS OF THE WESTERN WORLD